Charlotte Perkins Gilman

and a Woman's Place in America

STUDIES IN AMERICAN LITERARY REALISM AND NATURALISM

Charlotte Perkins Gilman

and a Woman's Place in America

Jill Bergman

THE UNIVERSITY OF ALABAMA PRESS
Tuscaloosa

The University of Alabama Press
Tuscaloosa, Alabama 35487-0380
uapress.ua.edu

Inquiries about reproducing material from this work should be addressed to
the University of Alabama Press.

Typeface: Garamond

Manufactured in the United States of America
Cover image: Gilman in Las Casitas, California, 1900; courtesy
of Walter Stetson Chamberlin
Cover design: Mary Elizabeth Watson

The volume editor and contributors wish to thank the Dorothy M. Healy
Endowment at the University of New England for providing financial assistance
toward the publication of this volume.

Library of Congress Cataloging-in-Publication Data

Names: Bergman, Jill, 1963– editor.
Title: Charlotte Perkins Gilman and a woman's place in America /
[edited by] Jill Bergman.
Description: Tuscaloosa : University Alabama Press, 2017. | Series: Studies in
American Literary Realism and Naturalism | Includes bibliographical references
and index.
Identifiers: LCCN 2016028743| ISBN 9780817319366 (hardback) |
ISBN 9780817390709 (e-book)
Subjects: LCSH: Gilman, Charlotte Perkins, 1860–1935—Criticism and
interpretation. | Place (Philosophy) in literature. | Women and literature—United
States—History—19th century. | Feminism and literature—United States—
History—19th century. | Women and literature—United States—History—20th
century. | Feminism and literature—United States—History—20th century. |
BISAC: SOCIAL SCIENCE / Women's Studies. | LITERARY CRITICISM /
Women Authors.
Classification: LCC PS1744.G57 Z59 2017 | DDC 818/.409—dc23
LC record available at https://lccn.loc.gov/2016028743

Contents

III. RECLAIMING AND REDEFINING A "WOMAN'S PLACE"

Illustrations

Acknowledgments

First and foremost I would like to thank all the contributors to *Charlotte Perkins Gilman and a Woman's Place in America* for their diligence, hard work, and faith in this project. Beyond being experts in the fields of Gilman studies and American literature, they have all been exemplary collaborators and generous colleagues in the development of this book.

Some of the chapters were originally presented at "Gilman Goes West: 5th International Conference on Charlotte Perkins Gilman," held at the University of Montana in June 2011. That conference—and subsequently this book—could not have happened without the goodwill and support of Royce C. Engstrom, the president of the University of Montana; Perry Brown, the provost and vice president for academic affairs; and Chris Comer, the dean of the College of Humanities and Sciences. My thanks as well, to Sarah Knobel, my research assistant, for her tireless work on the conference.

I would also like to thank Dan Waterman and Vanessa Rusch, our editors, and the anonymous readers for their time, energy, and expertise. The book is much stronger and smarter for their guidance and careful criticism; they have been the best sort of participants in the growth and development of this collective study of Gilman and place. Moreover, I am grateful for the professionalism and skill of the staff at the University of Alabama Press; this book would not exist without you.

The editor and authors would like to thank the following organizations and publications for permission to reprint earlier versions of chapters included in this work:

Peter Betjemann's "Eavesdropping with Charlotte Perkins Gilman: Fiction, Transcription, and the Ethics of Interior Design" first appeared in *American Literary Realism* 46, no. 2 (Winter 2014): 95–115.

Gary Scharnhorst's "Charlotte Perkins Gilman's 'The Giant Wistaria': A Hieroglyph of the Female Frontier Gothic" originally appeared in *Frontier Gothic: Terror and Wonder at the Frontier in American Literature*, ed. David Mogen, Scott P. Sanders, and Joanne B. Karpinski (Rutherford, NJ: Fairleigh Dickinson University Press, 1993): 156–64.

Portions of "Charlotte Perkins Gilman and the US West" first appeared in Jennifer S. Tuttle's "'New England Innocent' in the Land of Sunshine: Charlotte Perkins Gilman and California," *Western American Literature* 48, no. 3 (Fall 2013): 284–311.

Charlotte Perkins Gilman

and a Woman's Place in America

Introduction

A Woman's Place Is *Not* in the Home

Jill Bergman

Since the publication of Gaston Bachelard's *The Poetics of Space* (1957; translated and published in English in 1964), space and place have become central concerns in the study of literary and cultural productions. Imagining a house, a physical structure, besieged by "the bestial hostility of the storm," Bachelard argued that, for the house's inhabitants, its "virtues of protection and resistance are transposed into human virtues. The house acquires the physical and moral energy of a human body." The roof, walls, and rooms of the house, he suggested, take on meanings beyond their mere physical existence, and in some of the most famous lines in the book he concluded that "in this dynamic rivalry between house and universe, we are far removed from any reference to simple geometrical forms. A house that has been experienced is not an inert box. Inhabited space transcends geometrical space."[1] The house, of course, is not alive—Bachelard was not telling an Edgar Allan Poe story. Rather, the house is shot through, in the experience of its inhabitants, with all the complexities of human emotions, desires, beliefs, values, ideologies, history, and more. In human terms, space must be understood as much more than the dimensions or floorplan of a building. As Joan Ockman writes of Bachelard's *Poetics*, "in lyrical chapters on the 'topography of our intimate being'—of nests, drawers, shells, corners, miniatures, forests, and above all the house, with its vertical polarity of cellar and attic—he undertook a systematic study, or 'topoanalysis,' of the 'space we love.'"[2] Bachelard, along with contemporaries such as Maurice Merleau-Ponty, Martin Heidegger, and others, fostered the exploration of the social dimensions of space and place in literary studies, philosophy, architecture, and other fields.

Since then, a number of scholars have continued and elaborated on the work of the 1960s, and have firmly established place studies. Among the most celebrated works—many of which are referenced or cited in this collection— are Yi-Fu Tuan's *Topophilia: A Study of Environmental Perception, Attitudes, and Values* (1974) and *Space and Place: The Perspective of Experience* (1977), Peter Jackson's *Maps of Meaning* (1989), Edward J. Soja's *Postmodern Geographies: The Reassertion of Space in Critical Social Theory* (1989), Henri Lefebvre's *The Production of* Space (1991), Gillian Rose's *Feminism and Geography: The Limits of Geographical Knowledge* (1993), Tim Cresswell's *In Place/Out of Place: Geography, Ideology, and Transgression* (1996) and *Place: A Short Introduction* (2004), Krista Comer's *Landscapes of the New West: Gender and Geography in Contemporary Women's Writing* (1999), Linda McDowell's *Gender, Identity, and Place: Understanding Feminist Geographies* (1999), Mona Domosh and Joni Seager's *Putting Women in Place: Feminist Geographers Make Sense of the World* (2001), and Wendy Harding's *The Myth of Emptiness and the New American Literature of Place* (2014).

In turn, and building upon these and other works, literary scholars have undertaken analyses of the construction, representation, and gendering—and more—of space and place in poetry, drama, fiction, memoirs, and other genres and forms. Yet for all of this work, not all writers have earned equal attention. In particular, for our purposes, the diverse and many works of Charlotte Perkins Gilman have not received their due in terms of place studies: our collection seeks to fill at least part of this critical gap.

If we return to Bachelard for a moment, we can perhaps see why place and space should be central categories of concern in the analysis of Gilman's oeuvre. He wrote that "a house is first and foremost a geometrical object, one which we are tempted to analyze rationally. Its prime reality is visible and tangible, made of well hewn solids and well fitted framework. It is dominated by straight lines, the plumb-line having marked it with its discipline and balance. A geometrical object of this kind ought to resist metaphors that welcome the human body and the human soul. But transposition to the human plane takes place immediately whenever a house is considered as space for cheer and intimacy, space that is supposed to condense and defend intimacy."[3] Houses, as homes, are supposed to be places of safety and warmth, good feeling and affection, but where in Gilman's works are such houses, such buildings, such places and spaces? They are not possible until the women shed themselves of men or enter, eyes wide-open, relationships with the proper sort of men, who understand that women possess rights and dreams apart from their husbands or lovers.

Bachelard did not offer a naive or single-mindedly optimistic take on the home; he cited, after all, "an unusually moving exhibition of drawings by Pol-

ish and Jewish children who had suffered the cruelties of the German occupa-
tion during the last war."[4] Yet he nonetheless read mostly male poets and did
not inquire too deeply into how a woman might otherwise view the home, the
legal and social possession—in most Western cultures—of men. As article after
article, poem after poem, story after story, novel after novel, and occasional
piece after occasional piece by Gilman demonstrates, she did not find houses
all that comforting, nurturing, progressive, or dedicated to the right sorts of
social arrangements or commercial enterprises. In most cases, the home, replete with the rules, prohibitions, and power of patriarchy, did not foster the
ambitions, desires, or freedom of wives, daughters, sisters, or mothers.

In Gilman's most famous story, "The Yellow Wall-Paper," we see how deeply
saturated place and space can be with male authority—backed up with such
forms of manipulation as "reason," "knowing what's best," and a few timely
commands. The rules, regulations, and laws of the father—almost by themselves, by their all-but-palpable presence—force the narrator into the nursery–
prison cell and otherwise assault her thoughts, creativity, and desire for freedom of expression and of the self. The narrator moves as if through a force
field of emotional and psychological violence and oppression, and even as she
gazes out the window at the "*delicious* garden"—or what she hopes to be a
more genial, open space—her plight seems hopeless. Who, after all, owns the
garden? Who rules the world beyond the gate? What sort of escape can she
actually achieve? Embodied in the form of "a physician of high standing, and
one's own husband," patriarchy—which also seems to depend upon the col-
lusion of women such as Jane—browbeats the would-be writer until she becomes a nightmarish animal figure, lost in her own fractured mind:

> I kept on creeping just the same, but I looked at him over my shoulder.
> "I've got out at last," said I, "in spite of you and Jane! And I've pulled
> off most of the paper, so you can't put me back!"
> Now why should that man have fainted? But he did, and right across
> my path by the wall, so that I had to creep over him every time![5]

In what must be one of the most harrowing stories and denouements in American fiction, Gilman left little doubt about the destructive powers of the world
of men—even a man who gets kneed occasionally as his wife crawls over him—
and about how encoded place and space can be with inimitable, even maddening, cultural, political, and economic forces beyond the individual woman's control.

This brings us to the title of our collection, *Charlotte Perkins Gilman and
a Woman's Place in America*. So much of Gilman's work stands in direct, and
sometimes not very subtle, contradiction of the Victorian notion of a wom-

an's place being in the home and not out in the larger cultural, economic, and political worlds. The "angel in the house," a phrase coined by Coventry Patmore (an English appellation, if there ever was one) in 1854, represented so much of what Gilman detested and battled against: docility, domesticity, acquiescence to male authority, a lack of intellectual curiosity, willful ignorance disguised as innocence, and no work outside the home. Gilman argued for new places and spaces for women, where women could earn their economic keep, be free of financial control and domination by men, and exercise their minds, bodies, and desires. She argued for the reformulation of the home as a work space, a place of industry, and not just an enclosed, routinized, tedious abode set up for social engagements and the care of the stomachs and morals of a husband and children.

Gilman wanted to revise the geography of the home: get rid of the kitchen and hire someone to provide the meals; get rid of the nursery and remake it as a room of one's own; get rid of the men and form a co-op with other women. She especially wanted to revise the social and cultural norms, expectations, and forces that filled each nook and cranny. Just as much, however, she wanted women *out* of the house, able to be active participants in many of the same realms as men. She wanted not the angel but the entrepreneur, activist, doctor, lawyer, and teacher; she wanted women to occupy the social, cultural, and political places, spaces, and jurisdictions appropriate to such professions and talents.

At this point, before we turn to a consideration of what our individual contributors have to say about place and space in Gilman, we need to address two further matters: First, are *place* and *space* synonymous, and what do we mean by them, anyway? Second, what sorts of places and spaces, in particular, do our contributors analyze in Gilman?

In response to the first question, we can say that although *place* and *space* are not perfectly synonymous, they can be interchangeable, and rather than attempt to resolve the issue, our authors do not seek to delimit the possibilities or suggestive qualities of either term. If by *place* we usually mean a specific location or a particular site, building, or town—the coffee shop, 2120 Columbia Avenue, or Boston—Bachelard has already demonstrated that places exist as more than geometrical shapes or geographical coordinates. *Place* resonates with all sorts of ideas, emotions, anxieties, and rules that cannot be fixed so easily as, for example, the longitude and latitude of one's dwelling. Place, we can say, exceeds its own dimensions. In "The Yellow Wall-Paper" we can pretty easily see how a specific place—in this case, the nursery—takes on depths and dimensions beyond the physical measurements of the room: as the narrator gazes at the horrible wallpaper, she finds that she sees past the plane of the wall into dark zones populated by creeping, almost human figures. The wall, a mere surface, seems more and more like a sort of nightmare portal leading to or from who knows where. In such an instance, place takes on a kind of nonspecific geography, a set of coordinates no longer quite locatable; and as the mansions and castles in tales like Virginia Woolf's *Orlando* (1928), Mervyn Peake's *Titus Groan* (1950), Italo Calvino's *Invisible Cities* (1972), and Salman Rushdie's *Shame* (1983) amply demonstrate, place can reach toward infinity and exceed the ability of the mind (or a GPS device) to map it. Place, in other words, can easily begin to seem like space.

By *space* we probably mean something like the three dimensions enclosed by the walls, ceiling, and floor of a room. Or we might mean something like the wide-open spaces of the American West or the vast reaches of the universe. *Space* seems to imply and require a higher mathematics than *place*— we need three rather than just two lines of measurement—and it may even exceed any form of calculation: How deep, how many cubic feet, is the blue sky? Space perhaps contains fewer physical limits than place (and therefore promises or seems to engage the imagination differently than place), but as soon as we take into consideration the human element, space is as brimming with desires, hopes, rules, and laws as any specific location. It becomes a sort of almost contained entity to be argued over and controlled. As William Kittredge's book title asks, *Who Owns the West?* (1996). Who, in other words, owns the land, but also who owns the idea, concept, or definition of the West? Who gets to say what the spaces of the West may be or become? Who gets to shape or imagine what sort of life a person may live in the West? Suddenly a space seems very much like a place, no matter how vast and difficult it may be to measure.

To turn to our second question, what sorts of places and spaces do our contributors analyze in Gilman, we can happily say that the authors explore and closely read a rather dizzying array of places and spaces in Gilman. In these pages—places and spaces of their own—readers will find considerations of Gilman's representations of California and Colorado; of Herland, a utopian realm ruled and occupied by women; and of a patriarchal, close-minded, and stagnant New England. In a fascinating approach to place, and especially to space, some of our authors analyze the images and worlds presented on a flat surface—the canvas—and find all sorts of complexities, depths, and meanings.

Others investigate the page itself as an intensely contested place and space, and they delve deeply into Gilman's notion of the news, particularly in the form of a periodical aimed at women and progressive readers, as a space dedicated to public business, politics, and that snow leopard of human affairs, the truth. Still others search the intricate, complex, and sometimes even malevolent interiors of the private homes and public buildings in Gilman's fiction and analyze her representations of the physical objects (e.g., rocking chairs) and byways (e.g., ducts and almost-hidden openings in walls) of these intimate places and spaces. One contributor even documents Gilman's posthumous literary emergence in Rome. As this brief list suggests, the study of place and space in Gilman leads to all sorts of fascinating settings and locations and to all sorts of insights into Gilman's politics, polemics, and literary art.

Let us now turn to an overview of the book.

Part I opens with a landmark essay on the intersecting disciplines of Gilman, place, and western studies. In chapter 1 Jennifer S. Tuttle and Gary Scharnhorst recall that Gilman lived in California for eight years, specifically in Pasadena, Oakland, and San Francisco. These cities provided the locales for her fiction, poetry, essays, and autobiographical writings, but more important, they helped to shape the intellectual underpinnings of Gilman's reformist ideals: "Gilman associated California (and the West in general) with health, freedom, beauty, and a potential for change; it was the site of a personal and professional transformation, inspiring and enabling her creative and intellectual work." Offering analyses of the places and cultural and political values exhibited in such western works as *The Crux* (wherein, they argue, Gilman revises and rewrites aspects of Owen Wister's *The Virginian*) and *What Diantha Did*, Tuttle and Scharnhorst provocatively argue that *Herland* can and should be read as part of Gilman's western body of work.

Having opened with Gilman's western experiences and works, we continue with biographical inquiry but turn to two sorts of seemingly much more enclosed, perhaps even claustrophobic, dominions: the canvas and the spaces of the interior self, the latter impossible to measure or gauge yet nonetheless conceivable. In chapter 2 Denise D. Knight examines a number of recently recovered images of Gilman produced between 1877 and 1919 and reexamines a handful of already famous renderings. Noting that portraits of Gilman (in a variety of media) have not received their critical due, Knight argues that such works give us access not only to the physical spaces that Gilman inhabited at various stages of her life (including the American West) but also, and perhaps more important, to the psychological spaces of moods, emotions, and thoughts. Just as we can read Gilman's antipathy toward domesticity and the submission of women to men in her writing, we can see her desire for new places and spaces for women through the eyes of those who sought to capture her likeness and provide glimpses of her inner self. In a similar manner, the paintings express many of the ideals, themes, and critiques that appear in her poetry and prose.

Like Knight, William C. Snyder explores the surfaces and depths of the canvas. In chapter 3 he offers a canny analysis of Gilman's visual performances, exploring how her representations of place and space—especially of the infamous wallpaper—suggest a number of affinities with innovations in the visual arts. He remarks that Gilman employed "verbal-visual constructs that simulate techniques of impressionism, cubism, and abstract expressionism—three modernist programs that arose during Gilman's lifetime," and he contends that the narrator "paints" the "canvas" of the wall with "emotion, anxiety, and obsession." Comparing Gilman's techniques with the work of such masters as Claude Monet, Paul Cézanne, Mark Rothko, Georges Braque, and Pablo Picasso, Snyder explores how and why Gilman reworked her early training as a painter into an acutely visual and psychologically powerful modernist verbal imagery.

From geography, biography, and the canvas, we turn to Part II. Both essays in this section return to the centrality of the places, spaces, and opportunities of the American West in Gilman's work and thought. In chapter 4 Brady Harrison draws on diverse debates among philosophers over the possibilities of individual freedom: Are we really free to think and act as we wish, or are we overprogramed by histories, forces, cultures, and ideologies beyond our control or understanding? He discusses *The Crux*, a polemic novel about sexually transmitted diseases that compares the plight of young women in the repressive patriarchal world of New England with the opportunities afforded by the open, less patriarchal spaces and possibilities of the West. Harrison, however, finds that while Gilman championed women's rights and the freedom of the West, she perhaps offered a too prescriptive determination of how young women should conduct their new lives and thereby skirts a deeper consideration of what it might mean to be free in early twentieth-century America.

Chapter 5 provides a contrast to the view of the liberatory places and spaces of the West. Gary Scharnhorst submits that Gilman, like many other American writers, "viewed the American West in paradoxical terms, as both promised land and howling wilderness." Taking up and reworking elements of frontier mythology and the western literary genre, Gilman, in her gothic masterpiece "The Giant Wistaria," countered the certainties of both male-dominated literary forms and male forms of narrative closure. Scharnhorst writes that like the narrator in "The Yellow Wall-Paper," the female protagonist of "The Giant Wistaria" refuses to "submit to the demands of male authority" and instead "devises a set of signs that defy patriarchal control." The tale becomes, in this way, a "type of open-ended riddle rather than a closed authorial monologue," and the West figures as a cursed and violent land.

Part III opens with Sari Edelstein's fascinating reading of yet another way of thinking about our notions of space, in this case the blank page, and about the possibilities that Gilman saw for influencing individual lives, and the lives of women in general, through the periodic journal. In chapter 6 she argues that Gilman was deeply "concerned with preserving the periodical as a space devoted to public affairs, not love affairs. . . . She understood the profound power of the media to direct readers and to transform public and private relationships, and she harnessed this power to upset, rather than affirm, existing social geographies." Focusing on stories that Gilman published in the *Forerunner*, and offering in particular an extended analysis of "When I Was a Witch," Edelstein explores how Gilman's female protagonists battle for physical and intellectual spaces in which to survive and even thrive. In "When I Was a Witch," Gilman attacked mainstream newspapers for what she saw as their spurious, even salacious, stories and offers a comic yet ultimately serious means to identify the failure of the press to offer any "true and necessary news." Through her witchcraft, the protagonist color-codes all the different sorts of lies and hypocrisies, thereby revealing the average newspaper to be a "crazy quilt" of bait, fabrications, and outright mendacities. With the magic of an honest publication, Gilman hoped to change the world.

Like Edelstein, Catherine J. Golden, in chapter 7, finds a sort of magic in material culture, this time in the form of a letter. Drawing on postal history, material cultural studies, Victorian iconography and letter-writing manuals, the work of Tim Cresswell, and more, Golden analyzes how two women of very different classes—one a well-to-do wife, the other an abused domestic servant living far away from her family—seize upon misaddressed letters as a means to reshape both their lives and the meaning of home. Home, the wife discovers, is not the happily domestic and inviting place she thought it was; rather, it is a space of adultery, male privilege, and violence, so she leaves her husband and takes the servant with her to a new place and space for women, for sisterhood, for new ways of being apart and free from the baleful control of men.

In chapter 8 Peter Betjemann, recalling the architectural and decorative styles and theories of Gilman's era, explores how a number of characters in Gilman's stories and novels make use of the architectural environment—particularly places or spaces of concealment, screens, apertures or holes in walls, pipes, speaking tubes, and telephones,—to spy on and record (on the then new and popular dictograph) or transcribe the actions and conversations of others. The characters do this in keeping with Gilman's ideals of freedom and opportunity for women and her concern, as Edelstein demonstrates, for truth-telling and accurate reporting as a means "to hear through the limits of conventional domesticity or patriarchal privilege." Although readers of today might find such spying unsettling—we live, after all, in an age of creeping surveillance and the breakdown of individual privacy—Gilman's female protagonists use the physical environment to turn the tables, rather homeopathically, on male power, secrecy, and the control of place: the duplicity, malfeasance, and power-hungry nature of men can be recorded and broadcast to the greater world, particularly women, as a means of raising consciousness and of rebalancing power inside and outside the domestic space. In this way, Betjemann suggests, Gilman likewise asked her readers to confront and come to terms with patrilineal authority and its play in so many places and spaces.

Part III, and our collection, closes with chapter 9. Jennifer S. Tuttle studies the historical and cultural forces at play in Italy in the last several years that have enabled, and perhaps even required, the translation of Gilman's major works into Italian and their dissemination in parts of the Italian academy and society. Recounting her keynote at a 2010 conference on Gilman held at the University of Rome III, Tuttle quotes the conference organizers on the purpose and the timing of the international gathering: "It is particularly timely and appropriate to reconsider Gilman's analysis of the social dynamics of power, gender, and sexuality today in Italy, given the . . . stereotyped representation of women in Italian culture and their virtual nonexistence in political and economic institutions." Moreover, Tuttle draws upon her experiences in Rome as a means to meditate on the recovery of Gilman's work in American culture and on issues concerning women's health, feminism, and the power and ability of women to speak for themselves and be heard by both men and other women. What places do we have, in our concluding chapter? Only places that are small and easy to grapple with and understand, such as Rome, Italy, the United States, and the pages of history—or, to put it another way, so many of the multitudinous sorts of places and spaces explored in our other chapters.

To close this introduction, we can make at least two observations. The first is that our contributors, as concerned as they are with the issues and problems of place and space, do not take up only those issues in Gilman. Rather, as experts in Gilman, American, and, in some cases, international literary studies, they bring into play a wide range of questions, ideas, and subjects at stake in the study of an important, even controversial, intellectual and writer. The chapters take up Gilman's attitudes toward sexuality and queerness; the complex and evolving (and sometimes disturbing) nature of her views on ethnicity, race, and class; her place in US literary and intellectual history, and much more. Our contributors, we are glad to report, do not hit just one or two notes.

The second observation stems very much from Gilman's ethos and productivity: our contributors, we hope, have added considerably to the fields of Gilman, place, feminist, and western studies, and more, but in good Gilman fashion, the work will, and must, continue.

NOTES

1. Gaston Bachelard, *The Poetics of Space*, trans. Maria Jolas (Boston: Beacon Press, 1964), 46–47.

2. Joan Ockman, "*The Poetics of Space* by Gaston Bachelard," *Harvard Design Magazine* 6 (Fall 1998).

3. Bachelard, *Poetics of Space*, 47–48.

4. Ibid., 72.

5. Charlotte Perkins Gilman, "The Yellow Wall-Paper," in *Herland, The Yellow Wall-Paper, and Selected Writings*, ed. Denise D. Knight (New York: Penguin, 1999), 167, 182.

WORKS CITED

Bachelard, Gaston. *The Poetics of Space*. Translated by Maria Jolas. Boston: Beacon Press, 1964.

Gilman, Charlotte Perkins. "The Yellow Wall-Paper." In *Herland, The Yellow Wall-Paper, and Selected Writings*, edited by Denise D. Knight, 166–82. New York: Penguin, 1999.

Ockman, Joan. "*The Poetics of Space* by Gaston Bachelard." *Harvard Design Magazine* 6 (Fall 1998).

I

Geography and Biography

Places in and of Gilman's Life

Charlotte Perkins Gilman and the US West

Jennifer S. Tuttle and Gary Scharnhorst

Charlotte Perkins Gilman is usually considered an easterner, the child of such distinguished families as the Beechers, the Perkinses, and the Westcotts. After all, she lived most of her life in the Northeast: in New England, where she spent her first twenty-eight years (largely in Hartford, Connecticut, and Providence, Rhode Island); in New York City, where she resided between 1900 and 1922; and in Norwich, Connecticut, where she lived from 1922 until 1934. But this long residence in the East belies a more complex regional affiliation. Certainly Gilman spent some nomadic years "at large," proudly claiming no fixed address.[1] More significant, she resided for a time in California: in Pasadena, Oakland, and San Francisco, where she lived off and on for eight years and visited on multiple occasions. She repaired to the West during two crises in her life: in 1885, in the midst of severe depression; and again in 1888, after her failed rest cure and as her marriage to Charles Walter Stetson was unraveling. She returned to the West in 1934 to be near her daughter and grandchildren in Pasadena as she was dying of cancer. The US West, particularly California, was significant to Gilman both biographically and intellectually, and its impact on her work merits greater critical scrutiny.

Recovering Gilman's affiliations with and relationship to the West complicates prevailing views of her as an easterner and yields a more accurate picture of her self-construction as an author. It also provides new and compelling contexts in which to interpret her writing and her social philosophy. For beyond its healthy climate and geographical distance from the oppressive duties of the East (as she described it), the West appealed to Gilman because of its supposed association with progressive values, the vanguard of women's suffrage, and new possibilities for social organization. It was no accident that the West was the region in which Gilman launched her career as the poet of the socialist movement known as Nationalism and found her voice as an author. Hence the West's preponderance in Gilman's creative output as a laboratory for social experimentation and a setting for utopian plots. We advocate here, then, a more expansive conception of Gilman's relation to place through illustrating how extensively and inextricably the West figures in her life and work. Understanding Gilman through this lens also makes possible a new reading of her best-known utopia, *Herland*, that ties the novel to a western locale.

Acknowledging the ways that the West informed and enabled Gilman's career as an early feminist philosopher has the power to shift our frames of reference in Gilman studies. In general, recognizing the western origins of Gilman's utopian texts and reformist ideals further elucidates her leadership in the turn-of-the-century US women's movement and therefore the West's role in shaping the movement's intellectual underpinnings. Finally, this work can further illuminate western literary studies and critical western regionalism, where the recovery of women's cultural production is still underway and where, despite promising and innovative recent work, a masculinist orientation still tends to remain unchanged.

Although a significant portion of Gilman's writing is implicitly or explicitly about the West, only one of her more than twenty-one-hundred published poems, stories, and essays contains the word *West* in its title, and that work illuminates her association of the region with progressive social change. "Woman Suffrage and the West" was published in the *Kansas Suffrage Reveille* in 1897; the single extant original copy of this essay resides in the archives of the Kansas Historical Society. Gilman was on a lecture tour in Kansas when it appeared. As she remarked in the article, the first four states to recognize the right of women to vote and run for public office, all between 1869 and 1896, were in the West: Wyoming, Colorado, Idaho, and Utah.

"It is a significant fact that the first state to adopt full woman suffrage [Wyoming] was a western one," Gilman wrote, "after long experience of its advantage in territorial government; and that all the three following states to set their women free are also western, and are in close geographical relation." (The first nine states to pass suffrage laws were, significantly, in the West.) In a comment that betrayed her tendency toward racial essentialism, she averred, "In China you should allow a thousand years for a new idea to take root and not look for a crop for another thousand. It takes longer to move an Oriental than a European, longer to move a European than an American, and in America the westerner moves faster than his grandfather 'back east.' . . . As American women are given higher place—have won higher place—than any women on earth, so the women of the west stand higher than any in America."[2] Seventeen years later, in her essay "Why Nevada Should Win Its Suffrage Campaign in November," she reiterated that "the Southern and Eastern states" are "the least progressive of the whole country" and called for "a 'Solid West' of courage, liberty, and justice—the land that is not afraid of its women."[3] That is, Gilman shared the conventional opinion, epitomized by Frederick Jackson Turner's essay "The Significance of the Frontier in American History," that western Americans, in her case especially western American women, were the most progressive people in the world. She was a believer not only in American exceptionalism but also in western American exceptionalism.

The Turnerian bent of Gilman's work undoubtedly was informed by her biographical experience, in which the West served as a zone of healing, regeneration, and intellectual progress. Although S. Weir Mitchell's rest cure failed to restore Gilman to health in 1887 after her now infamous nervous breakdown, she twice recovered her health in the 1880s by self-administering what modern critics Barbara Will and Jennifer S. Tuttle have called the West Cure, which Mitchell often prescribed for men, a treatment that embraced the masculine prerogatives of freedom and independence and contributed to the West's preeminence as a popular site for health tourism. Like Mitchell's West Cure practitioners, Gilman healed and revitalized herself in the West repeatedly throughout her long life. The West, not rest, rejuvenated her.[4] Echoing promotional language commonly used about the region, Gilman opined of her first journey to Pasadena in 1885, "This place did not seem like earth, it was paradise." Her use of a religious trope to describe the West was quite deliberate; in her poem "In Mother-Time" she touted California as a prelapsarian Eden, "the Garden of the Lord"—a characterization that would fuel her portrayals of the West throughout her career. During her first use of the West Cure, she reported, she recovered her health "so fast" that she "was taken for a vigorous young girl." When she returned to Providence and to her husband and her daughter after several months, however, she relapsed. Soon after welcoming his wife home from Pasadena, Walter observed that "it is pretty hard to see what real good her winter's sojourn did her." Gilman herself confirmed, "I saw the stark fact that I was well while away [in the West] and sick while at home [in the East]."[5]

In 1888, after Mitchell failed to help her, Gilman separated from her husband, left Providence with her daughter in tow, and moved west to California, where she lived until 1895. This move signified her embrace "of the principles of the West Cure not as a temporary salve, but as a way of life." Coincident with (and, as she suggested, enabled by) the move to California, Gilman inaugurated her career as a professional writer, lecturer, reformer, and activist. "Before that there was no assurance of serious work," she wrote in her autobiography. "To California . . . I owe much. Its calm sublimity of contour, richness of color, profusion of flowers, fruit, and foliage, and the steady peace of its climate were meat and drink to me. . . . Everywhere there was beauty, and the nerve-rest of steady windless weather." Her husband Walter, who traveled West in vain seeking a reconciliation, confirmed in a letter to R. S. Stetson in July 1889, "It is astonishing how much she has changed for the better in every way. She never was so well or so calm. She is doing lots of good work and making no end of friends without any effort."[6] During these years Gilman became a member and the president of the Pacific Coast Women's Press Association and edited its magazine, the *Impress*. She helped organize a pair of Women's Congresses in the Bay Area and became active in the women's club movement. Gilman was mentored by Charles Fletcher Lummis, the editor of *Land of Sunshine* magazine (later called *Out West*), and regularly published work in his magazine as well as in the *Pacific Monthly*, the *Pacific Rural Press*, the *California Nationalist*, the *San Francisco Star*, the San Francisco *Wasp*, the *San Francisco Call*, the *Oakland Enquirer*, the *Stockton Mail*, and the *Californian Illustrated Magazine*. The first edition of *In This Our World*, a collection of her poetry and her first important book, was issued by an Oakland press in 1893, and this was followed by a second American edition issued by a San Francisco press in 1895.

It is understandable, then, that Gilman associated California (and the West in general) with health, freedom, beauty, and a potential for change; it was the site of a personal and professional transformation, inspiring and enabling her creative and intellectual work.[7] "Almost all of my descriptive poetry is about California," she allowed. "To this day, when in that lovely country, the verses come of themselves."[8] She wrote lyrics with such titles as "Thanksgiving Hymn for California," "Christmas Carol for Los Angeles," and "Our San Francisco Climate." She wrote "Powell Street," the free-verse dramatic monologue of a passenger on the Powell Street cable car in San Francisco. A good deal of this work conveys a promotional tone and is written from the perspective of a blue-blooded New Englander making herself at home in the Edenic West.

"Thanksgiving Hymn for California," which first appeared in the *Pacific Monthly*, imagines that the poet and the reader share a Puritan ancestry, which survived legendary hardship in that first New World settlement and now enjoys "a land all sunny with gold,— / A land by the summer sea; / . . . Comfort, and plenty, and beauty, and peace, / From the mountains down to the sea," In "The Changeless Year—Southern California," which appeared in *Harper's Bazar* in the midst of winter, the speaker beckons: "Come here, where the West lieth golden / In the light of an infinite sun, / Where Summer doth Winter embolden / Till they reign here as one!" Gilman's poetic boosterism continued well beyond her departure from California in 1895. "An Invitation," for example, encourages the beleaguered eastern reader, "tired of the doctoring and nursing, / Of the 'sickly winters' and the pocket pills," to come West.[9]

Despite her cultural and familial allegiances with New England, Gilman wrote frequently and satirically on eastern snobbery. Take, for example, "Our East":

> Our East, long looking backward over sea,
> In loving study of what used to be,
> Has grown to treat our West with the same scorn
> England has had for us since we were born.
>
> You'd think to hear this Eastern judgment hard
> The West was just New England's back yard!
> That all the West was made for, last and least,
> Was to raise pork and wheat to feed the East!
>
> A place to travel in, for rest and health,
> A place to struggle in and get the wealth, . . .
> Our Western acres, curving to the sun,
> The Western strength whereby our work is done.[10]

Gilman expressed the same point more succinctly in the epigraph to chapter 5 of *The Crux*: "Old England thinks our country / Is a wilderness at best— / And small New England thinks the same / Of the large free-minded West." However hackneyed such lyrics may be, Gilman's western writings in general were no more or less didactic than her other work. (Even "The Yellow Wall-Paper," after all, was written while she was living in Pasadena.) What is significant is her repeated self-assertion as a champion of the West and that much of her writing was fueled and shaped by her life there. Throughout her life, her verse expressed such praise of the region. The final poem she is known to have composed pays homage to the California Grapevine, the "long and winding" mountain pass leading to the "paradise" of California.[11]

While the West inspired Gilman's poetry, it also served as the stage for her rise to fame.[12] Gilman launched her public career by writing and speaking around California on behalf of Nationalism, the socialist movement inspired by Edward Bellamy's 1888 utopian romance *Looking Backward*, which contrasted the class conflict and cutthroat competition of the Gilded Age with the commonwealth of the imagined twenty-first century. In this utopia all industries have been nationalized (hence the name of the movement), and all citizens enjoy equal economic and political rights. Female readers were attracted by the promise of the abolition of sexual slavery, and from the beginning Nationalism thrived in California even more than in its native New England. About sixty-five Nationalist Clubs had been organized in the state by November 1890, according to the movement's publication.

Gilman noted, "California is a state peculiarly addicted to swift enthusiasms. . . . In 1890 the countryside was deeply stirred" by *Looking Backward*. She joined the movement, and her poem "Similar Cases," composed in March of that year, was published in the leading Nationalist magazine and won her immediate celebrity. William Dean Howells, the most prominent American man of letters at the time, wrote to her, "We have nothing since [James Russell Lowell's] Biglow Papers half so good for a good cause," and Lester Ward hailed the poem as "the most telling answer that has ever been made" to Social Darwinians. Even Gilman's bête noir, Ambrose Bierce, conceded in his weekly column in the *San Francisco Examiner* that "Similar Cases" was a "delightful satire upon those of us who have not the happiness to think that progress of humanity toward the light is subject to sudden and lasting acceleration." By the summer of 1890, Gilman had begun to lecture regularly around central and southern California on such topics as "What Is Nationalism?," "Nationalism and the Virtues," "Nationalism and the Arts," "Nationalism and Love," "Nationalism and Religion," and "Why We Want Nationalism." "It was pleasant work," she later recalled. "I had plenty to say and the Beecher faculty for saying it."[13] Soon after joining the lecture circuit, Gilman also helped organize a Social Purity society in Pasadena—which, in her view, was allied with the Nationalist cause. From the beginning, her feminism was inextricable from her advocacy of socialist principles, women's sexual education and self-determination, and eugenics. Through her activism she met Edwin Markham and other progressives. More than any other figure active in the movement, Gilman built her career by espousing its platform while she lived in the West, and to the end of her life Nationalism was the source of her utopianism.[14]

For many months after she left California in the summer of 1895, Gilman continued to position herself within the state's literary and reform establishment. In 1896 she attended a suffrage convention in Washington, DC, as well as the International Socialist and Labor Congress in London. On both occasions she registered as a delegate from California. In February 1896 she expressed the hope to return eventually to California—"my dear Southland"— to live. Two years later she went so far as to berate Lummis for not including her in his New League for Literature and the West, a joint-stock company of "recognized Western writers who would be listed on the masthead of *Land of Sunshine*." Melody Graulich has rightly labeled this an "insist[ent] claim" to the title of "Western writer," and it was effective: Lummis included Gilman's name in the magazine's next issue, formalizing her status as a California writer and legitimizing her as an authority on the state's curative and progressive potential. Although her career eventually drew her far afield from California, she arguably never let go of her desire to associate herself with the West—this despite her deep bitterness at her harsh treatment by the San Francisco press and Bay Area society as a result of her very public divorce and the scandal over her parenting arrangements. As late as January 1935, seven months before her death, she wrote Alice Stone Blackwell that "I love California, and this beautiful city [Pasadena] is more like home to me than any place on earth."[15]

Gilman's attraction to the West is evident as well in her tastes as a reader: she was a fan of western novels, just as she was fond of detective stories. Certainly she read the western writings of Jack London, Hamlin Garland, and Helen Hunt Jackson, including *A Century of Dishonor* and *Ramona*. She also read Owen Wister's bestseller *The Virginian* immediately upon its publication in 1902, and her copy of the novel survives among her books in the Walter Stetson Chamberlin Collection.[16] She even references it in her autobiography, where she both highlights the western's masculinist orientation and claims for herself the West's curative powers that Wister reserved for men (a gesture she had made in her fiction as well). Discussing "a ball" she attended in Utah in 1885—and archly describing the social milieu as one in which "the leading lady . . . was the wife of a railroad conductor"—she compares the entertainment to a similar scene in Wister's novel: "The bedrooms were all occupied by sleeping babies, as described in *The Virginian*." This episode in Wister's novel is certainly not a crucial moment in its plot, yet Gilman "singles [it] out for special mention."[17] The reason, we believe, may be explained through consideration of its intersections with her own work. In Wister's novel the hero and his partner, Lin McLean, move around the sleeping babies and dress them in each other's clothes so than none of the families leave with the right children at the end of the evening. Predictably, this infuriates the mothers, who are thirsty for revenge. The hero implicates McLean in this "crime against society," and a search party sets out to capture him but instead finds a sarcastic and incendiary note that Lin has pegged to a tree: "God bless our home."[18] What the hero regards as a mere prank becomes nothing less than a threat to the sanctity of the domestic sphere.

Gilman invokes this scene in her trademark superior tone "because, by permitting his hero to disrupt a [figurative] kindergarten, Wister mocked the practice of efficient and cooperative child care" that had been growing in popularity since the late nineteenth century and that "was a centerpiece of her reform agenda."[19] She had advocated shared nurseries, or "baby gardens," in such books as *Concerning Children* (which she had published in 1900, two years before *The Virginian* appeared) and *The Home: Its Work and Influence* (1903) and in dozens of magazine articles. There was no reason for her to reply directly to Wister's antediluvian views in her autobiography (the bulk of which was composed years later, in the 1920s) because she had already responded to them many times before in her fiction.

Although she vacillated on the question of whether to associate herself with California literary culture, Gilman undeniably *was* the author of a sheaf of western stories, through which she engaged with the themes and conventions of western writing at the time. "In her art no less than in her life, . . . Gilman revised the traditional pattern of male flight to the geographical frontier." This modification of the formula was a constant undercurrent in her western fiction. Her heroines, unlike Huck Finn, do not merely "light out for the territory" but struggle there for freedom and independence.[20] As early as 1891, in "The Giant Wistaria," Gilman related a tale, set in the late eighteenth century, of an unwed mother who escapes censure in England by fleeing west to New England. (As western historians have long understood, "the West" is a relative term. New England was "the West" to British colonists.) The tormented mother in "The Giant Wistaria" has landed on the "luxuriant" frontier and yearns to walk in the "green fields" of the virgin land, although as the result of her father's persecutions she ultimately fails to realize the promise of liberty and self-reliance. Instead, she presumably drowns her child and hides in a cellar until she too dies.[21]

In the western stories Gilman wrote for the *Forerunner* about twenty years later, her leading women were more successful. It is telling that of all of her western stories (and we include *Herland* in this category), only one was set in a western state that had not yet granted women the right to vote: *What Diantha Did* (1909-10), originally serialized in the *Forerunner* a year before California became a suffrage state. Of the others, *The Crux* (1911) is set in Colorado (which adopted women's suffrage in 1893) and "Girls and Land" (1915) in Washington (which became a women's suffrage state in 1910). All the other tales are set in California. Gilman located her western stories only in the most progressive states in what she believed was the most progressive region in the world: the West was a literal and figurative setting both for Gilman's own quest for self-determination and for mobilizing her vision of human progress.

A recurring motif appears in all these tales: the West as a laboratory for social experimentation and women's concomitant self-realization. These stories are populated by white women, often hailing from New England, who travel west to find health, independence, and an opportunity to contribute meaningfully to the commonwealth. In 1898 Gilman had forecast this work to Lummis: "I have been hovering for years over a series of little stories all set in Pasadena—not of the scenery, nor the history, nor the local character, but of the new life which that great country can so well let grow at last."[22] (She set these stories in California, but also elsewhere in the far West.)

A western setting was a key element of her didactic project, in which she urged social reform through literary exemplars. The enterprising heroine of *What Diantha Did*, for example, establishes a restaurant, a cooked-food delivery service, a cleaning service, a cluster of kitchenless homes, and an apartment hotel in the pastoral town of Orchardina in southern California, modeled on Pasadena. It is a success story in which Diantha rises, if not from rags to riches, then from maid to manager. Diantha's California is a land of opportunity, "good for nervous complaints, too."[23]

In "Girls and Land" the heroine grows up in the state of Washington, where she founds a "chain of R[est] & P[leasure] Clubs" for women. "The idea spread," we're told. "Tacoma took it up, and Portland, Bellingham, Everett and Spokane." Similarly, in "Bee Wise" (1913) Gilman depicted a pair of progressive communities in California where, as her heroine declares, "We can make a little Eden!" In "Dr. Clair's Place" (1915) Gilman described a female physician's treatment for neurasthenia in sharp contrast to Mitchell's rest cure. At a "psycho-sanatorium" situated on the "southern face of the Sierra Madres," the doctor prescribes a regimen of work and amusement. Her patients weave, read, swim, dance, and garden. In "My Poor Aunt" (1913) the heroine aspires to a literary life upon attaining her majority, but her mother and an aunt conspire to marry her to the first eligible suitor who happens along until, at a propitious moment, another aunt who owns a western newspaper arrives to offer her a job and freedom.[24] In "Joan's Defender" (1916) a nine-year-old girl lives with her aunt and uncle for two years on their California ranch and returns to her eastern home "a very different looking child from the one who left it so mournfully. She was much taller, larger, with a clear color, a light, firm step, a ready smile" and "no shadow of timidity." And in "Fulfilment" (1914) the self-made heroine immigrates to California at the age of twenty-one and, as she boasts, prospers in the West: "I'm a hundred per cent stronger and more efficient than I used to be. I've trained—years and years of it—in sunlight and mountain air. It's not just strength, but skill. I can climb mountains, ride, shoot, fence, row, swim, play golf, [play] tennis, [play] billiards, dance like a youngster—or a professional. I'm more *alive*, literally, than I was at twenty. . . . I belong to clubs, classes, societies. I'm a citizen, too—I can vote now." Lest there be any doubt that she has been rejuvenated by moving to the West, the story ends as a character asks, "Which is the quickest route to Southern California?"[25]

The most telling and most fully developed example of such a plot appears in her novel *The Crux*, wherein Gilman rewrote the formulaic western from the eastern belle's point of view. As Tuttle has noted, seven years earlier Gilman had published an essay that was in effect a concise summary of the novel in the *Woman's Journal* under the title "Woman's 'Manifest Destiny.'" In it Gilman echoed Horace Greeley's purported admonition to the "young man" to "go west and grow up with the country"—except that in this case, of course, she urged the young woman to go to the woman-hungry West.²⁶ "Why do not the women who really believe that marriage is their mission," she asked, "go forth in bands of maiden emigration to the frontier, where lonely men grow hard and bad for lack of 'women's influence'?" These women could have their pick of suitors—according to Gilman, in the West "intelligent, educated women" could both vote and exercise the prerogative of sexual selection and so change the "character of several States and territories. . . . Let the conscientious surplus of women go West," she concluded. "They would carry benefit to the lands adopted."²⁷

In *The Crux* Gilman advanced an alternative tradition of women's western writing similar to that of contemporaries such as B. M. Bower, Willa Cather, Caroline Lockhart, and Vingie E. Roe, who also could be said to have adopted and subverted the "formula western."²⁸ Just as the generic western can be considered "a cowboy novel without cows," Scharnhorst posits, Gilman writes "a western . . . without a male hero." Morton Elder, the character who might have filled that role, is instead a rake and syphilitic coward. Nor does Gilman's western feature either adventure or a compelling love story, staples of the formula. The fair New England heroine, Vivian Lane, like Wister's Molly Stark Wood, has certainly inherited "a store of quiet strength from some Pilgrim Father or Mother." If Molly is "Wister's type" of new woman, Scharnhorst argues, "then Vivian is Gilman's. . . . Molly and the Virginian eventually marry" and bring closure to Wister's plot through their anticipated Anglo-Saxon offspring; however, "Vivian eventually breaks off her romance with Morton Elder when she discovers he is afflicted" with a sexually transmitted disease.²⁹

Her doing so reflects not only her liberated, newly enlightened status but also her recognition of her duty to a eugenic ideal in support of which she must save herself for a more suitable mate with whom she may "save the race." Here and elsewhere in Gilman's work (and in the public discourse of her time, we should add), the term *race* was ambiguous; there was a certain amount of slippage, telling in and of itself, between *race* as in *human* and race as in *white*. Gilman biographer Cynthia J. Davis nicely summarizes how this problem manifests in Gilman studies. Although it is true that when Gilman used the term *race* she "usually meant 'the human race,' . . . as the years passed, her notions of both 'civilization' and 'race' became less abstractly human and more concretely Anglo-Saxon, and her images of the men and women involved grew uniformly fairer and more European in feature."³⁰ By the *Forerunner* era, especially given her embrace of eugenics, Gilman had begun to shift to the latter scenario. Moreover, she tended to idealize New England in racial and ethnic terms: proud of her own "pure New England stock," she transferred this blue blood to many of the heroines with whom she populated her western stories. Gilman advertised *The Crux* as "a novel along eugenic lines"; it is no accident, then, that Vivian's education and reproductive empowerment—and her new understanding of her duty in that regard—occur in the West.[31]

Certainly both Wister and Gilman presume the white-conquest model of Old West history. As Scharnhorst puts it, "Both the Virginian and Vivian are agents of 'civilization'. . . . They even have similar names—both begin[ning] with a 'Vi' and ending with 'ian,' . . . their names are alliterative and they rhyme. Each of them 'wins' the West, but in distinctively different ways—the Virginian with revolver and rope, Vivian with pencil and pen. Gilman described not a 'regeneration through violence' as in the typical male narrative of the period . . . but a 'regeneration through literacy.'"[32] Tuttle puts it another way: *The Crux* is "a middle-class white woman's answer to the Western"—Wister's in particular. On the suggestion of Dr. Bellair, a female physician, Vivian and a cohort of other women leave New England for Colorado. "Break away now, my dear, and come West," Bellair tells Vivian. "You can get work—start a kindergarten, or something." (Both Molly Wood and Vivian are teachers. "Come out to Colorado with me—and Grow," the doctor insists. "You'll have a thousandfold better opportunities in Colorado than you will here."[33]

As the doctor's surname indicates, the West promises myriad "health benefits to women, . . . and she diagnoses the medical conditions from which the women in New England suffer": "arrested development" and "*arthritis deformans* of the soul." Tuttle argues, "Vivian experiences the kind of personal transformation in the West that Wister had reserved for his male narrator. . . . Vivian's West Cure and new life in Colorado are central to Gilman's plot and are clear rewritings of Molly Wood's role in Wister's Western."[34] "Dr. Bellair's role as the heroine's mentor in Gilman's novel," Scharnhorst notes, "is analogous to the role of Judge Henry in *The Virginian*." Whereas Henry runs a ranch and authorizes the Virginian "to lynch a gang of cattle rustlers, however, Dr. Bellair leads women to a peaceful West" hungry for settlement, where they establish a flourishing, cooperative community epitomized by the boardinghouse.[35] Governed by liberated, educated, independent, and healthy eastern women, the Colorado boardinghouse models the kind of socialized housekeeping that Gilman advocated throughout her career, just as Vivian's new career running a western kindergarten embraces Gilman's vision of socialized child care.

In keeping with their shared Turnerian vision, Scharnhorst notes, "Wister and Gilman depict the West in similarly racialized terms." Like the male-authored western, Gilman's work reinscribes "conventional ideas about race" and western conquest. "Their Wests are dominated by Anglo-Saxons"—Wister once compared cowboys to medieval knights and the gunfight to the joust.[36] Both novels erase the presence of ethnic minorities in the West: Hispanics, African Americans, and Asian Americans do not appear, except for Chinese

American servants in Gilman's work. *The Virginian* mentions a couple of Jewish drummers in passing, and there are some offstage Indians who practice thievery and worse, but Wister's West, like Gilman's, is almost lily-white and nominally Protestant. Tuttle observes that "the reinvigorated 'race' of Americans in Gilman's Edenic West is white . . . and is to be saved and 'improved' by 'clean' New England women—the 'good people' and 'best civilization' Gilman cites in 'Woman's "Manifest Destiny."'" As elsewhere in her work, Gilman thus aligned her support of eugenics with her feminist rhetoric. Gilman's portrayal of the West is intertwined with her belief in Anglo-Saxon superiority and with her project for social reform that was based on that belief.[37] The key to reforming both US culture and the human race, in her view, was the reproductive capacity of empowered, educated white women. The western setting of *The Crux* was ideal for this purpose, combining what Gilman saw as a socially progressive milieu in terms of gender and a Turnerian vision of health, progress, and regeneration.

The model society that Gilman envisions in *The Crux*, like that in much of her other western fiction, can be understood as what Riane Eisler has called a "pragmatopia," a utopia that is "realizable": her western stories offer a blueprint for achieving, as Gilman promised to Lummis, "the new life which that great country [of the West] can so well let grow at last." Judith Allen has noted that Gilman "often locat[ed] her utopian explorations in a treasured topos—the West."[38] In looking broadly at Gilman's reformist fiction, set in the West or elsewhere, Carol Farley Kessler has established that Gilman combines utopian and realistic elements in order to inspire readers to enact her feminist reformist goals. In *The Crux*, white New England women in the West achieve Gilman's ideal of civilization through sexual and reproductive self-determination—exercising the prerogative of sexual selection to choose as mates those men best suited to yield superior, "clean" offspring. Elsewhere in her work, Gilman advocated a similar vision of maternalist feminism, the best-known example being *Herland*, a utopian novel in which an all-female population of "pure stock" has reproduced through parthenogenesis for "two thousand uninterrupted years." Sandra Gilbert and Susan Gubar note, "Divorced from heterosexuality, the private family, and economic dependence, a fully liberated maternal feeling flows through the Amazonian society of Gilman's parthogenetic women" in *Herland*.[39]

Composed while Gilman's address of record was in New York City and published in the *Forerunner*, *Herland* is not conventionally interpreted in relation to the US West; as a utopia, after all, the story is set in "no place"—by definition in an imaginary locale. But recovering the western identification that runs through so much of Gilman's work, and recognizing the centrality of the West (and particularly California) to her vision for social reform, provides an interpretive context that demands we rethink our critical framework for *Herland*. Although we are not arguing here that the novel is actually supposed to take place in California, we do assert that its setting suggests an idealized version of the state, particularly that presented at the 1915 Panama-Pacific International Exposition (PPIE) in San Francisco, a world's fair celebrating the completion of the Panama Canal.[40]

This interpretation overlaps (rather than conflicts) with the suggestion made by some critics that the novel's setting evokes South America: such references, after all, remind readers of the fair's namesake; they also call to mind the fair's centerpiece exhibit—a replica of the canal itself.[41] Understanding the novel's reliance on the PPIE for its sense of place not only expands our understanding of Gilman's western orientation but also illuminates the imperialist strain that runs throughout her social philosophy. Although it partakes of other major strands of Gilman's theory and literary output, *Herland* can and should be read as part of her western body of work.

Herland features a long-isolated society of women and girls who have survived through selective asexual reproduction: only those who can pass on desired characteristics allow themselves to become pregnant, which allows Herlanders to "breed out . . . the lowest types." This lost civilization is discovered by three male explorers who represent a spectrum of masculine attributes and who share assumptions about women and gender that Gilman knew to be typical of her day. Filtering the story through the men's point of view, Gilman critiques their reductive views of women, gender, sexuality, and reproduction, "confront[ing] the real-life intransigence of normative masculinities" that their attitudes represent. Having heard legends of a "strange and terrible 'Woman Land' . . . . where no men lived," the explorers are baffled by the "large-minded women" they encounter who are uniformly lacking in all trappings of femininity. They "had expected hysteria," the narrator admits, "and found a standard of health and vigor" they would not have believed possible.[42] Herland's matriarchal society is harmonious and hygienic, free of sex, desire, war, aggression, and the bugbear of individualism.

Gilman advocated for a world in which women and men reject gender differences in recognition of their common humanity, share power and responsibility, and thus enjoy a cooperative existence, and Herlanders embody a level of maternal achievement that Gilman believed was necessary to achieve this end. The utopian women of Herland exemplify (if taken to an unrealistic extreme) what Gilman called social motherhood, a calling wherein the maternal impulse is mobilized to benefit society as a whole and children are raised by experts in a socialized fashion, in "baby gardens" like those pilloried by Wister. Through long exposure to Herlanders, the narrator, Vandyke Jennings—and through him, Gilman's hoped-for readers—eventually begins to understand that gender is socially constructed and thus malleable; through recognizing the superiority of Herland's way of life, Van, as he is called, comes to recognize some of the flaws in his own (i.e., Gilman's) society.

If this utopia is meant to inspire readers to enact the principles of Gilman's social philosophy, then its western setting is key to the novel's success. The most explicit comparison of Herland to California in the novel is made directly by the narrator, Van: the most liberal of the three men who discover the country and the one most sympathetic to the Herlanders' experiments, he hails from that state. He observes that the climate of Herland, which he describes as "first-rate" and semitropical, "was like that of California, and citrus fruits, figs, and olives grew abundantly." Van's language echoes the promotional tracts that had long been used to lure eastern settlers to the state, and it also contributes to the idealized setting that Gilman constructed for her utopia. The male interlopers describe Herland in language that echoes Gilman's own praise for California: it is "a heavenly country" and "a paradise." Insisting that "there's no country lovelier" than California, Van admits that Herland surpasses it in its well-designed towns. As "a land in a state of perfect cultivation," Herland "looked like an enormous park" with "clean, well-built roads, . . . attractive architecture, . . . [and] ordered beauty." The men marvel at the "towering trees [that] were under as careful cultivation as so many cabbages." The "perfect road" is well designed, "with every curve and grade and gutter as perfect as if it were Europe's best. . . . Everything was beauty, order, perfect cleanness."[43]

This language of perfection and carefully cultivated nature is amplified in Van's labeling of the Herlanders as "lady Burbanks" for their meticulous breeding of cats; here he alludes to California horticulturalist Luther Burbank, who was known for his application of Darwinian principles to the breeding of edible and decorative plants. From here it is no great leap for the reader to learn that Herlanders were of "Aryan stock" and had bred themselves to a "new race." Having reproduced in isolation by parthenogenesis for two millennia, the inhabitants of Herland "had no enemies; they themselves were all sisters and friends; the land was fair before them, and a great Future . . . [had formed] itself in their minds."[44]

Although this idealized portrait of Herland is obviously what Gilman considered utopian and was clearly influenced by her love affair with California, it has, as we indicated above, an even more specific referent. Upon entering Herland for the first time, the three men exclaim that it is "like an Exposition. . . . It's too pretty to be true." It is no accident that this comparison to an exposition occurs in the novel's second installment in the *Forerunner,* in February 1915—the same month that the PPIE opened in what is now the marina district on San Francisco Bay (see figure 1.1). In order to grasp the full

Figure 1.1. Grounds of the 1915 Panama Pacific International Exposition, featuring the Tower of Jewels and Festival Hall (PAM PPIE Collection, GOGA 22023; courtesy Golden Gate National Recreation Area, Park Archives)

significance of Gilman's allusions to the fair, it will be helpful to briefly tour some of its highlights.[45]

The exposition championed what it proclaimed as San Francisco's phoenix-like reemergence after the 1906 earthquake and fire. Typically for a world's fair, it presented visitors with a "sanitized" and "idealized consumer city," a model of innovation and beauty in architecture and urban planning that little resembled the real city (and nation) beyond. This idealized San Francisco (and, by extension, California) was portrayed as the culmination of the preceding century's territorial expansion as well as the gateway to extending US influence abroad. As "the apotheosis of empire on the Pacific Rim," the fair paid tribute to both "the Aryan advance to the West" and an emerging "internationalist nationalism."[46] In part this vision was articulated through works of visual art featuring stock characters in the drama of Manifest Destiny.

Some of the sculptures created for the fair, for example, clearly followed the common attitude of celebrating "the advance of civilization into the new American Eden." Solon Hamilton Borglum's statue *The Pioneer: A Reverie* depicted this central figure in American mythology, tellingly described by Gray A. Brechin as "an archetype of 'the race' advancing westward with his rifle erect."

Figure 1.2. Alexander Stirling Calder, Leo Lentilli, and Frederick G. R. Roth, *The Nations of the West*, 1915, with Calder's "Mother of Tomorrow" at the center (BANC PIC 1959.087-ALB. V. 3, p. 108; courtesy of the Bancroft Library, University of California, Berkeley)

This statue was paired with James Earle Fraser's *The End of the Trail*, featuring the long-familiar Vanishing American whom the artist characterized as standing for "a weaker race . . . steadily pushed to the wall by a stronger [one]." Yet another sculpture, *The Nations of the West*, by Alexander Stirling Calder, Leo Lentilli, and Frederick G. R. Roth, assembled the entire cast: a white man on horseback, Native Americans, trappers, farmers, a prairie schooner with oxen, and a white pioneer woman at the center dubbed the "Mother of Tomorrow" (see figure 1.2).[47]

Many of the sculptures at the fair "embodi[ed] . . . the concept of racial progress [that] permeated the . . . Exposition as a whole," a fact made explicit by the preponderance of educational displays and scholarly meetings at the fair having to do with so-called race betterment, or eugenics, and by the fair's commodification of fertile white womanhood.[48] At the fair as elsewhere, then, US imperialism went hand in hand with the race- and gender-coded discourses of progress and domination, in which both men and women played important roles.

An important function of these sculptures, of course, was to put "into grandiose historical context" the exposition's most prominent aim: to hail the

Figure 1.3. Perham W. Nahl, "The Thirteenth Labor of Hercules," PPIE promotional poster (Markwyn, *Empress San Francisco*, plate 7)

completion of the Panama Canal and with it the achievement of "U.S. hemispheric domination."[49] The centerpiece of the fair was a replica of the canal itself, located in the sixty-five acre Joy Zone. A $250,000 project, the feted miniature canal represented the apex of the fair's more generalized celebration of American technological innovation, from the steam locomotive, the automobile, and the airplane to high-tension electrical current and transcontinental telephone service.

As marvels of "time-space compression," these new technologies "mediate[d]," as Brown has put it, "between a residual and an emergent, prosthetic mode of imperialist perception." The iconic photograph of Teddy Roosevelt perched "at the controls of the Bucyrus shovel at Pedro Miguel, the startlingly white American in control of, but miniaturized by, the gargantuan, dark prosthetic machine" used to carve the canal announces this tension, for the faded image of Roosevelt's now-residual Rough Riders surely still lingered in the American imagination. "America's new empire," writes Moore, "was recreated in miniature" by the canal exhibit and the fair more generally.[50]

The canal's symbolic importance to US assertions of power on the world stage is made clear in the official poster of the fair, Perham Nahl's "The Thirteenth Labor of Hercules" (see figure 1.3). The poster features a hypermasculine nude colossus "thrusting apart," as the fair's official historian put it, "the continental barrier at Panama to let the world through to the Pacific." This image certainly partakes of the sexualized violence that is central to westward expansion and to imperialist discourse in general. "Embod[ying] a dialectic of the national and the international," the poster presents an "imperialist physique": it invokes the strenuous masculinity advocated by Wister, Mitchell, and the young Roosevelt in service of a newer, mechanized, eugenic form of masculine embodiment.[51]

Sarah J. Moore describes it succinctly: Nahl's Hercules combines "the history of the United States' taming of the frontier and its imperialist future, . . . offer[ing] visual evidence of the inevitability of American progress." Like Hercules, the exposition itself embodied the transition in the US national imagination from a Turnerian model of continental expansion to a vision of unbounded American influence made possible by the opening of an "imperial frontier."[52]

Just as Gilman appropriated and intervened in the masculinist discourse of the US West, her writing also makes clear her familiarity with the cultural function and significance of world's fairs like the PPIE; as we argue here, Gilman mobilized the fair's eugenicist, imperialist discourses to advance her own vision of social reform, rejecting the prevailing Herculean model for one favoring white women's central role. Gilman recognized the utopian, didactic nature of world's fairs, which rendered them an ideal setting for visionary work such as *Herland*. Gilman's innovative proposals for domestic architecture and urban planning underlay model societies in both her fiction and her nonfiction on social reform; in an essay in the same issue of the *Forerunner* wherein Van likens Herland to an exposition, Gilman hopefully remarked, "Since the World's Fair at Chicago in 1893, we have had our dream cities. Soon we can have them real." She was alluding to the Columbian Exposition, the so-called White City along the lakefront in Chicago.[53] For Gilman, as for others in her time, world's fairs were a foretaste of utopia.

In the coming months, as *Herland*'s installments continued to appear in the *Forerunner*, Gilman visited the PPIE. She shared her impressions of the fair in the magazine's May issue; significantly, her essay "The Gorgeous Exposition" was printed so that it immediately preceded that issue's installment of *Herland*. Gilman gloried in the "dream city," built "on one of the loveliest sites in all the world." Her central concern in the essay was to maximize the fair's potential for "social education": "the human race," she asserted, "is *a stock to be improved!*" The fair has the potential to model "a clean well-ordered world," which, she argued, could be achieved through both a cultivation of beauty and a deployment of "scientific ingenuity" such as that exemplified in the canal replica, "a wonder of relief-map work and marvelous mechanics."[54] The fair's official historian expressed the aims of the PPIE in terms that could apply equally, in every respect, to Gilman's agenda in *Herland*. The exposition, he averred, "will generate fresh ambitions, awaken new motives, and give that practical turn to thought which brings the vision and the dream into the realm of reality, and directs them to the service of human welfare."[55]

The feats of engineering that Gilman praised in her review of the fair "mark the utopian vision of the times, that humans had control over the environment and could manipulate it at will with the aid of technology and science"; the "race betterment" movement similarly "supported a utopian vision that both nature and nurture could be manipulated by humans." In his cultural history of the fair, Alexander Missal explores how early twentieth-century writers, artists, and policymakers, inspired (like Gilman) by Bellamy's *Looking Backward*, transformed the "Canal Zone . . . into an American utopia" in their works, a tendency concretized in the fair itself. Although Missal does not include *Herland* in his analysis, Gilman's novel exemplifies many aspects of his thesis: "the expansionists' program" that he describes "was based on the decidedly modern, neo-Lamarckian belief that bodies, people, and nations could be remade in an evolutionary, transformative, and ultimately technological act."[56] Gilman departed from this program primarily, of course, in her deployment of gender, for although a powerful and authoritative masculine ideal was central to this expansionist discourse, Gilman explicitly repudiated this patriarchal model in *Herland* as primitive and passé, asserting instead that the new society could be achieved only through the maternalist feminism outlined above.

Bridget Bennett frames this repudiation in Gilman's novel as a parody of popular tales featuring male adventurers "in contemporary literature and journalism." Noting *Herland*'s appearance in the same year as the PPIE, Bennett highlights the ways that the canal exhibit invoked recent advances in aviation to signal "the possession of land and of a land- and water-based colonial dominance," for it "presented the visitor . . . with what appeared to be an aerial view of" the canal zone. In Bennett's reading, Gilman used the male interlopers' initial flyover of Herland, along with the later scene in which the Herlanders prevent their escape by encasing their plane in neatly sewn cloth, to "parody . . . masculine adventure stories" and "subver[t] . . . colonial myths" in which the airplane represents "masculine and imperial values" that "appropriate[ed] . . . technology by and for patriarchy." Rather than noting Herland's likeness to the fair itself, Bennett argues that the land (as part of Gilman's parody of the men's "project[ed] . . . fantasies") is "figured as the gigantic body of a woman, fertile, nurturing and unknown and thrilling," much as the masculinist discourse of Manifest Destiny relied on a "virgin land" ripe for mastery. As such, *Herland* "should be read as the antithesis to Hercules[;] . . . not precisely virgin," Herland is "a womb-like kindergarten, a gigantic and fertile place filled with women and female children who make a cult of maternity and celebrate motherhood."[57]

Bennett's analysis of Herland's geography and her reading of the novel as parody are persuasive and can certainly be understood in tandem with Gilman's appropriation of the formula western in *The Crux*. As Kristin Carter-Sanborn rightly points out, however, the "resistance" of the Herlanders to being colonized by the men belies "an imperializing tendency within the world of Herland itself," to which we have alluded here. Carter-Sanborn notes the close correspondence of Gilman's utopian aims "to those of American political discourse during the era of U.S. hemispheric domination, exemplified by American interventions in Cuba, the Philippines, and Panama"; "Gilman fully appropriates the American 'masculine' colonial fantasy for her own tale of the white imperial mother."[58]

Like Gilman's other work on the West, *Herland* exemplifies white, native-born women's "double positioning" in relation to conquest and empire: excluded or objectified by masculinist narratives, such women are nonetheless implicated in and benefit from the imperial project. Gilman, like other reformers and feminists of her day, mobilized her own such project for the "Mothers of Tomorrow" concretized in Calder, Lentilli, and Roth's statue *The Nations of the West*. If, as Moore suggests, the fair's canal exhibit had a "self-conscious pedagogical function," inviting viewers "to cast an imperial gaze over the landscape," then the model society so didactically conjured in *Herland* surely invites such a vision of the future—to be realized not with Herculean prosthetics such as the rifle or the Bucyrus shovel but through empowered white motherhood (see figure 1.4). Herlanders, having mastered the reproductive technology of parthenogenesis, eschew individualism for the collective good: as "Mother[s] of a Race that is judged in terms of the racial purity of an Aryan stock," they are meant to lead the world by eugenic example.[59]

In the view of many promoters of the PPIE, then, "Americans were destined to remake the world . . . and would do so beginning in California"; Gilman proceeded exactly in this fashion. In *Herland* and the other *Forerunner* stories set in the West, Gilman "posed her most detailed visions of new sexual and reproductive arrangements required to anchor the new human world" for which she advocated. Recognizing the western elements of *Herland's* setting and reading the novel as part of Gilman's body of work set in the West are necessary for a full grasp of the novel's reformist aims and mechanisms. In general, reading *Herland* in this way further illuminates the western American exceptionalism that not only fueled Gilman's utopian and pragmatopian work but also shaped her role as the "leading intellectual in the women's movement" at the turn of the last century.[60]

A typical observation was made by Nora Stanton (Blatch) Barney, the granddaughter of Elizabeth Cady Stanton and a 1905 graduate in civil engineering from Cornell University, who wrote of her "college days" that Gilman's early manifesto "'Women and Economics' was to our young souls like a beacon to a

Figure 1.4. Promotional postcard for the PPIE signaling the imperial potential of fertile white womanhood (Jennifer S. Tuttle personal collection)

ship. How far and immeasurably in advance of her times [Gilman] was." Gail Bederman writes, "From 1898 to the mid-1910s, Gilman was the most prominent feminist theorist in America. . . . No woman of her time wrote with more insight about the very real barriers white women faced in their quest to participate productively in the world outside their homes. Few proposed more sweeping and innovative reforms to make that participation possible. Probably no feminist theorist of her day was more influential or convinced more American women to embrace the cause of women's advancement." If, as Rebecca Mead has argued, historical accounts of the US women's movement have not accounted for the realities and contributions of the western United States, then recognizing how the West shaped and fueled Gilman's intellectual leadership of that movement will surely be of value.[61]

Attention to Gilman's western orientation can also contribute to the important work ahead for critics of western literatures. Krista Comer has recently called for feminist scholarship in western studies, including a variety of texts; claiming Gilman for this field will contribute to this effort. How, for example, might we read Gilman alongside the "Anglo expatriate women" whom Lois Rudnick has argued viewed the West as a land of "utopian promise"?[62] Melody Graulich, who has insightfully compared Gilman with Mary Austin, models in her work how critics might undertake the project that Comer calls for: "redirecting a critical regionalism informed by gender." It is noteworthy how Gilman's writing both appropriates and challenges a western masculinist regional orientation—what Comer calls the "Stegnerian spatial field" that has "enable[d]" so many male authors "to conceive of themselves *as* writers, enable[d] them to write out their own relationships to western history, mythology, gender relations, the environment, and, significantly, to national literary culture at large." Reading Gilman's utopian writing through a western lens may also contribute to recent critical efforts in postwestern studies to "work against a narrowly conceived regionalism . . . that restricts western cultures . . . to some predetermined entity with static borders and boundaries."[63]

Within Gilman studies, attention to issues of place might enhance a biographical interpretation of Gilman's work for critics who are so inclined. How is it relevant, for example, that Gilman was residing in California—not only visiting the PPIE in San Francisco but also spending time at Las Casitas resort in the Sierra Madre—in early 1915 when she composed part of *Herland*?[64] We have attempted here to highlight the importance of the West to Gilman's life and work, suggesting, in fact, that reorienting her in this way is necessary for an accurate understanding of her contributions. But place has meaning beyond the purely geographical; we argue as well for greater critical attention to the material and literary contexts of Gilman's writing. *Herland* was never published in a freestanding edition during her lifetime; rather, it appeared in monthly installments in the *Forerunner*. Attending to its placement in that magazine, to Gilman's understudied short fiction published there, and to the other work she published in close proximity to *Herland*—such as her writing on the PPIE and on urban design—restores the novel to its original placement in print and thereby enables new lines of critical interpretation. There is much still to be done on the question of Gilman and place, imagined or real, geographical or literary—and we hope that our recovery of Gilman's western orientation will fuel such work in the years to come.

ACKNOWLEDGMENTS

Portions of this essay were originally delivered as the keynote address (by Scharnhorst) and the plenary address (by Tuttle) at the 2011 Fifth International Gilman Conference, "Gilman Goes West," at the University of Montana, Missoula. Because Tuttle's address was subsequently published in *Western American Literature* as "'New England Innocent' in the Land of Sunshine: Charlotte Perkins Gilman and California," there is a small amount of overlap with that essay, indicated in the notes. Tuttle's research for this essay was made possible by a research support grant from the Schlesinger Library for the History of Women in America, Radcliffe Institute, Harvard University. The authors are grateful to Hollis Haywood at the University of New England and Amanda Williford at the Park Archives and Records Center, Golden Gate National Recreation Area, National Park Service, for their help obtaining the illustrations. Most of all we thank Jill Bergman for her myriad efforts to encourage new scholarship on Gilman and the West.

NOTES

1. Charlotte Perkins Gilman, *The Living of Charlotte Perkins Gilman* (1935; repr., New York: Harper Colophon, 1975), 181.

2. Charlotte Perkins Gilman, "Woman Suffrage and the West," *Kansas Suffrage Reveille*, June 1897.

3. Charlotte Perkins Gilman, "Why Nevada Should Win Its Suffrage Campaign in November," *Out West*, August 1914.

4. For a more detailed discussion of Gilman's use of the West Cure, see Jennifer S. Tuttle, "Rewriting the Rest Cure: Charlotte Perkins Gilman, Owen Wister, and the Sexual Politics of Neurasthenia," in *The Mixed Legacy of Charlotte Perkins Gilman*, ed. Catherine J. Golden and Joanna Schneider Zangrando (Newark: University of Delaware Press, 2000), 103–21.

5. Gilman, *Living*, 93–95; *Charlotte Perkins Gilman, In This Our World and Uncollected Poems*, ed. Gary Scharnhorst and Denise D. Knight (Syracuse, NY: Syracuse University Press, 2012), 85–86; Jennifer S. Tuttle, "'New England Innocent' in the Land of Sunshine: Charlotte Perkins Gilman and California," *Western American Literature* 48, no. 3 (Fall 2013): 287.

6. Tuttle, "Rewriting," 112; Gilman, *Living*, 107; Tuttle, "New England Innocent," 290.

7. For Gilman's career launch in the West, see Gary Scharnhorst, "Making Her Fame: Charlotte Perkins Gilman in California." *California History* 64 (Summer 1985): 192–201. Although our focus here is her strong and sustained connection to the West, her feelings about California and her place there appear to have been deeply conflicted. See Tuttle, "New England Innocent."

8. Gilman, *Living*, 111.

9. Gilman, *In This Our World*, 31–32, 47, 70; Tuttle, "New England Innocent," 295–96. Other poems, too—such as "Our Tomorrow" and "Our Sky," both first published in *Land of Sunshine*—feature a speaker with eastern origins who has manifested her destiny to lay claim to the West.

10. Gilman, *In This Our World*, 69.

11. Charlotte Perkins Gilman, *The Crux*, ed. Jennifer S. Tuttle (1911; repr., Newark: University of Delaware Press, 2002), 130; Charlotte Perkins Gilman, *The Later Poetry of Charlotte Perkins Gilman*, ed. Denise D. Knight (Newark: University of Delaware Press, 1996), 170.

12. Gary Scharnhorst, *Charlotte Perkins Gilman* (Boston: Twayne, 1985), 11–33.

13. Gilman, *Living*, 113, 122; Lester Frank Ward, *Glimpses of the Cosmos: A Mental Autobiography* (New York: G. P. Putnam's Sons, 1917), 5: 336.

14. Scharnhorst, *Charlotte Perkins Gilman*, 27, 30–31.

15. Gilman, *Living*, 187, 198; Charlotte Perkins Gilman, *The Selected Letters of Charlotte Perkins Gilman*, ed. Denise D. Knight and Jennifer S. Tuttle (Tuscaloosa: University of Alabama Press, 2009), 294; Charles Fletcher Lummis, "The New League for Literature and the West," *Land of Sunshine*, April 1898; Melody Graulich, "Creating Great Women: Mary Austin and Charlotte Perkins Gilman," in *Charlotte Perkins Gilman and Her Contemporaries: Literary and Intellectual Contexts*, ed. Cynthia J. Davis and Denise D. Knight (Tuscaloosa: University of Alabama Press, 2004), 144; Tuttle, "New England Innocent," 293–94.

16. This is the private collection of Gilman's grandson in Los Alamos, New Mexico.

17. Gilman, *Living*, 93; Gary Scharnhorst, *Owen Wister and the West* (Norman: University of Oklahoma Press, 2015), 162.

18. Owen Wister, *The Virginian*, ed. Gary Scharnhorst (1902; repr., New York: Pocket Books, 2002), 105, 107.

19. Scharnhorst, *Owen Wister*, 162.

20. Gary Scharnhorst, "Charlotte Perkins Gilman's 'The Giant Wistaria': A Hieroglyph of the Female Frontier Gothic," in *Frontier Gothic: Terror and Wonder at the Frontier in American Literature*, ed. David Mogen, Scott P. Sanders, and Joanne B. Karpinski (Rutherford, NJ: Fairleigh Dickinson University Press, 1993), 159.

21. Charlotte Perkins Gilman, "The Giant Wistaria," in *Herland, The Yellow Wall-Paper, and Selected Writings*, ed. Denise D. Knight (New York: Penguin, 1999), 154, 155.

22. Gilman, *Selected Letters*, 248.

23. Charlotte Perkins Gilman, *What Diantha Did*, ed. Charlotte J. Rich (1909-10; repr., Durham, NC: Duke University Press, 2005), 44.

24. Charlotte Perkins Gilman, "Girls and Land," in *The Yellow Wall-Paper and Other Stories*, ed. by Robert Schulman (New York: Oxford University Press, 2009), 289; Charlotte Perkins Gilman, "Bee Wise," in *Herland, The Yellow Wall-Paper, and Selected Writings*, ed. Denise D. Knight (New York: Penguin, 1999), 266; Charlotte Perkins Gilman, "Dr. Clair's Place," in *Herland, The Yellow Wall-Paper, and Selected Writings*, ed. Denise D. Knight (New York: Penguin, 1999), 282; Charlotte Perkins Gilman, "My Poor Aunt," *Forerunner*, June 1913.

25. Charlotte Perkins Gilman, "Joan's Defender," in *Herland, The Yellow Wall-Paper, and Selected Writings*, ed. Denise D. Knight (New York: Penguin, 1999), 295, 296; Charlotte Perkins Gilman, "Fulfilment," in *The Yellow Wall-Paper and Other Stories*, ed. Robert Schulman (New York: Oxford University Press, 2009), 251, 252.

26. Jennifer S. Tuttle, ed., "Introduction," in *The Crux*, by Charlotte Perkins Gilman (1911; repr., Newark: University of Delaware Press, 2002), 40. Whether Greeley uttered these exact words, and whether he was the first to do so, is a matter of some debate; see Coy F. Cross, *Go West, Young Man! Horace Greeley's Vision for America* (Albuquerque: University of New Mexico Press, 1995), 136.

27. Charlotte Perkins Gilman, "Woman's 'Manifest Destiny,'" *Woman's Journal*, June 1904.

28. Norris Yates, *Gender and Genre: An Introduction to Women Writers of Formula Westerns, 1900–1950* (Albuquerque: University of New Mexico Press, 1995). In her forthcoming book, *Westerns: A Women's History* (University of Nebraska Press), Victoria Lamont argues that recovering more women's contributions to western literature calls into question the widespread assumption that the western genre was exclusively masculinist at all.

29. Scharnhorst, *Owen Wister*, 163.

30. Gilman, *Crux*, 202; Cynthia J. Davis, *Charlotte Perkins Gilman: A Biography* (Stanford, CA: Stanford University Press, 2010), 272.

31. Gilman, *Selected Letters*, 56; Gilman quoted in Davis, *Biography*, 303.

32. Scharnhorst, *Owen Wister*, 163. For more on Gilman and the discourse of civilization, see Gail Bederman, *Manliness and Civilization: A Cultural History of Gender and Race in the United States, 1880–1917* (Chicago: University of Chicago Press, 1995), 121–69.

33. Jennifer S. Tuttle, "Gilman's *The Crux* and Owen Wister's *The Virginian*: Intertextuality and Woman's Manifest Destiny," in *Charlotte Perkins Gilman and Her Contemporaries: Literary and Intellectual Contexts*, ed. Cynthia J. Davis and Denise D. Knight (Tuscaloosa: University of Alabama Press, 2004), 127; Gilman, *Crux*, 110, 113, 117.

34. Scharnhorst, *Owen Wister*, 163; Gilman, *Crux*, 109, 114; Tuttle, "Gilman's *The Crux*," 131, 133.

35. Scharnhorst, *Owen Wister*, 163–64.

36. Ibid., 164. See also Gary Scharnhorst, ed., "Introduction," in *The Virginian*, by Owen Wister (1902, repr., New York: Pocket Books, 2002), xvii; and Owen Wister, "The Evolution of the Cow-Puncher," *Harper's Monthly*, September 1895.

37. Tuttle, "Introduction," 40. See also Dana Seitler, "Unnatural Selection: Mothers, Eugenic Feminism, and Charlotte Perkins Gilman's Regeneration Narratives," *American Quarterly* 55 (March 2003): 81. She notes, "In Gilman's brand of eugenic feminism . . . it is the duty of white people (male or female) to expand, extend, colonize, and reproduce."

38. Eisler quoted in Carol Farley Kessler, *Charlotte Perkins Gilman: Her Progress toward Utopia with Selected Writings* (Syracuse, NY: Syracuse University Press, 1995), 7; Gilman, *Selected Letters*, 248; Allen, "Reconfiguring Vice," 176.

39. Kessler, *Charlotte Perkins Gilman*, 8; Charlotte Perkins Gilman, *Herland*,

in *Herland and Related Writings*, ed. Beth Sutton-Ramspeck (Buffalo: Broadview, 2013), 141; Sandra M. Gilbert and Susan Gubar, "'Fecundate! Discriminate!': Charlotte Perkins Gilman and the Theologizing of Maternity." *Charlotte Perkins Gilman: Optimist Reformer*, ed. Jill Rudd and Val Gough (Iowa City: University of Iowa Press, 1999), 205, 207. Gilbert and Gubar make the important point that the apparent idealization of motherhood in *Herland* is balanced elsewhere in Gilman's writing by a "generalized horror of the maternal."

40. Still another possible referent for Herland is the mythological island of California, as imagined by Garcí Ordoñez de Montalvo in *Las sergas del muy esforzado caballero Esplandian* (1508). Writing during the age of discovery, Montalvo transforms older myths of Amazons to portray "an island called California, very near to the region of the Terrestrial Paradise," surrounded by "steep rocks" and inhabited by black women "of vigorous bodies and strong and ardent hearts" who are ruled by Queen Calafia; these women reproduce through "carnal unions" but otherwise expel or kill all men. See Dora Beale Polk, *The Island of California: A History of the Myth* (Lincoln: University of Nebraska Press, 1991), 125. We thank Andrea Dominquez for reminding us of this myth. Although there are obviously telling differences between Montalvo's California and Gilman's Herland, it is very likely that she was familiar with Montalvo, because it was her own uncle, Edward Everett Hale, who was the first to suggest Montalvo as the source for California's name. Asserting that Hernán Cortés (credited by some for naming the region) would surely have known Montalvo's work, Hale affirms that "from the romance, the peninsula, the gulf, and afterwards the State, got their name." Edward Hale, Everett, "The Queen of California," *Atlantic Monthly*, March 1864.

41. See, e.g., Charlotte J. Rich, "From Near-Dystopia to Utopia: A Source for *Herland* in Inez Haynes Gillmore's *Angel Island*," in *Charlotte Perkins Gilman and Her Contemporaries: Literary and Intellectual Contexts*, ed. Cynthia J. Davis and Denise D. Knight (Tuscaloosa: University of Alabama Press, 2004), 166. Rich has written that "Herland's vague location in a 'semitropical' region . . . , in the 'enormous hinterland of a great river' . . . , suggests it to be somewhere in South America, a continent where American capitalists were heavily investing in agricultural and natural resource industries in the late nineteenth and early twentieth centuries." See also Kristin Carter-Sanborn, "Restraining Order: The Imperialist Anti-Violence of Charlotte Perkins Gilman," *Arizona Quarterly* 56, no. 2 (2000): 14.

42. Gilman, *Herland*, 34, 106, 107 120; Judith A. Allen, *The Feminism of Charlotte Perkins Gilman: Sexualities, Histories, Progressivism* (Chicago: University of Chicago Press, 2009), 232.

43. Gilman, *Herland*, 42, 44, 48, 49, 104, 154.

44. Ibid., 76, 81, 84, 86.

45. Ibid., 49. In *Herland*'s sequel, *With Her in Ourland*, serialized the next

year in the *Forerunner*, Van and his Herlander wife, Ellador, even attend the PPIE, along with other world's fairs. It is not surprising that the reality of Ourland does not measure up to the fair or to Herland.

46. Burton Benedict, ed., "The Anthropology of World's Fairs," in *The Anthropology of World's Fairs: San Francisco's Panama Pacific International Exposition of 1915* (Berkeley, CA: Scolar Press, 1983), 60; Gray A. Brechin, *Imperial San Francisco: Urban Power, Earthly Ruin* (Berkeley: University of California Press, 1999), 246; Bill Brown, "Science Fiction, the World's Fair, and the Prosthetics of Empire, 1900–1915," in *Cultures of United States Imperialism*, ed. Amy Kaplan and Donald Pease (Durham, NC: Duke University Press, 1993), 149.

47. Wayne Craven, *Sculpture in America*, rev. ed. (Newark: University of Delaware Press, 1984), 132, 493; Brechin, *Imperial San Francisco*, 246. This eugenic maternalism was expressed even more famously at the fair in Charles Grafly's pronatalist *Pioneer Mother* statue. See Brenda D. Frink, "San Francisco's Pioneer Mother Monument: Maternalism, Racial Order, and the Politics of Memorialization, 1907–1915," *American Quarterly* 64, no. 1 (March 2012): 85–113; and Abigail M. Markwyn, "Encountering 'Woman' on the Fairgrounds of the 1915 Panama-Pacific Exposition," in *Gendering the Fair: Histories of Women and Gender at World's Fairs*, ed. T. J. Boisseau and Abigail M. Markwyn (Urbana: University of Illinois Press, 2010), 180–83.

48. Sarah J. Moore, "Manliness and the New American Empire at the 1915 Panama-Pacific Exposition," *Gendering the Fair: Histories of Women and Gender at World's Fairs*, ed. T. J. Boisseau and Abigail M. Markwyn (Urbana: University of Illinois Press, 2010), 87; Robert W. Rydell, John E. Findling, and Kimberly D. Pelle, *Fair America: World's Fairs in the United States* (Washington, DC: Smithsonian Institution Press, 2000), 65; Markwyn, "Encountering 'Woman,'" 172. A telling example of such commodification, notes Markwyn, were the "orange girls," the "young, attractive, white women" who "showcased local produce" and "represented California's fecundity" to "potential [white] settlers" concerned about the state's ethnic diversity.

49. Elizabeth E. Armstrong, "Hercules and the Muses: Public Art at the Fair," in *The Anthropology of World's Fairs: San Francisco's Panama Pacific International Exposition of 1915*, ed. Burton Benedict (Berkeley, CA: Scolar Press, 1983), 125; Brown, *Science Fiction*, 141. It is not insignificant that another of the fair's aims was to observe the four hundredth anniversary of Vasco Nuñez de Balboa's "discovery" of the Pacific Ocean.

50. Brown, *Science Fiction*, 139, 142, 145; Moore, "Manliness," 76.

51. Frank Morton Todd, *The Story of the Exposition: Being the Official History of the International Celebration Held at San Francisco in 1915 to Commemorate the Discovery of the Pacific Ocean and the Construction of the Panama Canal* (New York: G. P. Putnam's Sons, 1921), 1:20; Brown, *Science Fiction*, 138, 146, 148. Like

the older model of manliness epitomized by the West Cure, which depended on the invisible labor of packers, guides, and servants, according to Brown, this new representation of American technological power, through an idealized corporeal form, "aestheticizes . . . into [an] abstraction" the actual labor performed by the close to forty thousand men, mostly West Indians, who worked with American-made machines to create the canal. For an excellent discussion of Roosevelt's significance to the fair, see Moore, "Manliness," 75–76.

52. Moore, "Manliness," 84. Indeed, Turner himself envisioned such a transition to overseas expansion in his 1896 essay, "The Problem of the West."

53. Charlotte Perkins Gilman, "Standardizing Towns," *Forerunner*, February 1915, 53.

54. Charlotte Perkins Gilman, "The Gorgeous Exposition," *Forerunner*, May 1915, 121, 122.

55. Todd, *Story of the Exposition*, 3:1.

56. Elisabeth Nicole Arruda, "The Mother of Tomorrow: American Eugenics and the Panama-Pacific International Exposition, 1915," master's thesis, San Francisco State University, 2004, 26; Alexander Missal, *Seaway to the Future: American Social Visions and the Construction of the Panama Canal* (Madison: University of Wisconsin Press, 2008), 123, 199.

57. Bridget Bennett, "Pockets of Resistance: Some Notes towards an Exploration of Gender and Genre Boundaries in *Herland*," in *A Very Different Story: Studies on the Fiction of Charlotte Perkins Gilman*, ed. Val Gough and Jill Rudd (Liverpool, UK: University of Liverpool Press, 1998), 42, 43, 47.

58. Carter-Sanborn, "Restraining Order," 2, 28.

59. Brigitte Giorgi-Findlay, *The Frontiers of Women's Writing: Women's Narratives and the Rhetoric of Westward Expansion* (Tucson: University of Arizona Press, 1996), 11; Moore, "Manliness," 89, 90–91. Moore notes that the canal exhibit's "pedagogical motivation . . . was formally recognized by its receipt of a grand prize under the Liberal Arts Section" of the fair. Susan Gubar, "*She* in *Herland*: Feminism as Fantasy," in *Charlotte Perkins Gilman: The Woman and Her Work*, ed. Sheryl L. Meyering (Ann Arbor: University of Michigan Research Press, 1989), 198.

60. Gregory Clark, *Rhetorical Landscapes in America: Variations on a Theme from Kenneth Burke* (Columbia: University of South Carolina Press, 2004), 143; Allen, *Feminism*, 214; Carl N. Degler, ed., "Introduction," in *Women and Economics: A Study of the Economic Relation between Men and Women as a Factor in Social Evolution*, by Charlotte Perkins Gilman (1898; repr., New York: Harper, 1966), xiii.

61. Nora Stanton [Blatch] Barney to Katharine Beecher Stetson Chamberlin, August 21, 1935, Katharine Beecher Stetson Papers, 1827–1956, 2011-M45, carton 3, folder 8, Arthur and Elizabeth Schlesinger Library, Radcliffe Institute, Harvard University, Cambridge, MA; Bederman, "Manliness," 122, 167; Rebecca J. Mead, *How the Vote Was Won: Woman Suffrage in the Western United States, 1868–*

1914 (New York: New York University Press, 2006), 76. Gilman was a vocal participant in the California suffrage campaign, which similarly entwined feminism with white supremacy. "Her arguments," writes Mead, "challenged many assumptions about gender but relied heavily upon prevailing racialist paradigms. Gilman did not challenge contemporary discourses about 'civilization' and 'race suicide.' Instead, she modified and reinforced these ideas for feminist purposes, helping to reinscribe nativist and racist prejudices in the public mind." See also Gayle Gullett, *Becoming Citizens: The Emergence and Development of the California Women's Movement, 1880–1911* (Urbana: University of Illinois Press, 2000), 31. For *Herland's* affinity with the broader purposes of the California suffrage movement, including its deployment of white supremacist rhetoric, see Darcie Rives-East, "Charlotte Perkins Gilman's *Herland* and the California Suffragist Movement, 1896–1911," paper presented at the American Literature Association Conference, San Francisco, May 24, 2012.

62. Krista Comer, "Exceptionalism, Other Wests, Critical Regionalism," *American Literary History* 23, no. 1 (Spring 2011): 159–73; Lois Rudnick, "Re-Naming the Land: Anglo Expatriate Women in the Southwest," in *The Desert Is No Lady: Southwestern Landscapes in Women's Writing and Art*, ed. Vera Norwood and Janice Monk (Tucson: University of Arizona Press, 1987), 11; see also Tuttle, "New England Innocent," 307n21.

63. Melody Graulich, "Creating Great Women: Mary Austin and Charlotte Perkins Gilman," in *Charlotte Perkins Gilman and Her Contemporaries: Literary and Intellectual Contexts*, ed. Cynthia J. Davis and Denise D. Knight (Tuscaloosa: University of Alabama Press, 2004); Comer, "Exceptionalism," 171; Krista Cromer, *Landscapes of the New West: Gender and Geography in Contemporary Women's Writing* (Chapel Hill: University of North Carolina Press, 1999), 42; Susan Kollin, ed., "Introduction: Postwestern Studies, Dead or Alive," in *Postwestern Cultures: Literature, Theory, Space* (Lincoln: University of Nebraska Press, 2007), xi.

64. Gilman wrote in a letter from Las Casitas, "I feel very much at home and welcome [at Las Casitas]. . . . I still think I should like to live in this part of the country, but not too near town!" Charlotte Perkins Gilman to Katharine Beecher Stetson Chamberlin, April 21, 1915, Katharine Beecher Stetson Papers, 2011-M45, carton 1, folder 6 .

WORKS CITED

Allen, Judith A. *The Feminism of Charlotte Perkins Gilman: Sexualities, Histories, Progressivism*. Chicago: University of Chicago Press, 2009.
———. "Reconfiguring Vice: Charlotte Perkins Gilman, Prostitution, and Frontier Sexual Contracts." In *Charlotte Perkins Gilman: Optimist Reformer*, edited by Jill Rudd and Val Gough, 173–99. Iowa City: University of Iowa Press, 1999.

Armstrong, Elizabeth E. "Hercules and the Muses: Public Art at the Fair." In *The Anthropology of World's Fairs: San Francisco's Panama Pacific International Exposition of 1915*, edited by Burton Benedict, 114–33. Berkeley, CA: Scolar Press, 1983.

Arruda, Elisabeth Nicole. "The Mother of Tomorrow: American Eugenics and the Panama-Pacific International Exposition, 1915," master's thesis, San Francisco State University, 2004.

Bederman, Gail. *Manliness and Civilization: A Cultural History of Gender and Race in the United States, 1880–1917*. Chicago: University of Chicago Press, 1995.

Benedict, Burton, ed. "The Anthropology of World's Fairs." In *The Anthropology of World's Fairs: San Francisco's Panama Pacific International Exposition of 1915*, 1–65. Berkeley, CA: Scolar Press, 1983.

Bennett, Bridget. "Pockets of Resistance: Some Notes towards an Exploration of Gender and Genre Boundaries in *Herland*." In *A Very Different Story: Studies on the Fiction of Charlotte Perkins Gilman*, edited by Val Gough and Jill Rudd, 38–53. Liverpool, UK: University of Liverpool Press, 1998.

Bierce, Ambrose. "Prattle." *San Francisco Examiner*, February 4, 1894.

Brechin, Gray A. *Imperial San Francisco: Urban Power, Earthly Ruin*. Berkeley: University of California Press, 1999.

Brown, Bill. "Science Fiction, the World's Fair, and the Prosthetics of Empire, 1900–1915." In *Cultures of United States Imperialism*, edited by Amy Kaplan and Donald Pease, 129–62. Durham, NC: Duke University Press, 1993.

Carter-Sanborn, Kristin. "Restraining Order: The Imperialist Anti-Violence of Charlotte Perkins Gilman." *Arizona Quarterly* 56, no. 2 (2000): 1–36.

Clark, Gregory. *Rhetorical Landscapes in America: Variations on a Theme from Kenneth Burke*. Columbia: University of South Carolina Press, 2004.

Comer, Krista. "Exceptionalism, Other Wests, Critical Regionalism." *American Literary History* 23, no. 1 (Spring 2011): 159–73.

———. *Landscapes of the New West: Gender and Geography in Contemporary Women's Writing*. Chapel Hill: University of North Carolina Press, 1999.

Craven, Wayne. *Sculpture in America*. Rev. ed. Newark: University of Delaware Press, 1984.

Cross, Coy F. *Go West, Young Man! Horace Greeley's Vision for America*. Albuquerque: University of New Mexico Press, 1995.

Davis, Cynthia J. *Charlotte Perkins Gilman: A Biography*. Stanford, CA: Stanford University Press, 2010.

Davis, Cynthia J., and Denise D. Knight, eds. *Charlotte Perkins Gilman and Her Contemporaries: Literary and Intellectual Contexts*. Tuscaloosa: University of Alabama Press, 2004.

Degler, Carl N., ed. "Introduction." In *Women and Economics: A Study of the Economic Relation between Men and Women as a Factor in Social Evolution*, by Charlotte Perkins Gilman, 1898, vi–xxxv. New York: Harper, 1966.

Frink, Brenda D. "San Francisco's Pioneer Mother Monument: Maternalism, Racial Order, and the Politics of Memorialization, 1907–1915." *American Quarterly* 64, no. 1 (March 2012): 85–113.

Gilbert, Sandra M., and Susan Gubar. "'Fecundate! Discriminate!': Charlotte Perkins Gilman and the Theologizing of Maternity." In *Charlotte Perkins Gilman: Optimist Reformer*, edited by Jill Rudd and Val Gough, 200–216. Iowa City: University of Iowa Press, 1999.

Gilman, Charlotte Perkins. "Bee Wise." In *Herland, The Yellow Wall-Paper, and Selected Writings*, edited by Denise D. Knight, 263–71. New York: Penguin, 1999.

———. *The Crux*. 1911. Edited by Jennifer S. Tuttle. Newark: University of Delaware Press, 2002.

———. "Dr. Clair's Place." In *Herland, The Yellow Wall-Paper, and Selected Writings*, edited by Denise D. Knight, 280–88. New York: Penguin, 1999.

———. "Fulfilment." In *The Yellow Wall-Paper and Other Stories*, edited by Robert Schulman, 244–52. New York: Oxford University Press, 2009.

———. "The Giant Wistaria." In *Herland, The Yellow Wall-Paper, and Selected Writings*, edited by Denise D. Knight, 154–62. New York: Penguin, 1999.

———. "Girls and Land." In *The Yellow Wall-Paper and Other Stories*, edited by Robert Schulman, 286–94. New York: Oxford University Press, 2009.

———. "The Gorgeous Exposition." *Forerunner*, May 1915.

———. *Herland*. In *Herland and Related Writings*, edited by Beth Sutton-Ramspeck, 31–163. Buffalo: Broadview, 2013.

———. *Herland, The Yellow Wall-Paper, and Selected Writings*. Edited by Denise D. Knight. New York: Penguin, 1999.

———. *In This Our World and Uncollected Poems*. Edited by Gary Scharnhorst and Denise D. Knight. Syracuse, NY: Syracuse University Press, 2012.

———. "Joan's Defender." In *Herland, The Yellow Wall-Paper, and Selected Writings*, edited by Denise D. Knight, 289–96. New York: Penguin, 1999.

———. *The Later Poetry of Charlotte Perkins Gilman*. Edited by Denise D. Knight. Newark: University of Delaware Press, 1996.

———. *The Living of Charlotte Perkins Gilman*. 1935. New York: Harper Colophon, 1975.

———. "My Poor Aunt." *Forerunner*, June 1913.

———. *The Selected Letters of Charlotte Perkins Gilman*. Edited by Denise D. Knight and Jennifer S. Tuttle. Tuscaloosa: University of Alabama Press, 2009.

———. "Standardizing Towns." *Forerunner*, February 1915.

———. *What Diantha Did*. 1909-10. Edited by Charlotte J. Rich. Durham, NC: Duke University Press, 2005.

———. "Why Nevada Should Win Its Suffrage Campaign in November." *Out West*, August 1914.

———. "Woman's 'Manifest Destiny.'" *Woman's Journal*, June 1904.

———. "Woman Suffrage and the West." *Kansas Suffrage Reveille*, June 1897.

Giorgi-Findlay, Brigitte. *The Frontiers of Women's Writing: Women's Narratives and the Rhetoric of Westward Expansion.* Tucson: University of Arizona Press, 1996.

Graulich, Melody. "Creating Great Women: Mary Austin and Charlotte Perkins Gilman." In *Charlotte Perkins Gilman and Her Contemporaries: Literary and Intellectual Contexts*, edited by Cynthia J. Davis and Denise D. Knight, 139–54. Tuscaloosa: University of Alabama Press, 2004.

Gubar, Susan. "*She* in *Herland*: Feminism as Fantasy." In *Charlotte Perkins Gilman: The Woman and Her Work*, edited by Sheryl L. Meyering, 191–202. Ann Arbor: University of Michigan Research Press, 1989.

Gullett, Gayle. *Becoming Citizens: The Emergence and Development of the California Women's Movement, 1880–1911.* Urbana: University of Illinois Press, 2000.

Hale, Edward Everett. "The Queen of California." *Atlantic Monthly*, March 1864.

Kessler, Carol Farley. *Charlotte Perkins Gilman: Her Progress toward Utopia with Selected Writings.* Syracuse, NY: Syracuse University Press, 1995.

Kollin, Susan, ed. "Introduction: Postwestern Studies, Dead or Alive." In *Postwestern Cultures: Literature, Theory, Space*, ix-xix. Lincoln: University of Nebraska Press, 2007.

Lummis, Charles Fletcher. "The New League for Literature and the West," *Land of Sunshine*, April 1898.

Markwyn, Abigail M. *Empress San Francisco: The Pacific Rim, the Great West, and California at the Panama-Pacific International Exposition.* Lincoln: University of Nebraska Press, 2014.

———. "Encountering 'Woman' on the Fairgrounds of the 1915 Panama-Pacific Exposition." In *Gendering the Fair: Histories of Women and Gender at World's Fairs*, edited by T. J. Boisseau and Abigail M. Markwyn, 169–86. Urbana: University of Illinois Press, 2010.

Mead, Rebecca J. *How the Vote Was Won: Woman Suffrage in the Western United States, 1868–1914.* New York: New York University Press, 2006.

Missal, Alexander. *Seaway to the Future: American Social Visions and the Construction of the Panama Canal.* Madison: University of Wisconsin Press, 2008.

Moore, Sarah J. "Manliness and the New American Empire at the 1915 Panama-Pacific Exposition." *Gendering the Fair: Histories of Women and Gender at World's Fairs*, edited by T. J. Boisseau and Abigail M. Markwyn, 75–96. Urbana: University of Illinois Press, 2010.

Polk, Dora Beale. *The Island of California: A History of the Myth.* Lincoln: University of Nebraska Press, 1991.

Rich, Charlotte J. "From Near-Dystopia to Utopia: A Source for *Herland* in Inez Haynes Gillmore's *Angel Island*." In *Charlotte Perkins Gilman and Her Contemporaries: Literary and Intellectual Contexts*, edited by Cynthia J. Davis and Denise D. Knight, 155–70. Tuscaloosa: University of Alabama Press, 2004.

Rives-East, Darcie. "Charlotte Perkins Gilman's *Herland* and the California Suffragist Movement, 1896–1911." Paper presented at the American Literature Association Conference, San Francisco, May 24, 2012.

Rudnick, Lois. "Re-Naming the Land: Anglo Expatriate Women in the Southwest." In *The Desert Is No Lady: Southwestern Landscapes in Women's Writing and Art*, edited by Vera Norwood and Janice Monk, 10–26. Tucson: University of Arizona Press, 1987.

Rydell, Robert W., John E. Findling, and Kimberly D. Pelle. *Fair America: World's Fairs in the United States*. Washington, DC: Smithsonian Institution Press, 2000.

Scharnhorst, Gary. *Charlotte Perkins Gilman*. Boston: Twayne, 1985.

———. "Charlotte Perkins Gilman's 'The Giant Wistaria': A Hieroglyph of the Female Frontier Gothic." In *Frontier Gothic: Terror and Wonder at the Frontier in American Literature*, edited by David Mogen, Scott P. Sanders, and Joanne B. Karpinski, 156–64. Rutherford, NJ: Fairleigh Dickinson University Press, 1993.

———, ed. "Introduction." In *The Virginian*, by Owen Wister, 1902, vii-xxii. New York: Pocket Books, 2002.

———. "Making Her Fame: Charlotte Perkins Gilman in California." *California History* 64, no. 3, (Summer 1985): 192–201.

———. *Owen Wister and the West*. Norman: University of Oklahoma Press, 2015.

Seitler, Dana. "Unnatural Selection: Mothers, Eugenic Feminism, and Charlotte Perkins Gilman's Regeneration Narratives." *American Quarterly* 55 (March 2003): 61–88.

Stetson, Katharine Beecher. Papers. 1827–1956. Arthur and Elizabeth Schlesinger Library, Radcliffe Institute, Harvard University, Cambridge, MA.

Todd, Frank Morton. *The Story of the Exposition: Being the Official History of the International Celebration Held at San Francisco in 1915 to Commemorate the Discovery of the Pacific Ocean and the Construction of the Panama Canal*. 5 vols. New York: G. P. Putnam's Sons, 1921.

Tuttle, Jennifer S. "Gilman's *The Crux* and Owen Wister's *The Virginian*: Intertextuality and Woman's Manifest Destiny." In *Charlotte Perkins Gilman and Her Contemporaries: Literary and Intellectual Contexts*, edited by Cynthia J. Davis and Denise D. Knight, 127–38. Tuscaloosa: University of Alabama Press, 2004.

———, ed. "Introduction." In *The Crux*, by Charlotte Perkins Gilman, 1911, 11–75. Newark: University of Delaware Press, 2002.

———. "'New England Innocent' in the Land of Sunshine: Charlotte Perkins Gilman and California." *Western American Literature* 48, no. 3 (Fall 2013): 284–311.

———. "Rewriting the Rest Cure: Charlotte Perkins Gilman, Owen Wister, and the Sexual Politics of Neurasthenia." In *The Mixed Legacy of Charlotte Perkins Gilman*, edited by Catherine J. Golden and Joanna Schneider Zangrando, 103–21. Newark: University of Delaware Press, 2000.

Ward, Lester Frank. *Glimpses of the Cosmos: A Mental Autobiography.* 5 vols. New York: G. P. Putnam's Sons, 1917.

Wister, Owen. "The Evolution of the Cow-Puncher." *Harper's Monthly*, September 1895.

———. *The Virginian.* 1902. Edited by Gary Scharnhorst. New York: Pocket Books, 2002.

Yates, Norris. *Gender and Genre: An Introduction to Women Writers of Formula Westerns, 1900–1950.* Albuquerque: University of New Mexico Press, 1995.

2
Artistic Renderings of
Charlotte Perkins Gilman

Denise D. Knight

Twelve days before her suicide at the age of seventy-five, Charlotte Perkins Gilman wrote to her literary executor and nephew, Lyman Beecher Stowe, that after her second husband, Houghton Gilman, died suddenly in 1934, she had casually discarded "some kind of plaster thing crated up," which she realized too late was the bust of herself that had been sculpted by her daughter, Katharine, years earlier. The loss of the bust, cast in 1917, was immeasurable to Gilman researchers. It captured Gilman's likeness at the pinnacle of her long career and replicated the contours, dimensions, and features of her head and face, which are lost in the one-dimensional flatness of even the clearest photographs. Seventy-three years later, in August 2008, when Gilman's great-granddaughter, Linda Chamberlin, was going through old boxes stored in her family's garage, she made a stunning discovery: a signed and dated plaster bust that was a duplicate of the original mold of Gilman. Chamberlin arranged to have the bust cast in bronze, and it now graces the second-floor reading room at the Arthur and Elizabeth Schlesinger Library on the History of Women in America at the Radcliffe Institute in Cambridge, Massachusetts, a fitting place for a woman who spent the better part of her life promoting the cause of women.[1]

Remarkably, Chamberlin's rescue of the bust is just one of a number of recently recovered renderings of Gilman produced by various artists between 1877 and 1919. Created in a variety of media (oil, plaster, charcoal, ink, pencil, and photography), the artistic renderings include a painting of Gilman breastfeeding her daughter, Katharine, by Gilman's first husband, artist Charles Walter Stetson, just before Gilman's nervous breakdown; a sketchbook of

Stetson's, which contains twelve drawings of Gilman from 1885 to 1887; early sketches of Gilman, drawn by Katharine, from around 1898 through 1906; a bas-relief cast by Gilman's son-in-law, artist F. Tolles Chamberlin, in September 1919; and several candid photographs of Gilman taken in Las Casitas, California, in 1900.[2] These works of art join other better-known renderings, including a portrait at age seventeen completed by Ellen Day Hale in 1877; an early Stetson painting from 1882; and a death mask of Gilman made by her Pasadena physician and cast by a local artist in August 1935.[3]

It is surprising that even the works that have long been known to exist have generated little critical commentary thus far. Their existence, however, along with the recently recovered works, is exciting; the visual art allows us to both "see" and "read" Gilman through the eyes of others. But they also illuminate the concept of place in its various forms: the concrete physical world that Gilman inhabited; the wide-ranging emotional space that she occupied; and her position in American literary history. Each rendering provides a snapshot of a particular moment, or even a chapter, in Gilman's life.

The earliest rendering to surface in the last thirty years is a portrait painted when Gilman was seventeen by her cousin Ellen ("Nellie") Day Hale, who later became an accomplished artist and author.[4] The typically hard-boiled Gilman was uncharacteristically fond of this particular painting; six weeks after Houghton's death, Gilman, who was packing up her Connecticut home to join Katharine in Pasadena, informed her daughter that she had made a will leaving to her what few items she was bringing: "a couple of trunks . . . a few boxes of books & mss.," and various paintings. The only painting Gilman identified specifically was the Hale portrait. "I want to leave you the [portrait that] Nellie Hale painted of me at seventeen," she wrote in June 1934.[5] Gilman apparently treasured the painting: a newly recovered photograph of the inside of Gilman's Pasadena home taken around 1890 shows the Hale portrait occupying a prominent place on the cottage wall.

On display at the National Portrait Gallery at the Smithsonian Institution in Washington, DC, Hale's painting of Gilman is in good company: portraits of Walt Whitman, Nathaniel Hawthorne, and Mark Twain occupy the same area of the museum. The Hale canvas is fairly small; it measures approximately twelve by sixteen inches and depicts the teenage Gilman seated in a casual pose (see figure 2.1). The eye is drawn immediately to the light on Gilman's face and right hand; her head is resting on her right fist. The illumination of not only her face but also her hand, cuff, and collar stands in contrast to the darkness of her hair and dress. The tension between light and darkness that Hale depicts anticipates the dichotomy in Gilman's life, which was marked by exhilarating highs and devastating lows.

Hale, the daughter of Unitarian minister and author Edward Everett Hale,

Figure 2.1. Gilman oil by cousin Ellen ("Nellie") Day Hale, 1877

produced this early portrait of Gilman when she was just twenty-two. As in many of Hale's earlier works, the influence of impressionism on this portrait is evident. Her technique became more refined with experience, but even this early work reveals not only technical skill but also an ability to capture the essence and mood of her subject, both through the expression on Gilman's face and through the use of color. The contrast of darkness and light evokes the duality in Gilman's nature that began to emerge as Gilman came of age; it is likely that she would have found Hale, five years her senior, to be a perceptive and sympathetic confidante. The seventeen-year-old Gilman had, for some time, struggled to determine her place in the world. It was incumbent on human beings, she wrote, to "find our places, our special work in the world, and when found, do it, do it at all costs."[6]

But her desire to be independent—to do her "special work in the world"—collided with her yearning to find happiness through conventional love. In 1882 she wrote to Charles Walter Stetson, "I knew . . . the time would come when I must choose between two lives, but never did I dream that . . . the struggle would be so terrible." The untitled portrait depicts a contemplative Gilman, pondering, perhaps, the possibility of integrating each part of her dual nature. Her face is elevated above the darkness, but Hale's rendering obscures the distinctness of her features and expression. Yet Hale draws attention to the part in Gilman's hair; it is well-defined and suggests, in a subtle way, the divide between her choices—her "vacillating nature" as she later characterized it.[7] It is a

Figure 2.2. Gilman oil by Charles Walter Stetson, 1882

painting that speaks of possibilities, as light pours in from an unseen window, representing the promise of life outside the realm of domesticity. But Gilman wears an expression of studied neutrality, and even though her face is bathed by warmth and sunlight, she is not looking through the window at the world outside; rather, the rendering suggests that she has yet to achieve the wisdom that would enable her to decide which of the "two lives"—representing vastly different places—would be the better choice.

Another early rendering of Gilman, the whereabouts of which are regrettably unknown, was painted by Walter Stetson in the autumn of 1882, at the Fleur-de-Lys, his Providence studio, when the two were nine months into their relationship (see figure 2.2). They had met at the Providence Art Club earlier that year, when Gilman attended a lecture by Stetson on etching. Stetson's star was rapidly rising; his work had caught the attention of such influential critics as Charles DeKay and artist George Whitaker. Yet the painting of Gilman's portrait did not go well. Stetson intended "to show the thoughtful side of [Charlotte's] nature," but, as he acknowledged in his diary, "I do not advance the portrait as I ought: her face is very difficult to paint. May be [because] it [is] hers I want to say it so well that at the thought of saying it I stammer." Stetson's metaphorical ascribing of speech to the process of painting illustrates his insecurities as a young artist; he relied on the more familiar convention of speaking than on the representation—even in the privacy of his diary—of himself as a painter. "No one need tell me how poor [my work] is," he wrote in his journal. "I never felt it more strongly than since I began to paint my love. . . . while I improved one part of the face I injured another so I can scarce see any progress." Like the experience of Anne Bradstreet's speaker in "The Author to Her Book," the more Stetson tried to improve the portrait, the worse it seemed to get.[8]

When on September 16, 1882, Gilman arrived at the Fleur-de-Lys for yet another sitting, Stetson tried to focus on her sensual nature. She "unbound her hair and let it fall over her shoulders," Stetson wrote in his diary; "it fell . . . in rich dark waves and framed her rich complexion and intensified the soft ivory of her neck! I have never seen her so beautiful."[9] This is the pose that we see in the portrait. Despite repeated attempts to render a likeness, however, Stetson continued to falter.

Three weeks into the project, he poured his frustration into two rather incondite sonnets, in which he lamented his inability to replicate Gilman's likeness. In the first poem he expressed his inability to "fix the face . . . on canvas." The word *fix* is interesting in this context; it means, among other things, to "secure," to "capture," to "take revenge upon," and to "repair." The first sonnet invokes many of the hyperbolic conventions that are common in romantic verse: it alludes to Gilman's "grace," her "marvellous . . . dark and bright" eyes, her "eloquent" red lips, her "delicate smooth chin," her "supple throat," and her "heaving breasts" with their "cream[y] white . . . mounds"—all features that Stetson tried to "fix" on the canvas. In the second sonnet Stetson chides himself while searching for the "fault" or "sin" that "dulls [his] sight or warps her image." He turns to the "Lord" for answers and questions whether "within [his] heart" he has "an image true" of his love. He wonders, too, whether he actually "know[s] her spirit [that] dwells therein" and even questions his aspirations to be an artist. He wrote, "What then the hope for eminence in Art / When what I love e'en as my very soul / Is not seen clear, is scarcely understood?" He ended the poem again bemoaning his inability to "fix [even] the smallest part" of Gilman's "great loveliness."[10]

Despite being a poor verse, the second sonnet is noteworthy because in it Stetson clearly wonders whether his rendering of Gilman is an illusion. He can't quite "read" her or "say" her face; when he tries, he "stammers." He questions whether he "know[s] her spirit [that] dwells" within her; he admits that he hasn't yet "seen [Gilman] clear[ly]" and that he "scarcely" understands her. Thus, the portrait Stetson created is both flawed and deficient—a reminder, he believed, of his inadequacies as an artist, as he strove, unsuccessfully, to situate Gilman in his life. In hindsight, of course, what he seemed to be witnessing was the wild and inevitable fluctuation in Gilman's mood as she struggled, much more openly than in her sitting with Hale, to reconcile what she referred to as the "wild unrest of two strong natures."[11]

After Gilman left Stetson's studio on September 28, he wrote, "I painted & painted but I *could not* get it to come [out] right." In "sheer desperation" Stetson abandoned his brushes and turned instead to a palette knife, and while he saw some improvement in the likeness, it was "still . . . far away from her loveliness," he wrote. And Stetson was correct: the portrait he rendered bears little resemblance to Gilman. She is positioned in profile with her head dipped; we see a demure and subdued young woman with hands clasped, quietly posing. But her pose and demeanor seem to be directed rather than natural; it is no wonder, then, that Stetson couldn't "fix" the portrait; the canvas as a place to capture or contain Gilman's essence is unsatisfactory because it is patently false. The painting that Stetson rendered is his idealized and romanticized vision of Gilman as a humble, yet sensual, young wife-to-be—a far cry from the burgeoning New Woman who was endeavoring to emerge from the cocoon of domesticity.[12]

In fact, Stetson's intensity as he tried to paint the portrait unnerved Gilman. To Grace Channing, who later became Stetson's second wife, Gilman confided that she "hated to have [Walter] paint . . . her; she said 'he looked at her as a stranger; something coldly impersonal came into his gaze.'" Channing sympathized with Gilman; she herself had witnessed Stetson's detachment when he was engaged in painting portraits. He would "go off into remote and superior spaces and gaze at you . . . with an awful *concentrated* vision . . . [which] made [the subject] for the time a part of his creation."[13] The place that Stetson inhabited in order to render his creation—those "remote and superior spaces"—effectively reduced his subject to object. But Stetson could not master Gilman, either literally or figuratively. By this point in their relationship, she was rapidly constructing both an independent identity and a philosophy by which she would live her life; while she loved Stetson, she refused to be "created" by him or by anyone, even on canvas.

Although we don't know how many paintings of Gilman Stetson completed before and during their marriage, we do know that at least one other major portrait of her survives. It was begun in 1886, during Gilman's breakdown, and completed in 1887. The recovery of this later portrait, purchased at an auction in 2008, is one of the most exciting developments in Gilman studies in recent years. Now in the private holdings of art collectors Christopher and Melinda Ratcliffe of Providence, Rhode Island, the portrait is a stunning oil on board depicting Gilman as she nurses daughter Katharine (see figure 2.3). The twelve-by-fifteen-inch painting was completed during the darkest period of Gilman's life, just two months before she received treatment for neurasthenia from Dr. S. Weir Mitchell. In his notes about the painting, Stetson proudly remarked, "I believe this [portrait] to be among the very best of my pictures to date."[14]

Figure 2.3. *Evening—Mother & Child*,
1886–1887, oil by Charles Walter Stetson

And, in fact, we do see growth and evolution in his style compared to the studio portrait of Gilman that he completed nearly four and a half years earlier.

Stetson began the portrait in 1886 from a sketch he had made of Charlotte and Katharine, and he completed it in February 1887. Titled *Evening—Mother & Child*, Stetson's painting, like Ellen Day Hale's, employs a contrast between light and darkness; half of Gilman's face is illuminated, as is her breast and the collar and trim of her gown. Unlike the earlier rendering, this painting shows that Stetson was able, finally, to "say" her face and to "fix" it on the canvas. The expression Gilman wears suggests despondency and sorrow; her face is both literally and figuratively downcast. She loosely cradles her daughter's head, which is also bathed in light. Her wedding ring is on her right hand rather than on her left; it is likely that weight loss during the months preceding her treatment for "exhaustion of the nerves" necessitated a switch from left to right, where the fit was more secure. In a document titled "Records of My Daughter Katharine Stetson," which, like the painting, was begun in August 1886, when her daughter was seventeen months old, Gilman wrote that Katharine "was nursed . . . under terrible nervous depression on my part, tears mingling with her milk."[15]

It is this tortured ritual—and Gilman's realization that "instead of [feeling] love and happiness" she felt "only pain"—that Stetson depicts in this portrait. The awareness, Gilman said, that "motherhood brought no joy" was "utterly bitter," and the emotional pain was a form of "mental agony" that propelled her into a "nightmare gloom"—an enormously dark place from which she saw no escape.[16] More than any other rendering, the painting serves as a visual companion to the written word; it is an arresting and authentic illustration of the emotional suffering that Gilman endured as she tried to conform to the socially prescribed expectations governing marriage and motherhood. And although Stetson had completed many other paintings by this time, he chose to display this portrait of his anguished wife at the Providence Art Club's annual exhibition in May 1887; ironically, the exhibition, held at the very place Stetson and Gilman had met, coincided with Gilman's treatment in Philadelphia by S. Weir Mitchell. Twelve days after she left Providence to undergo the rest cure, this very intimate portrait, depicting Gilman at her lowest point, was being scrutinized by friends and strangers alike, just a short walk from the home she shared with Walter Stetson.

One of Stetson's surviving sketchbooks contains a likely study for the painting. Although some of the illustrations from the summer and fall of 1886 have been removed from the tablet, there is a simple pencil sketch titled "Bedtime Aug. 1886" (see figure 2.4). It depicts Gilman attired in the same robe, apparently, and in what appears to be the same chair as the one depicted in Stetson's second painting. In the sketch Gilman's eyes are closed, and her face reflects the "constant dragging weariness," the "absolute misery" and the "helpless shame" that she describes in her memoir. One of the most intriguing features in the study is what appears to be a halo around Gilman's head—a common convention in Christian iconography that signifies divine motherhood. In his diary, Stetson complained bitterly about Gilman's desire to break free from the cult of domesticity. He wrote, "It is sin—surely sin—anything that takes woman away from the beautifying and sanctifying of home and the bearing of children must be sin. . . . She little knows what she does." Clearly, Gilman could not assume the role of angel in the house as her husband demanded. The domestic sphere was simply not a place she felt at home. Shortly after her release from Mitchell's care, Gilman began to lay the groundwork for a separation and eventual divorce.[17]

Katharine Stetson followed in her father's footsteps and also became an artist, who actively practiced her craft before the birth of her children. In her teens, she produced a series of early sketches of her mother, which were probably drawn sometime between 1898 and 1900 (see figure 2.5). Although the sketches do not reflect a high degree of artistic merit, they do offer a glimpse of Gilman, who relinquished custody of her daughter when she was nine, through Katharine's eyes. What is noteworthy about the drawings—and allowing for the fact that these are early sketches—is that Katharine engaged in a careful observation of her mother and depicted her as variously drowsy, squinting,

Figure 2.4. "Bedtime"—pencil sketch
by Charles Walter Stetson, August 1886

Figure 2.5. Pencil sketch by Katharine,
ca.1898–1900

Figure 2.6. Pencil sketch by
Katharine, 1904

or frowning in each of the illustrations. Motherhood was not a role that Gilman could gladly embrace. As she confided in a letter to Houghton Gilman, whom she would marry in 1900, "when [Katharine] was little [she was] . . . so lovely!—and I *knew* it, but couldn't *feel* it! And it aches and aches."[18]

Two additional sketches from the fall of 1904, when Katharine was nineteen, also survive. The first, rendered on October 16, is again not a close likeness of Gilman; Katharine struggled to capture her mother's features, particularly her nose and lips. The second rendering, drawn from a different angle than the first, again depicts a frowning figure, who appears to be cross and weary (see figure 2.6). Walter Stetson once wrote of Gilman, who was herself artistic, that she had produced a powerful painting of a "wan" and "worn out" figure who was facing an "insurmountable wall." Stetson characterized the painting as a "literal transcript of her mind."[19] The same might be said of Katharine's renderings of her mother; the two women had a thorny relationship that worsened when Katharine ultimately rejected her mother's leanings toward public service and instead, like her father, became an artist.

Much to Gilman's disappointment, Katharine also embraced the domestic sphere by becoming a housewife and mother, who painted and sculpted only as time allowed, even while acknowledging that female artists often subordinated their own work in order to attend to domestic chores. She wrote that "married women, unless wealthy[,] cannot devote themselves to art[,] as someone must care for the children and run the house."[20] While Gilman campaigned for socialized motherhood and professionalized housekeeping that would free

Figure 2.7. Charcoal sketch by Katharine, ca.1906

women to work outside the home, Katharine was willing to place traditionally feminine responsibilities ahead of her artistic ambitions.

Before her marriage in 1918 to fellow artist F. Tolles Chamberlin, Katharine studied art for five years in Italy, where she lived with her father and Grace Channing; there she exhibited a series of drawings at the American Pavilion of the Roman International Exposition. She began exhibiting her work nationally when she was twenty-one.[21] At some point, possibly as early as 1906, when she was a resident of the MacDowell Colony, a working retreat for artists in Peterborough, New Hampshire, Katharine produced two additional portraits of her mother. Although the original renderings are lost, photographs of the works have survived, and they document the evolution in Katharine's skills as an artist. It is difficult to define her style, but she was certainly influenced by her father's portraiture from this period, which often depicted the subject in a "rigid pose and isolate[ed] . . . against a uniformly dark [back]ground"[22]

One of the works (see figure 2.7) is a charcoal sketch with a background veiled in darkness, which provides a noticeable contrast to the illumination on Gilman's face. For the first time, the subject, facing three-quarters to the right, stares back at the artist. The likeness in this drawing is more evolved than in Katharine's earlier works, and although we don't know what Gilman's reaction was to the rendering, it is likely that she would have been pleased.[23] Gilman is in full possession of the face that Charles Walter Stetson tried unsuccessfully to "fix." There is a strength—a bold, defiant, unflinching, and steely gaze—a subtle suggestion of the strong will borne of Gilman's New England heritage, of which she was enormously proud.[24] We also see more fidelity in the rendering of Gilman's features than in earlier portraits: Katharine depicted the straightness of her mother's nose, the frown lines that were starting to emerge, and the cleft in her chin.

In contrast to the image of the stern New Englander, there are several newly recovered photographs of Gilman taken at Las Casitas Sanitarium in California in January 1900. (The photographer is unidentified.) More than any other rendering of Gilman, these photographs illustrate the impact of place on Gilman's joie de vivre, on her outlook, and on her physical and mental health. Freed from the shackles of domesticity, Gilman appears ready, both literally and metaphorically, to climb mountains. Taken just two years after she had achieved international acclaim for her book *Women and Economics* (1898), these photographs are remarkable not only for their quality—they score fairly high on clarity—but also because, unlike most of the other images, they are candid shots that depict a cheerful, radiant, and unguarded Gilman taking pleasure from the beauty of the idyllic setting in the foothills of the Sierra Madre.[25] It was also in the Sierra Madre that Gilman chose to have her ashes scattered upon her death about thirty-five years later. The turn-of-the-century equivalent of today's spa resorts, Las Casitas Sanitarium—or the "charming retreat," as it was dubbed in Charles F. Lummis's magazine, *The Land of Sunshine*—was touted as a place to which people who were "physically and mentally weary . . . [could] turn . . . for rest."[26]

Health-care professionals, including Dr. O. Shepard Barnum, who founded the sanitarium, believed that clean mountain air had the ability to heal both body and mind. *Land of Sunshine* contributor Elizabeth A. Graham remarked that in Las Casitas "one basks in the sunshine, drinks in the pure, bracing air, strolls through the canyons, roams over the trails, and life is one long summer dream." Likewise, Grace Channing's brother, Harold, a longtime acquaintance of Gilman's, wrote in a tourists' guide to Southern California that the remedial facility "offers to invalids a beautiful home, . . . picturesque walks . . . excellent cuisine[,] and skilled medical attendance." Although Gilman stayed in the adjacent boardinghouse, she was photographed in front of the sanitarium's main building, where she was accompanied in some of the images by two canine companions, a "big bull-dog [named] Jack" and "Tommy, a little Skye terrier."[27]

As Gilman noted in her autobiography, the winter that she spent at Las Casitas—where she drafted much of her 1904 book, *Human Work*—was among her happiest. She had her upcoming marriage to Houghton Gilman to look forward to in June, and she spent quality time with Katharine, who was living at the time with Walter and Grace in Pasadena. At Las Casitas, mother and daughter "tramped the hills together, read, played games—it was a joy,"

Figure 2.8. Gilman in Las
Casitas, California, 1900

Gilman wrote in her memoir. The extant photographs capture her exuber-
ance. Away from the public eye, Gilman is relaxed and smiling, armed with
a walking stick for climbing, a blanket for sitting, sturdy boots for hiking,
and a tablet for writing. The mountains, broad and majestic, serve as a backdrop (see figure 2.8). To Houghton, Gilman waxed lyrical about the beauty
and color of the landscape, describing the "flaming rose color [of the moun-
tains] in the sunset light," the "delicate brilliant green" of the meadows, the
"sea of splendid color" in the valley, and the emergence at night of "the big
liquid stars." She was also proud of her physical prowess and routinely hiked
six miles a day.[28]

The written discourse describing her stay in Las Casitas is noteworthy: "You
[should] see me prancing about these mountains. I'm not past being nimble
yet—if I am [almost] forty! The folks here gaze at me in amazement," Gilman
bragged to Houghton. "This splendid air, the peace and stillness and beauty,
are balm and strength to me."[29] Her language is striking: "prancing" is play-
ful, and the "gaze [of] amazement" from onlookers contrasts sharply with
the depiction of the anguished mother in Stetson's rendering of Gilman thirteen years earlier. The visitors at Las Casitas Sanitarium in January 1900 saw
in Gilman a woman who was at the pinnacle of health and happiness. Unless
they were familiar with her background, they would not have seen what we
see: a woman who teetered on the brink of insanity and found her way out.

Of particular note is how Gilman described her heightened senses during
her stay at Las Casitas—not only the visual but also the olfactory and auditory senses: "I am spending all day and every day out in the sweet high air

and blessed sun," she wrote to Houghton, adding that "the fruit buds swell, almonds are long in flower. . . . The wood doves are calling to each other all up and down the shadowy wooded canyons." At other points in her life—most notably during her breakdown years—she complained about hypersensitivity to sound, about having "wilted nerves" and "no 'appetite' in the mind," when the effort "to see, to hear, to think" was like "wad[ing] in glue" and there was "an irritable unease[,] which finds no rest."[30]

Gilman's experiences at Las Casitas, which she again visited in the spring of 1915, surely served as the foundation for her story "Dr. Clair's *Place*" (emphasis added), which offered an alternative to S. Weir Mitchell's rest cure by promoting the therapeutic benefits of a mountain resort. The story was published in the June 1915 issue of the *Forerunner*, and its title not only emphasizes the importance of physical space but also identifies the location of the fictional "psycho-sanatorium" as "the southern face of the Sierra Madres." The title also indicates that the female Dr. Clair has earned her "place" as a physician in what was then a traditionally male field; moreover, it suggests her psychological state: Dr. Clair is, as we would say today, in "a good place" emotionally. The name Clair, a fusion of the words *clear* and *air*, reflects the pristine environment that greeted new patients at the "sanatorium," where they were urged to climb hills, go swimming, and sleep outdoors. Gilman's own experience at Las Casitas certainly informed the creation of her fictional counterpart, Octavia Welch, whose treatment for neurasthenia at Dr. Clair's Place saves her from her "proposed suicide." Also significant is that Gilman described the interior space at the sanitarium—when Welch arrives, she is placed in a "quiet fragrant rosy room" with a "rose-draped balcony"—much like the one that the narrator longed for in Gilman's chilling story, "The Yellow Wall-Paper."[31]

Another image of Gilman that was recovered at the home of her grandson is a bas-relief that was sculpted by Gilman's son-in-law, F. Tolles Chamberlin, in New York in September 1919, the year after his marriage to Katharine.[32] The relief, in the Gilman Papers at the Schlesinger Library, was cast using plaster of Paris and measures approximately twenty-one by fourteen inches (see figure 2.9). In this rendering too we see a smiling Gilman, at the age of fifty-nine, whose expression suggests serenity and peace.

In fact, in 1919 Gilman was in a happy place; for the first time in her life she had a steady income as a contributor to the *New York Tribune* syndicate, where she turned out nearly 250 columns. The bas-relief, however, is not a precise likeness of Gilman; when we compare it to a photographic portrait of Gilman that was shot nine years earlier, it appears as though Chamberlin performed a cosmetic "lift" on her profile, softening the sharpness of her nose and reducing the beginnings of a double chin (see figure 2.10). Indeed, Gilman was consciously trying to soften her image; after a year of em-

Figure 2.9. Bas-relief by F. Tolles Chamberlin, 1919

Figure 2.10. Gilman, ca.1910

ployment as a syndicated writer, she was let go because her column could no longer "hold the popular taste." In order to earn a living, she again turned to the lecture circuit.[33]

As Gilman biographer Cynthia Davis points out, Gilman's "lecture opportunities had dwindled by the late teens," in part, Gilman insisted, because the nation was focused on the threat posed by World War I; as a result, her lecture bookings declined precipitously, and her income was reduced, she estimated, "by as much as 80 percent." Gilman's response, Davis notes, was to remake her image, to "[play] up her physical charms," and to downplay "her reputation as a 'radical.'" Davis also points out that "the word 'gentle' appears in nearly all" of the promotional materials that Gilman wrote and marketed, and she also borrowed language from favorable reviews that commented upon her "engaging smile and general charm of manner," as well as those that characterized her as "perfectly delightful," "gentle," and "feminine."[34] In a word, Gilman reinvented herself to appeal to a larger audience. We don't know whether she was complicit in the sculptural makeover or Chamberlin made the image more flattering in an attempt to win the approval of his mother-in-law, who could, at times, be more than a little hard to please.

After Houghton's death from a massive stroke in 1934, Gilman returned to Pasadena to die. The breast cancer that had been diagnosed two years earlier was inoperable, and Gilman resolved that "when all usefulness is over, when one is assured of unavoidable and imminent death, it is the simplest of human rights to choose a quick and easy death." To a friend she wrote, "I love California, and this beautiful little city is more like home to me than any place on earth." She described the beauty of the natural surroundings: "[I] spend my afternoons under a tall orange tree. . . . The white petals drift down softly. A large back garden; plenty of roses and other flowers." When Gilman was ready to "exit" the world, as she referred to her suicide, she inhaled chloroform, preferring it, she said, to cancer.[35]

When the coroner arrived to pronounce the death, Katharine informed him "that [she would] probably . . . want to make a death masque." There is no evidence that Gilman herself had requested that a mask be made, nor is there anything to suggest that she would have opposed such a plan. The mask, made by the family physician, Dr. Henry G. Bieler, was cast the next day by Sherry Peticolas, a local sculptor and a friend of Katharine and Tolles. It is a remarkable—and final—rendering of Gilman; every pore, line, and eyelash is preserved (see figure 2.11). To her cousin Lyman Beecher Stowe, Katharine wrote that "there was an air of peaceful triumph in her quiet figure," and, indeed, the barest hint of a smile appears on her emaciated face; the breast cancer that she had been fighting for three years had clearly had taken its toll.[36]

Five weeks before her death, Gilman had complained to Stowe, "I'm noth-

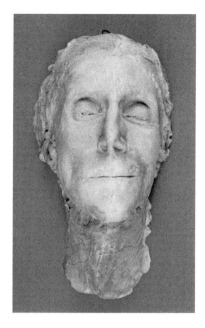

Figure 2.11. Gilman death mask cast by
Sherry Peticolas, August 1935

ing but bones and wrinkles—and to my disgust, I weigh [only] 100 [lbs.]!"
Likewise, to her old friend, Edward Alsworth Ross, she remarked, "I'm just
bones and drapery! and can't sit up long. Comfortable & happy all the same."
She no longer "walked," she told long-time friend Zona Gale; she "totter[ed]."
Paraphrasing Walt Whitman, she wrote to Gale that she was "absolutely at
peace . . . about God and Death," and just two days before she inhaled the
lethal vapors, she said to Ross, "I'm getting 'fed up' with sheer weakness . . .
so I'm going to go peaceably to sleep with my beloved chloroform."[37] Made
just hours after Gilman's death, the mask serves, in effect, as her final portrait. It reflects serenity and triumph, self-determination and freedom. Her
friend Hattie Howe observed, "Death did not seize her, an unwilling victim.
She went resolutely to meet it . . . as she met all things, gallantly, like a soldier on the field of battle."[38]

Howe's metaphor was appropriate in many ways. Gilman found deep within
herself a well of courage that allowed her to soldier on through a number of
battles: poverty, depression, censure, and loss. Collectively, the recovered works
are emblematic of Gilman's voyage through life. The early Hale painting and
the first Stetson portrait suggest the youthful Gilman at a crossroads, as she con-
templated the choices before her; the second Stetson painting, along with the
Stetson sketches, depicts Gilman's pain as she nursed Katharine and struggled
with the realization that "even motherhood brought no joy."[39] Katharine's early
drawings reflect her mother's reserve as the two tried to navigate their way

Figure 2.12. Gilman bust by Katharine Beecher Stetson Chamberlin, 1917

through what was sometimes a complicated mother-daughter relationship. The photos taken in Las Casitas, California, in 1900 capture a radiant and optimistic Gilman looking forward to the promise that the new century would bring. The bas-relief reveals a softer Gilman as her career begins to wane, and the death mask illustrates her determination to exercise her right to die. Examining the artistic renderings against the backdrop of Gilman's biography allows us to view them not solely as objects but also as tools in discovering how the various works inform our study of Gilman's life.

I will close this essay where I began it: with the recovered bust (see figure 2.12). Once fragile and now resilient, the bust symbolizes not only Gilman's recovery from her breakdown, but also her enduring impact. She began her life in the East, settled in the West (California) after her separation from Charles Walter Stetson, made her way back East after she married Houghton Gilman, and ventured West again after his death to live out her days—as, she said, a "Distinguished Invalid" in a "little house" with a "big green yard— flowers—. . . a blossoming orange tree, bees & birds and sunshine."[40]

Gilman loved the sensual appeal of the West: the floral fragrance in the air, the chirping birds in the boughs, and the warmth of the sun on her skin. But her intellectual and emotional ties were deeply rooted in New England. In 1972, thirty-seven years after her death, the first installment of Gilman's papers arrived, back East, at Harvard University's Schlesinger Library in Cambridge, Massachusetts.[41] The original cast of Gilman's bust was inadvertently discarded in the East; the duplicate was discovered in the Southwest, after its long storage in Katharine's Pasadena garage. The bust was finally cast in bronze and shipped to Cambridge, Massachusetts, where it joined the collection of Gilman artifacts at the Schlesinger Library.

The youthful Gilman, captured in Ellen Day Hale's 1877 portrait, could not have foreseen the journey that her life would take, from East to West and back again. Nor could she have known that she would one day be famous enough not only to occupy a prominent place in the annals of the American literary landscape but also to have her bust—an enduring image of her legacy—securely installed in a library that is dedicated to the preservation and study of women's history.

There is no place more fitting for it to be.

NOTES

1. Charlotte Perkins Gilman to Lyman Beecher Stowe, August 5, 1935, Charlotte Perkins Gilman Papers, Arthur and Elizabeth Schlesinger Library, Radcliffe Institute, Harvard University, Cambridge, MA. As has been well documented, much of Gilman's rhetoric promoted the cause of middle-class women but largely ignored the plight of working-class and minority women.

2. The oil painting by Stetson, *Evening—Mother & Child*, 1886–1887, is in the private art collection of Christopher and Melinda Ratcliffe, Providence, RI; Stetson's sketchbook was purchased by me at an auction in 2005 and is in my private collection in Cortland, NY; the early sketches of Gilman by her daughter, Katharine Beecher Stetson Chamberlin, are in the Walter Stetson Chamberlin Family Papers, the private collection of Gilman's grandson, as are the photographs of Gilman taken in 1900; and the bas-relief by F. Tolles Chamberlin is in the archives, Arthur and Elizabeth Schlesinger Library, Radcliffe Institute, Harvard University, Cambridge, MA.

3. The location of the 1882 painting, if it survives, is unknown. A photograph of the painting is in the Walter Stetson Chamberlin Family Papers. The painting by Hale is in the National Portrait Gallery at the Smithsonian Institution in Washington, DC. The death mask is in the Gilman Papers.

4. Ellen Day Hale (1855–1940) studied painting both in the United States with William Morris Hunt and in Europe under the tutelage of a number of artists. She had her first exhibition in 1876. Her portrait of Gilman was donated to the Smithsonian by Gilman's heirs in 1983.

5. Charlotte Perkins Gilman, *The Selected Letters of Charlotte Perkins Gilman*, ed. Denise D. Knight and Jennifer S. Tuttle (Tuscaloosa: University of Alabama Press, 2009), 202.

6. Charlotte Perkins Gilman, *The Living of Charlotte Perkins Gilman: An Autobiography* (New York: Appleton-Century, 1935), 43.

7. Gilman, *Selected Letters*, 29; Charles Walter Stetson, *Endure: The Diaries*

of Charles Walter Stetson, ed. Mary A. Hill (Philadelphia, PA: Temple University Press, 1985), 121.

8. Stetson, *Endure*, 99, 100, 104; Anne Bradstreet, "The Author to Her Book," http://www.annebradstreet.com.

9. Stetson, *Endure*, 101.

10. Charles Walter Stetson, "The Painting of *The Portrait*," in *The Diaries of Charlotte Perkins Gilman*, ed. Denise D. Knight (Charlottesville: University Press of Virginia, 1994), 1: 876–77. The sonnets are written in Stetson's hand on loose paper that was inserted in Gilman's diary for 1882, and the title is from this copy. The sonnets are also included in Stetson's diary, *Endure*, but there they are untitled. In full, the sonnets read as follows:

The Painting of *The Portrait*
These many days I've tried to fix the face
Of her I love on canvas, that it might
Remain to tell of her and glad the sight
Of those to come with intellectual grace.
Most patiently did she sit, and I did trace
And study the marvellous eye that's dark and bright,
The curve from the wide clear brow's fair height
Along the cheek to the eloquent lips' red place;
And then adown the delicate smooth chin
To the supple throat, until it was so lost
In the hid and heaving breasts' cream white high mounds.
But Oh! today 'tis not more like to her within
My soul, nor like to what her soul surrounds,
Than 'twas when first my brush the canvas crossed.
II
O what in me the fault, or what the sin,
That dulls my sight or warps her image fair
Until my hand may not her lovliness [sic] declare—
For which I've prayed e'er since I did begin?
Ah, Lord, and hath it always suchwise been,
That ne'er within my heart I yet did bear
An image true of all her shape so rare,
Tho' sure I know her spirit dwells therein?
What then the hope for eminence in Art
When what I love e'en as my very soul
Is not seen clear, is scarcely understood?
And while I cannot fix the smallest part
Of her great loveliness what can console,
And what of all my life and Art is good?

11. Charlotte Perkins Gilman, *The Diaries of Charlotte Perkins Gilman*, ed. Denise D. Knight (Charlottesville: University Press of Virginia, 1994), 1: 882.

12. Stetson, *Endure*, 106. The timing here is also important; the portrait was completed just three days before Gilman's closest friend, Martha Luther, was married—an occasion that brought a sense of loss, sadness, resignation, and rebellion into Gilman's life. Gilman's romantic friendship with Luther has been well documented by biographers; see, e.g., Cynthia J. Davis, *Charlotte Perkins Gilman: A Biography* (Stanford, CA: Stanford University Press, 2010), 48–56.

13. Stetson, *Endure*, 93.

14. Charles Walter Stetson, "Opera Book," 1881–1908, 77, Charles Walter Stetson Papers, Smithsonian Archives of American Art, Smithsonian Institution, Washington, DC. Stetson finished the painting on February 5, 1887; he exhibited it in May of that year at the Providence Art Club, and in October 1888 the portrait was purchased by Mrs. George V. Cresson of Philadelphia. The Ratcliffes purchased the painting in 2008 from the John Moran Auction House in Altadena, CA. "Opera Book" is a treasure trove of information about the various drawings, sketches, and paintings that Stetson created. It contains dates, titles, sales, exhibition information, and personal reflections about the works.

15. Charlotte Perkins Gilman, "Records of My Daughter Katharine Stetson," Chamberlin Family Papers.

16. Gilman, *Living*, 91, 92, 96.

17. Gilman, *Living*, 91; Stetson, *Endure*, 148. We know that one additional portrait of Gilman and Katharine has survived, but its whereabouts are unknown. Titled *From My Window after Rain, Pasadena*, (1889–1890), the portrait depicts the two walking through an orange grove. In a letter to Gilman dated July 9, 1894, Stetson wrote that Katharine, who was living with him at the time, "*loves* that [painting] & finds in it the 'Mama' you desired as being in it." Cynthia J. Davis, "The Two Mrs. Stetsons and the 'Romantic Summer,'" in *Charlotte Perkins Gilman and Her Contemporaries*, ed. Cynthia J. Davis and Denise D. Knight (Tuscaloosa: University of Alabama Press, 2004), 9.

18. Charlotte Perkins Gilman, *A Journey from Within: The Love Letters of Charlotte Perkins Gilman, 1897–1900*, ed. Mary A. Hill (Lewisburg, PA: Bucknell University Press, 1995), 65. Katharine's sketches are in the Chamberlin Family Papers. On one of them, Katharine wrote in green pencil that the sketches "are all Drawn from my mother[—]not a likeness[.]"

19. Stetson, *Endure*, 244.

20. Katharine Beecher Stetson Chamberlin, "MacDowell Colony Questionnaire," n.d., 2, Chamberlin Family Papers.

21. Ibid. Katharine also studied for a year (1906) at the Pennsylvania Academy of the Fine Arts, where she further refined her skills.

22. Charles C. Eldredge, *Charles Walter Stetson: Color and Fantasy* (Lawrence, KS: Spencer Museum of Art, 1982), 95.

23. Throughout the years Gilman was told that she bore a resemblance to a number of famous women: the French writer George Sand (1803–1876), the English novelist George Eliot (1819–1880), the biblical matriarch Rachel, and the English poet Christina Rossetti (1830–1894)—a "noble list," she remarked in 1894. Gilman, *Diaries*, 576.

24. For a discussion of Gilman's allegiance to her New England roots, see Denise D. Knight, "'That Pure New England Stock': Charlotte Perkins Gilman and the Construction of Identity," in *Charlotte Perkins Gilman: New Texts and Contexts*, ed. Jennifer S. Tuttle and Carol Farley Kessler (Columbus: Ohio State University Press, 2011), 27–43.

25. "Gilman . . . vacillated dramatically in her views on California and her place in its literary pantheon." Jennifer S. Tuttle, "'New England Innocent' in the Land of Sunshine: Charlotte Perkins Gilman and California," *Western American Literature* 48, no. 3 (Fall 2013): 286–87. Indeed, Gilman was captivated by the natural beauty of the Golden State, yet she felt an allegiance to New England, where she was born and raised. She was also bitter about the sensationalized coverage in the California newspapers of her divorce in 1894 from Stetson and the public condemnation that followed.

26. Elizabeth A. Graham, "Las Casitas—A Charming Retreat," *Land of Sunshine*, April 1895.

27. Ibid.; Harold S. Channing, "To Health Seekers," in *B. R. Baumgardt & Co's Tourists' Guide Book to South California*, ed. George Wharton James (Los Angeles: B. R. Baumgardt, 1895), 444; Gilman, *Living*, 276.

28. Gilman, *Living*, 278; Gilman, *Journey*, 334.

29. Gilman, *Journey*, 336, 338.

30. Ibid., 345, 347; Gilman, *Living*, 102.

31. Charlotte Perkins Gilman, "Dr. Clair's Place," *Forerunner*, June 1915, 141, 142, 144.

32. Katharine makes several references to her mother coming for sittings for a bas-relief, sometimes for as long as two and a half hours. Katharine Beecher Stetson Chamberlin, "Journal," August and September 1914, Katharine Beecher Stetson Papers, 1827–1956, Correspondence, Gilman Papers, Arthur and Elizabeth Schlesinger Library, Radcliffe Institute, Harvard University, Cambridge, MA.

33. Gary Scharnhorst, *Charlotte Perkins Gilman: A Bibliography* (Metuchen, NJ: Scarecrow Press, 1985), 157–75; Gilman, *Living*, 310.

34. Davis, *Biography*, 322.

35. Gilman, *Living*, 333, 334; Gilman, *Selected Letters*, 294, 299.

36. Katharine Beecher Stetson Chamberlin to Lyman Beecher Stowe, August 20, 1935, Beecher-Stowe Family Collection, Arthur and Elizabeth Schlesinger Library, Radcliffe Institute, Harvard University, Cambridge, MA; Walter Stetson Chamberlin, e-mail to author, February 24, 2011.

KNIGHT / 69

37. Gilman, *Selected Letters* 302, 303, 305; Chamberlin to Stowe, August 20, 1935, Beecher-Stowe Family Collection. According to Walter Stetson Chamberlin, Gilman started stockpiling small amounts of chloroform in the final months of her life. She visited various pharmacies, asked for just enough chloroform to "kill a cat," and was able to collect a sufficient amount. She carried out her suicide on August 17, 1935. Many of the specific details about the aftermath of Gilman's suicide are contained in the August 20 letter from Katharine to Lyman Beecher Stowe, three days after her mother's death. The letter reveals just how strong-willed Gilman was in terminating her life. Gilman's doctor had cautioned her that self-administration of chloroform would probably fail since "the average person fights the effects when going under." Katharine surmised, however, that "the first few whiffs must have carried her off." She wrote to Stowe that "there was an air of peaceful triumph in her quiet figure—she had carried out her plan in all details as she had wished" and that she "had failed very fast" during her last week and was so "feeble" and "weary" that she welcomed death. "She was happy in the thought—she just longed for it," Katharine wrote, "so we feel that it was better—far[—]for her to go." Gilman's will, which Gilman had updated in 1934, began with a clause addressing the disposition of her remains: "I wish to be cremated and that my ashes be disposed of as convenient to my heir, with no funeral services of any kind." Gilman Papers, folder 284. Katharine honored Gilman's wishes.

38. Harriet Howe, "Charlotte Perkins Gilman—As I Knew Her," *Equal Rights: Independent Feminist Weekly*, September 1936.

39. Gilman, *Living*, 92.

40. Ibid., 297.

41. Katherine Beecher Stetson Chamberlin to Jeannette Cheek, September 13, 1972, Gilman Papers, Office Correspondence. Katharine insisted that her decision to provide the library with her mother's papers was not driven by the fact that it specialized in "women's archives," but rather because it had "made the first offer."

WORKS CITED

Beecher-Stowe Family Collection. Arthur and Elizabeth Schlesinger Library, Radcliffe Institute, Harvard University, Cambridge, MA.
Bradstreet, Anne. "The Author to Her Book." http://www.annebradstreet.com.
Chamberlin, Walter Stetson. Family Papers. Private collection.
Channing, Harold S. "To Health Seekers." In *B. R. Baumgardt & Co's Tourists' Guide Book to South California*, edited by George Wharton James, 437–44. Los Angeles: B. R. Baumgardt, 1895.
Davis, Cynthia J. *Charlotte Perkins Gilman: A Biography*. Stanford, CA: Stanford University Press, 2010.

———. "The Two Mrs. Stetsons and the 'Romantic Summer.'" In *Charlotte Perkins Gilman and Her Contemporaries*, edited by Cynthia J. Davis and Denise D. Knight, 1–16. Tuscaloosa: University of Alabama Press, 2004.

Eldredge, Charles C. *Charles Walter Stetson: Color and Fantasy*. Lawrence, KS: Spencer Museum of Art, 1982.

Gilman, Charlotte Perkins. *The Diaries of Charlotte Perkins Gilman*. 2 vols. Edited by Denise D. Knight. Charlottesville: University Press of Virginia, 1994.

———. "Dr. Clair's Place." *Forerunner*, June 1915.

———. *Human Work*. New York: McClure, Philips, 1904.

———. *A Journey from Within: The Love Letters of Charlotte Perkins Gilman, 1897–1900*. Edited by Mary A. Hill. Lewisburg, PA: Bucknell University Press, 1995.

———. *The Living of Charlotte Perkins Gilman: An Autobiography*. New York: Appleton-Century, 1935.

———. Papers. Arthur and Elizabeth Schlesinger Library, Radcliffe Institute, Harvard University. Cambridge, MA.

———. *The Selected Letters of Charlotte Perkins Gilman*. Edited by Denise D. Knight and Jennifer S. Tuttle. Tuscaloosa: University of Alabama Press, 2009.

———. *Women and Economics: A Study of the Economic Relation between Men and Women as a Factor in Social Evolution*. Boston: Small, Maynard, 1898.

———. *The Yellow Wall-Paper*. 1892. Edited by Elaine R. Hedges. New York: Feminist Press, 1973.

Graham, Elizabeth A. "Las Casitas—A Charming Retreat." *Land of Sunshine*, April 1895.

Howe, Harriet. "Charlotte Perkins Gilman—As I Knew Her." *Equal Rights: Independent Feminist Weekly*, September 1936.

Knight, Denise D. "The Dying of Charlotte Perkins Gilman." *American Transcendental Quarterly*. 13, no. 2 (June 1999): 137–59.

———. "'That Pure New England Stock': Charlotte Perkins Gilman and the Construction of Identity." In *Charlotte Perkins Gilman: New Texts and Contexts*, edited by Jennifer S. Tuttle and Carol Farley Kessler, 27–43. Columbus: Ohio State University Press, 2011.

Scharnhorst, Gary. *Charlotte Perkins Gilman: A Bibliography*. Metuchen, NJ: Scarecrow Press, 1985.

Stetson, Charles Walter. *Endure: The Diaries of Charles Walter Stetson*. Edited by Mary A. Hill. Philadelphia, PA: Temple University Press, 1985.

———. "The Painting of *The Portrait*." In *The Diaries of Charlotte Perkins Gilman*, Vol. 1, edited by Denise D. Knight, 876–77. Charlottesville: University Press of Virginia, 1994.

———. Papers. Smithsonian Archives of American Art, Smithsonian Institution, Washington, DC.

Stetson, Katharine Beecher. Papers. 1827–1956. Arthur and Elizabeth Schlesinger Library, Radcliffe Institute, Harvard University, Cambridge, MA.

Tuttle, Jennifer S. "'New England Innocent' in the Land of Sunshine: Charlotte Perkins Gilman and California." *Western American Literature* 48, no. 3 (Fall 2013): 284–311.

Tuttle, Jennifer S., and Carol Farley Kessler, eds. *Charlotte Perkins Gilman: New Texts, New Contexts*. Columbus: Ohio State University Press, 2011.

3
"The Yellow Wall-Paper" as Modernist Space

William C. Snyder

As a social reformer from the 1890s until her death in 1935, Charlotte Perkins Gilman is appropriately categorized as a modern writer for advancing progressive ideas about female psychology and domestic economy. Although scholars have shown how her reformist themes were ingeniously incorporated into "The Yellow Wall-Paper" (1892), the story breaks ground on another level: its radical visuality allows us to consider Gilman as a modern *artist*. An exercise in ekphrasis (the literary description of a visual work of art) from the first sentence to the last, "The Yellow Wall-Paper" treats space through semiotic play in text that is an experiment against the conventions of perception and depiction, suggesting a number of affinities to innovations in the visual arts that occurred near the time of the author's early adulthood.

Throughout the story, Gilman requires us to engage several different sets of visual fields. The ancestral home rented for the summer offers a piazza with clusters of roses, pleasing grounds, and gratifying third-floor views. The top-floor nursery can be troped as a gallery, the windows providing scenes of a delighting natural world from an elevated point of view. The wallpaper in this room is essentially a canvas, its fluctuating images drawing the protagonist and the reader into a peculiar and then grotesque experience. Whereas the first section of the narrative compares and contrasts indoor and outdoor scenes, the latter part is dominated by idiosyncratic forms and nonlinear sequences provided exclusively by the wall.

Familiar with and fluent in perceptual process, the narrator in the story represents a new kind of character. Gilman, synthesizing her own training in the arts, her repression as a young girl, and her depression as a new mother, created a unique persona: a sensitive, creative woman constantly striving to understand her environment, made up entirely of her marriage, her mother-hood, and her confinement, with no occasion to pursue her art. By delving into the less coherent, more fragmentary, and disturbed recesses of the mind, Gilman invented an imagery for the forced isolation of body and a constraint on vivid imagination. This convergence of unusual sensibilities and perceptions breaks from traditional modes of characterization, making the wife in "The Yellow Wall-Paper" a modern antiheroine.

Elements of Gilman's autobiography figure heavily in a mode of composition that introduces us to new ways of correlating physical spaces to figurations of the female. Although the protagonist's sensibilities are implicit in *The Living of Charlotte Perkins Gilman*, her perceptual process can be traced in Gilman's diaries and letters—literary performances all pointing to the author's persistent and strong sense of physical location.

While attending Providence's Rhode Island School of Design (1878–1880), Gilman cherished the one-mile walk along the campus of Brown University, and when she arrived at the art school she had a place where eye and imagination could be indulged and where she could fully feel "twenty-one. My own mistress at last." She reported being very pleased with her third-floor room on Manning Street, which provided a vista of the town:

From my high window the outlooker sees
The whole wide southern sky;
Fort Hill is in the distance, always green,
With ordinary houses thick between,
And scanty passers by.
Our street is flat, ungraded, little used,
The sidewalks grown with grass;
And, just across, a fenceless open lot,
Covered with ash-heaps, where the sun shines
On bits of broken glass.

In this space of her own, Gilman enjoyed Providence's panorama on a daily basis and was so enamored of fresh air that she attempted to bring the outdoors inside. Just after moving in, she performed an unusual action: "The window I promptly took out of the casing, it stayed out for the three years we lived there. In very stormy weather I used to stand one of the spare leaves from the dining-table against it; that and closed blinds kept out most of the snow."[1]

Clearly, being able to see beyond her own bodily situation and being able to connect with visual elements far and near were important to Gilman. More-over, her freedom to set her own schedule, take students according to her own volition, and walk anywhere without reporting her whereabouts made her feel "a tremendous sense of power, clean glorious power, of ability to do whatever I decided to undertake." At this time of her life, Gilman could enjoy a residence that offered a sense of liberation and connection so critical to defining a home space, which Gaston Bachelard has said should contain "the psychological elasticity of an image that moves us at an unimaginable depth."[2] Also noteworthy is Gilman's practice in her autobiography of upholding physical movement as complementary to perceptual nimbleness and creative motility.

The time after Gilman's short formal education soon began to contrast with her time as a student. The years after 1884 brought a reluctant marriage, immediate motherhood, postpartum stress, and a new residence—not far from her location on Manning Street, but worlds apart in atmosphere. The division of these two periods was pronounced in Gilman's own mind; her move to Humboldt Street upon her marriage to Walter Stetson was made for traditional and domestic purposes, and Gilman wrote that she was provided "a charming home" with "a loving and devoted husband; an exquisite baby, healthy, intelligent and good; a highly competent mother to run things, a wholly satisfactory servant." But even though she could acknowledge the comforts of these trappings, she "lay all day on the lounge and cried." In this space she was mainly stationary, and clearly she could no longer enjoy any of the virtues of her single existence. The small third-floor room that she had called her own was immensely more satisfying than living in an expansive house owned by someone else—a role played by the colonial mansion of "The Yellow Wall-Paper."[3]

In 1888, after having tried S. Weir Mitchell's rest-cure for neurasthenia, Gilman relocated to her friend Grace Ellery Channing's home in Pasadena, California. Having escaped Providence and the therapy, Gilman wrote to her closest confidante, Martha Luther, and shared a positive verbal sketch of her new surroundings: "I am really quite happy. I ought to be. The great blue periwinkles crowd around my little piazza, the roses are coming out by the hundreds—(two great vines that shade and sweeten the whole front of the house); the Banksia rose flourishes from ground to ridgepole on the South, and is myriad budded now; the oranges hang ever ready and the orange blossoms make a dreamland all about me, and then there are mockingbirds and moonlight galore."[4]

Gilman's letters from Pasadena reveal an attention to spaces whose descriptions reclaim her love of openness, airiness, color, and human situation in nature. They provide a record of a creative mind settling into writing as a self-cure, with the Channing house and grounds supplying pleasures and comforts that flash in and out of the letters—quick sensory notes embedded among sketches of pleasant familial activity, such as drying her hair in the piazza or watching her daughter, Katharine, swinging in a hammock.[5] With more than a dozen descriptions like these, written just a few months before Gilman composed "The Yellow Wall-Paper," the letters clearly provided some of the spatial references in the story where the protagonist enjoys natural views supplied by the windows.

While Gilman's biography and correspondence offer clues to the relation of place to the emotional disposition of the story's protagonist, Gilman's paintings produced throughout the 1880s connect to the visual performances prevalent in the "The Yellow Wall-Paper." Art school provided Gilman with a sense of structure and perceptual discipline, and her canvases reveal not only a love of pattern but also a proclivity to experiment with modes of execution within a two-dimensional medium. The collection of her drawings and paintings at Harvard University's Schlesinger Library reveals a focus on natural objects, including flower drawings with intense colors and a few landscapes with a strong sense of perspective.

Gilman's background in the arts, the vicissitudes of her twenties, and perhaps her exposure to modernist literature put her in the category of late nineteenth-century artists who felt the limitation of traditional courses of creativity and opted for originality in seeing and composing.[6] The themes of isolation and fragmentation, along with the shifting of perspective and attention to oddity and absurdity, render "The Yellow Wall-Paper" Gilman's greatest artistic breakthrough. It is, ostensibly, the first modernist work of fiction by a woman, appearing a generation before the works of Mina Loy, Gertrude Stein, and Virginia Woolf.

The definition of the term *modernism* may have loose boundaries, but its core terminology applies to "The Yellow Wall-Paper." Chris Baldick states that modern writing represents a "wide range of experimental and avant-garde trends in the literature (and other arts) of the early 20th century" in which literary texts are "characterized chiefly by a rejection of 19th-century traditions and of their consensus between author and reader: conventions of realism or traditional meter." Modernist writers are "disengaged from bourgeois values," disturbing "their readers by adopting complex and difficult new forms and styles." Concerning style, modern texts include "techniques of juxtaposition and multiple points of view" that "challenge the reader to reestablish a coherence of meaning from fragmentary forms." Christopher Butler observes that modern imagery follows an "aesthetic of an evolutionary or disruptive tradition" and participates "in the migration of innovatory techniques and their associated ideas. In this period, concepts like 'intuition' and 'expression,' or 'subjectivity' and 'inner division,' or 'harmony' and 'rhythm,' are parts of a changing framework of ideas which inspired stylistic change in Modernist work in all the arts."[7]

"The Yellow Wall-Paper" disturbs the traditional interplay of language and narrative to pioneer new ways in which fiction can portray action in static space. Modern artists—both writers and painters—reflect perceptual process and psychological states that cannot be captured through standard artistic modes. Gilman employed both conventional and eccentric sensory references to deepen plot and define her main character, whose descriptions of the spaces in the story "give an exterior density to the interior being."[8] Her consciousness fluctuates according to the number of stimuli: external, providing a sense of pleasure originating in the freedom to perceive, recognize, act, and react; and internal, enclosing the protagonist and relegating her to a fixed, constrictive space.

From the beginning to the end, the narrative rests on two visual frames: (1) the windows out of which the woman can enjoy the pastoral spaces beyond the house, and (2) the wall, an antinature, two-dimensional "canvas" on which she ends up "painting" with emotion, anxiety, and obsession. Seeking ways to narrate a mind that vacillates among active, creative, and dissociative modes of observation, Gilman composed "The Yellow Wall-Paper" by maneuvering verbal-visual constructs that simulate techniques of impressionism, cubism, and abstract expressionism—three modernist programs that arose during Gilman's lifetime. She brought her familiarity with visual art, chromatics, and design to the pen and page to convey one woman's new way of seeing by means of optical fusion, juxtaposition, collage, color fields, and "ready-mades"—modernist modes of engaging place and space.

I wish to emphasize here that Gilman's method in composing in "The Yellow Wall-Paper" has *affinities* with the work of other modernists; I do not mean to argue that Gilman influenced, or was influenced by, the visual artists of her lifetime. Rather, my assertion is that Gilman's story discloses a mind that produces images that participate in a modernist mode of perceiving and executing. The writing of "The Yellow Wall-Paper" in the early 1890s is a nascent expression of the modernist argument, a work that contributes a number of images that fit into the modernist catalog.

Forty percent of "The Yellow Wall-Paper" consists of reactions to visual stimuli: the windows of the wife's bedroom provide pleasant scenes and vistas, and the wall provides a field for free play, confabulations, and, ultimately, bizarre apprehensions. The rising action of the narrative follows the process of wider perspectives becoming closed off, accompanying the woman's increasingly frustrated attempts to excavate meaning from the wallpaper. The middle and end of the story force the reader-perceiver to deal with smaller subsections of her terrible space, and as the protagonist gets closer to the paper, it pushes her deeper into her anxieties by overwhelming her visually, the way that viewers might feel when sitting too close to a movie screen. Rational forms are camouflaged because they are viewed too intimately.

The first section of "The Yellow Wall-Paper" suggests methods of perception found in impressionist painting, which was gaining renown when Gilman was an art student. The features of impressionism—the emphasis on the impermanence of a scene, the effects of lighting, the interplay of color, and the materiality of atmosphere—are evident until the mention of Weir Mitchell. These techniques, apparent in French artists including Claude Monet, Auguste Renoir, and Camille Pissarro, announced a break from traditional modes of visual representation.

Gilman's story starts with positive descriptions of the new space of the mansion. Her journal entries, made in a hasty manner, are a series of impressions of objects that are standard imagery in impressionist views: flowers, gardens, lanes, trees, water, pathways, shade, and light. A particular delight provided by impressionist canvases is optical fusion: a process in which the eye (and the mind) merge components, fragments, and segments to create a comprehensible scene. Because the image is not fully given to the viewer as an object, active perception is required to provide recognition, which emphasizes an imaginative mediation that initiates pleasure. Although many impressionist paintings rely on optical fusion, like Monet's *Antibes Seen from La Salis* (see figure 3.1), Gilman's 1884 botanical painting (see figure 3.2) reveals the same artistic approach of integrating independent optical components that depend on one another to define an object or to convey a certain atmosphere, almost always a pleasing one.

This way of seeing—involving an act of creation by the viewer—offers a layer of pleasure that complements the delightful subjects that typically occupy impressionist scenes. In the story, impressionist references occur between the wife's initial attempt to describe the house and the passing of the Fourth of July. Gilman spends nearly eight hundred words setting the story and conveying the wife's initial state of mind, her optimism and felicity, through her ability to perceive and imagine. The narrator's first reaction to her new space, the large old mansion with expansive grounds, is an enthusiastic report that conveys a marked sense of delight at the home's site and attributes:

> The most beautiful place! It is quite alone, standing well back from the road, quite three miles from the village. It makes me think of English places that you read about, for there are hedges and walls and gates that lock, and lots of separate little houses for the gardeners and people.

Figure 3.1. Claude Monet, *Antibes Seen from La Salis*, 1888 (Toledo Museum of Art)

Figure 3.2. Charlotte Perkins Gilman, botanical painting, 1884 (Gilman Papers, 1846–ca.1975, Series 6, 323a–323c, seq. 88)

There is a *delicious* garden! I never saw such a garden large and shady, full of box-bordered paths, and lined with long grape-covered arbors with seats under them.

There were greenhouses, too, but they are all broken now.[9]

This excerpt interrupts concerns about her husband John's opinion of her condition and the legal status of the house; the report is the first place in the story where the artist is able to separate from the wife. The interlude is a celebration of the senses. The rest cure, designed to numb the mind, is thwarted by metaphors and synesthesia: the phrases "*delicious* garden," "box-bordered paths," and "grape-covered arbors" confirm the efficacy of the viewer's senses and avow an active pleasure principle. But the passage is hardly an exposition, a full and measured illustration: the narrator's lines are akin to the author's California journal—a glance, an impression. In addition, the phrase "standing well back from the road" establishes depth of field; the hedges, walls, and "separate little houses for the gardeners and people" provide leading lines to the house, as in a painting.

Each grammatical component, each phrasal brushstroke, moves to a new object, accompanied by transitory judgments; objects are "beautiful" and "delicious," blending sight with taste as the fusion of her senses evokes a pleasure that yields exclamation. However, the narrator also points out "broken" greenhouses, conjuring a picturesque scene inviting completion by readers: we participate and we integrate, invited to imagine metal skeletons holding up shattered calcified windows, weeds growing out of fallen pots, perhaps, and rusted pumps. The broken glass and frames of the greenhouses signify the breaking of the perception, as delicate as it is momentary.

This scene through the window, infused with enjoyment, fits Robert Hughes's definition of impressionism as a "landscape of pleasure" whose view "represented one thing at a given moment in time, an effect of light and colour that was by definition fugitive." Not only are the narrator's attentions on the same elements habitually found in impressionist works—trees, arbors, paths, people—they are rendered with a mixture of excitement and elation, with details only sketched, as in a typical impressionist scene, "which should have taken only as long to paint as it took to see."[10]

The second visual bracket is antithetical to the window. When the wife first sets eyes on the wallpaper, her aesthetic sense is immediately violated. She claims that she "never saw a worse paper in [her] life," describing the space not through sense references but through negative subjective judgments: "lame," "uncertain," "outrageous," "unclean," "dull," "sickly." The "artistic sins" of the wallpaper are in its "flamboyant patterns," which stifle her from the pleasures of recognition so nimbly evoked by her perceptions of the world outside. The passage is laden with imagery of rejection: "contradiction," "repellant," and "revolting" show that she detests and resents the wall. The two spaces, window and wall, form a contradiction that will initiate a key tension: faraway scenes captivate her; spaces near repulse her.[11]

The story's second impressionist-like composition is a follow-up to the wife's first encounter with the wallpaper. After rationalizing John's absences and her separation from her child, and after undertaking a survey of the interior space, the protagonist moves her eye across the room. The new perception prompts another drastic mood shift:

> Out of one window I can see the garden, those mysterious deepshaded arbors, the riotous old fashioned flowers, and bushes and gnarly trees.
> Out of another I get a lovely view of the bay and a little private wharf belonging to the estate. There is a beautiful shaded lane that runs down there from the house. I always fancy I see people walking in these numerous paths and arbors, but John has cautioned me not to give way to fancy in the least.[12]

The shapes that the protagonist describes here still derive from the storehouse of impressionist painting; she moves quickly from garden to bay to land. But the arbors—now "deepshaded"—are "mysterious," the flowers "riotous," and the trees "gnarly." Within this perception we detect the wife's struggle between sense and sensibility, for the delights of the views are darkened by John's distrust of imagining, of "giv[ing] way to fancy." While these window frames open the narrator to the joys of the outside world, they are also delimiting structures, visually, psychologically, and corporeally: the gardens and countryside that supply her contentment and bliss are on the other side of the frame—spaces beyond, outward and other.

The word *gnarly* in reference to the trees has visual, narrative, and subtextual significance. Gilman is probably referring to a coast live oak (see figure 3.3), whose branches can curve like a corkscrew.[13] The adjective introduces a new kind of shape, indicating a modulation in the feelings of the woman as she discovers that the world of nature includes striking asymmetry. In addition, the term denotes a shift in the narrator's point of view, foreshadowing the irregular and fantastic shapes that emerge later in the story. It is at this point that the wife begins to recognize the deep-shadedness of the human mind, the riotousness of a strained marriage, and the gnarled emotions caused by these forces.

The leitmotif of duress, however, does not affect the protagonist's awareness of design and composition. There is a discernible line of perspective—the lane running from the wharf to the house—and her "fancy[ing]" seeing "people walking in these numerous paths and arbors." Her faculties intact, she

Figure 3.3. Coast live oak, Descanso Gardens, Pasadena, CA

is in touch with herself as a person and as a perceiver, circumstances that Gilman conveys through her own ability to see as a painter would: in fugitive accounts that associate the summer landscape with figures of joy, harmony, and satisfaction. The difference between the author and the protagonist is articulated by the difference in the spaces each occupies. Gilman's biography celebrates the ability to spend time in the piazza—to walk in the lanes, breathe the scent of roses, and watch a daughter frolic. That the story's narrator cannot experience these connections with nature suggests that "The Yellow Wall-Paper" represents Gilman's imagining of the fate that awaited her if not for her twenty-one-month stay at the Channings.[14]

The mention of John terminates the composition before it is complete, and her creative effort fades into resignation as the woman goes back to his advice to use her "will and good sense." As the thought of her husband infiltrates her mind, the wall again catches her eye; from this point, John and the paper are linked for the rest of the story. After recognizing the "vicious" influence of the paper, she grows angry at its "impertinence," as John's sister, the housekeeper, seems to be approaching. The caregiver's complicity in the oppression is acknowledged: "I must not let her find me writing," for "she thinks it is the writing which made me sick!" However, knowing her sister-in-law's routine allows the narrator the freedom to think, to view, and to compose:

But I can write when she is out, and see her a long way off from these windows.

There is one that commands the road, a lovely shaded winding road, and one that just looks off over the country. A lovely country, too, full of great elms and velvet meadows.[15]

This report is the last time in the story that the protagonist's attention is drawn outside. The three views out the windows—her three quick impressions of life outside the room—move from near to far, from the piazza below to the roads and houses to the horizon. The window overlooking the "lovely shaded winding road" supplies the notion that the woman longs to escape and be among the bright things in nature. The window that "just looks off over the country" reminds her that the "great elms" and "velvet meadows" cannot be part of her direct experience. The diversions of sunny landscapes and alluring colors fade and cease to be part of the story. After this last panorama, she recognizes that the room is a barrier between her and the prospects she loves to look upon. The narrator realizes that her remaining companion of any consequence is the wallpaper. After this passage, the narrative line of development moves from the light, airy, and transitory effects of impressionism to a less rational and less representational series of images.

As impressionist painters were probing the interfusion of light and object and were recording the process as sensuous pleasure, Paul Cézanne, in the 1880s, was changing the relationship between color and structure, reprioritizing ways of seeing: from a fixed vantage point he could create manifold views, within the same canvas or in a succession of canvases. He wrote, "The same subject seen from a different angle gives a motif of the highest interest, and so varied that I think I could be occupied for months without changing my place—simply bending a little more to the right or left."[16] Cézanne's paintings of Mont Sainte-Victoire (see figure 3.4), done in a series in the 1880s and 1890s, emphasize the role of geometric shapes occupying a panoramic natural space.

The mountain and its environs (trees, buildings, roads, and an aqueduct) insinuate basic geometric forms (rectangles, triangles, circles, ovals, and cubes), steering later painters such as Georges Braque and Pablo Picasso toward cubism. Cézanne's view of Mont Sainte-Victoire from 1885 shows how a canvas with various colors and myriad objects creates an inviting depth of field that accentuates the pleasure of a natural landscape: we see familiar shapes in proportion, but the particular vision of the artist emphasizes underlying forms. This technique emerges in the story where Gilman mentions an "outside pattern," a "top pattern," and a "sub-pattern," often noting the structures suggested by them, such as a front design, columns, bars, and a frieze (see figure 3.5).[17]

In a later (1887) view of the mountain, Cézanne illustrates how a more monochromatic execution can force a flatter, and less obliging, viewing experience when the canvas is less of a scene and more of a screen (see figure 3.6).

Figure 3.4. Paul Cézanne, *Mont Sainte-Victoire and the Viaduct of the Arc River Valley*, 1882–1885 (Phillips Collection, Washington, DC)

Figure 3.5. Charlotte Perkins Gilman, detail from lake watercolor, 1884 (Gilman Papers, 1846–ca.1975, Series 6, 323a–323c, seq. 124, detail)

Figure 3.6. Paul Cézanne, *Mont Sainte-Victoire from near Gardanne*, 1887 (National Gallery of Art, Washington, DC)

One tactic within modern art is to limit the use of color, with the goal of featuring other visual elements such as action, superstructure, or the effects of color temperature. Since yellow is the dominant color of the space in "The Yellow Wall-Paper," the narrator is constrained to seeing and creating in two dimensions; the minimal palette forces attention to contours and entropy over images. There is no depth of field, no correlation among objects. At this advanced point in the story, the wife can only integrate shades of the color and a fascination with amorphousness and broken pattern. Her projection of emotions onto the wall, or the pulling of emotions from it, allows us to read an erratic, and eventually frenetic, transaction between perceiver and perceived. Confronted by a hostile space, the woman forgets the satisfying curvilinear outdoor world.

The protagonist's interior landscape—her most immediate surroundings (the room, her bed, and the wallpaper), alien to nature and pleasure—compel verbal descriptions from visual encounters. When she looks out the window, her eye is free and her perceptions are gratified. Inside the room, her eye is forced to see and to play within limitations, so she reports juxtapositions, color shifts, free associations, and dynamic interplay of virulent shapes. At this point Gilman is providing a narrative-based study on the evolution of a

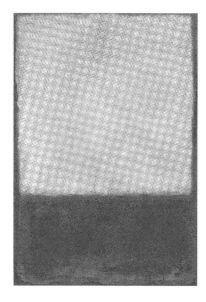

Figure 3.7. Mark Rothko, *Ochre and Red*, 1954 (Phillips Collection, Washington, DC)

perceiving subject whose mind becomes less and less dependent on external or objective reference points. The author is integrating text and image to depict neurasthenia.

For part of the story the wall acts as a color field, a minimalist space in which the principal value is communicated through blank space, which announces itself exclusively through tone and tint. The featuring of a large, two-dimensional space with a dominant color brings to mind the color-field paintings of Mark Rothko, Clyfford Still, and Helen Frankenthaler, who sacrificed form in favor of hue and experimented with the vibration of color on a larger than usual scale. The method won such painters the label of abstract expressionists, and they were noted for revealing a visual experience beyond the recognition, or even the suggestion, of objects.

Rothko declared, "We no longer look at a painting as we did in the nineteenth century; we are meant to enter it, to sink into its atmosphere of mist and light or draw it around us like a coat—or a skin. . . . These silent paintings with their enormous, beautiful, opaque surfaces are mirrors, reflecting what the viewer brings with him. In this sense, they can even be said to deal directly with human emotions, desires, relationships, for they are mirrors of our fantasy and serve as echoes of our experience."[18] Rothko's battle with his own demons gave rise to a series of bi- or tri-colored canvases, typically about ninety by seventy inches (see figure 3.7). Although his color fields are contemplative, the quality of the viewer's reception can shift from work to work, led by choice of hue, which may provide pleasure or passion, tension or peace.

Although Rothko insisted that his canvases did contain images, the expansive space of a color field always remains open to the imaginative and emotional condition of the perceiver.

The narrator of the story remembers that she "used to lie awake as a child and get more entertainment and terror out of blank walls and plain furniture than most children could find in a toy-store."[19] Faced with the field of yellow presented by the wall, the woman encounters a minimalist surface; with objects wiped away, emotions can play, unfiltered by conscience. Although she will spend the final part of the story describing chimeras and patterns that emerge from the paper, we discover through her that a spectrum of emotions can be elicited from vacant space. She spends time "trying to decide whether that front pattern and the back pattern really did move together or separately. . . . On a pattern like this, by daylight, there is a lack of sequence, a defiance of law, that is a constant irritant to a normal mind."[20] As her mental state becomes more and more dominated by anxiety, the woman surveys the room and is disposed to uncover metaphors in the "wallscape." Shortly after the mention of Weir Mitchell, the minimalist wall takes on a new life, as she starts to project ideas onto the plane, or draw emotions from it, yoking abstractions into an uneasy hyperbolic existence. The apparitions lurking in the wall behave differently from the forms outside the windows, causing frustration, the inverse of delight.

Once the narrator's anxieties overtake the perceptual momentum, representation is not possible. What she sees in the wall is rendered to us in free-associated juxtaposition, irregular lines and shapes contesting one another. In this part of the story the narrative gains greater psychological weight. The woman cannot write in her journal, yet her creative impulses begin to come at a frequency that she cannot manage. She feels "a steady brain-ache that fills the conscious mind with crowding images of distress."[21] As a wife she despises the paper as a symbol of her confinement, but as an artist she is transfixed by its visual potentialities:

> I know a little of the principle of design, and I know this thing was not arranged on any laws of radiation, or alternation, or repetition, or symmetry, or anything else that I ever heard of.
>
> It is repeated, of course, by the breadths, but not otherwise.
>
> Looked at in one way each breadth stands alone, the bloated curves and flourishes—a kind of "debased Romanesque" with *delirium tremens*—go waddling up and down in isolated columns of fatuity.
>
> But, on the other hand, they connect diagonally, and the sprawling outlines run off in great slanting waves of optic horror, like a lot of wallowing seaweeds in full chase.

The whole thing goes horizontally, too, at least it seems so, and I exhaust myself in trying to distinguish the order of its going in that direction.

They have used a horizontal breadth for a frieze, and that adds won-
derfully to the confusion.[22]

Her comments accentuate the difference from the scenes outside: the wall-
paper, and her oppression, are rudely unnatural. On the wall, all principles of
design are violated; all connections haphazard—"waddling," "sprawling," and
"slanting." The "optic horror" challenges her; the disorder "exhaust[s]" her.

In shifting, sometimes radically, from representational to nonrepresenta-
tional imagery, modern painters jumbled the roles of perceiver and perceived.
The single-perspective painting was explored as new subject matter, and intense emotions were applied to the canvas. Picasso declared, "I paint forms as
I think them, not as I see them."[23] As the narrator feels less and less control
over her body and thus her fate, her relation to the familiar world is snapped:
finding so many points of observation, she attempts to handle multiple spaces
at the same time, changing point of view suddenly—coming at the reader from
the bed and then from the paper, then dashing across the room to repeat the
confusion: "There is one end of the room where it is almost intact, and there,
when the crosslights fade and the low sun shines directly upon it, I can almost
fancy radiation after all,—the interminable grotesques seem to form around
a common centre and rush off in headlong plunges of equal distraction."[24]

As the wife's psychological condition becomes more precarious, the readers rely on a visual sense, employing modernist perspectives in constructing
the perception, and thus intimately experience the writer's development of the
protagonist through tropes of psychic change. In an analysis of "neuroaesthet-
ics," Barbara Maria Stafford describes an "echo object" as a perceived entity
whose "meshlike styles challenge the viewer to fit them together," producing
"genres where it is impossible to separate thought from object."[25]

The wallpaper, therefore, becomes more a part of the woman even as her
mind struggles to resist it. The narrator divulges her feeling that the spaces
in her room are interesting enough to "provoke study." She is startled by the
ability of the wall to "confuse the eye" with "unheard-of contradictions" and
"uncertain curves"—characteristics that suggest works of cubism, which teases
logic by presenting different planes of visual objects simultaneously, using lines
that "plunge off at outrageous angles" and force the viewer to understand the
subject as wayward geometry, where layers of "sub-patterns" scuffle for attention and lead to a new stratum of presences. Just after her last view from the
window, the narrator starts to synthesize the angles and patterns to introduce a
startling new character into the story: "But in the places where it isn't faded and

Figure 3.8. Georges Braque, *Woman with a Guitar*, 1913 (Musée National d'Art Moderne, Paris)

where the sun is just so I can see a strange, provoking, formless sort of figure, that seems to skulk about behind that silly and conspicuous front design."[26]

This amorphous being, this echo object born of angled sunlight, assumes greater definition as the text moves forward: "There are things in that paper that nobody knows but me, or ever will. Behind that outside pattern the dim shapes get clearer every day. It is always the same shape, only very numerous. And it is like a woman stooping down and creeping about behind that pattern. I don't like it a bit." The woman inside the paper is an echo of the wife, a concealed personification of immurement. The visitor keeps appearing as a "sub-pattern," "shaking" the paper by crawling within the space, grabbing the "bars" like an incarcerated person, and unsettling the narrator, who wishes to "astonish" John by "getting out." But the bars on the windows are too strong, and the wallpaper is the only "escape"—from John, and from the many "women" outside (representing, perhaps, all the females enshrouded by Mitchell's theory), and from the bedroom.[27]

Georges Braque's *Woman with a Guitar* (see figure 3.8) presents a human form drawn underneath, a puzzle to be stared at and discovered, the gender of the person not readily recognizable. Her identity is subjected to an arrangement of disheveled quadrangles, "dim shapes" amid a selection of colors that might be sensed as "lame." Her life is behind the surface of the canvas, and

Figure 3.9. Pablo Picasso, *Guernica*, 1937 (Museo Reina Sofia, Madrid)

her chief identifier is her art: her guitar. Yet she moves and appears to be smiling and strumming; the image approximates a musical measure, denoting an asymmetrical sequence of staff and ledger lines—a modernist rhythm.

After we are introduced to the figure on the wallpaper, the narrator describes a number of compositions indicating modern vision and technique that take us to the end of the story. The most important of these bears a strong affinity to a motif that appears in the greatest modernist mural of the twentieth century: Pablo Picasso's *Guernica* (see figure 3.9).

Presenting a series of panels conveying a narrative about the suffering of war, Picasso registers a protest through images of innocents reacting to the disintegration of their bodies. The narrator of "The Yellow Wall-Paper" is an early figure of such a use of artistic space to articulate distress. The wife increasingly perceives parts of others, and herself, in the wall. In the final phase of the story, her identity is constructed by conflict, and her status as the perceiver is overturned to reveal another role: "There is a recurrent spot where the pattern lolls like a broken neck and two bulbous eyes stare at you upside down." To escape the surveillance, she resorts to tearing off the wallpaper, and thus takes an active hand in creating new shapes: "Then I peeled off all the paper I could reach standing on the floor. It sticks horribly and the pattern just enjoys it! All those strangled heads and bulbous eyes and waddling fungus growths just shriek with derision!"[28]

Picasso's mural is filled with "strangled heads and bulbous eyes," some of them "upside down" with their open mouths ostensibly "shriek[ing]." The modernist type of the disembodied human being may be rooted in European wars, but the concept can be read back to encompass T. S. Eliot's Prufrock or Emily Dickinson's recluse—souls fragmented by a failure to connect with traditional and institutional values and ideals, creative minds wrestling with alien spheres of existence. Here the wife's unsheathing of the eyes allows her to expose her real nemesis: the watchful other. While the eyes in *Guernica* are dead and cannot see, they are still open, can still make a statement, and can still make the perceiving subject feel like the perceived object—and disturbingly so. Although the visual arts have routinely produced figures who gaze back, before 1900 the images rarely conveyed a modern anxiety—triggered by rude surveillance, the watched space turning inside out to watch the watcher.

The eyes on the wallpaper are the wife's and the author's translation of the eyes of John, Jennie (John's sister), and Weir Mitchell. They are ever present, vexing, and infuriating: "Up and down and sideways they crawl, and those absurd, unblinking eyes are everywhere. There is one place where two breadths didn't match, and the eyes go all up and down the line, one a little higher than the other."[29]

The protagonist, certain that she is seen in a distorted way, paints the distortion onto the wall to tell the readers that her caregivers, like the eyes and the fungus, are dead wrong: "upside down," lolling, "waddling," "bulbous," and derisive. This recognition is the woman's most infuriating circumstance. The absurdity of the entire process—the convoluted switching from gazer to gazed-upon—prevents the narrator's consciousness from pursuing any line, or developing any momentum, of rational perception of physical space. The story shifts into a radical modernist mode when gaze becomes scrutiny, when the masks and signs take on a life of their own, holding power over the person perceiving them. The final section of the story is filled with surprise, declaration, and frenzy, as nearly every sentence ends with an exclamation point, disclosing her anger, pleasure, frustration, and "triumph" over John and Jennie.

For minds that found romanticism, realism, and Victorian idealism obsolete and mute, new lexicons for artistic expression were overdue. By 1890, shifts in ideas about sexuality, class, and gender were imminent. Gilman's adulthood was witness to the tectonic shocks delivered by the forces that urged modernity: photography, electricity, evolution, suffrage, psychoanalysis, and existentialism. Artists were experimenting with ways of seeing that were emancipated from institution and academy. Inner space, complete with angst and phobias, became a new field for aesthetic inquiry. Modern visual artists revealed a startling yet compelling nature through a new perceptual process; modern writers illustrated the behavior of creative powers turning back upon an isolated self rather than launched into a receptive and rational world.

The modernist encounters a stimulus, and instead of urging it toward recognition by employing the cultural consciousness, allows the secret or suppressed impulses of the individual mind to come to light, through viewings and figures that often challenge and agitate us. The power and longevity of

"The Yellow Wall-Paper" reside in Gilman's genius to make us see and feel a two-dimensional space through the imaginative fusion, randomness, dis-association, optical anarchy, and angst that characterize so much modern art.

NOTES

1. Charlotte Perkins Gilman, *The Living of Charlotte Perkins Gilman: An Auto-biography* (1935; repr., New York: Arno Press, 1972), 68, 69, 70.

2. Ibid., 71; Gaston Bachelard, *The Poetics of Space* (Boston: Beacon Press, 1969), 6.

3. Gilman, *Living*, 89. Because Gilman's writing became so intermittent dur-ing her illness and rest-cure treatment, details about the Humboldt Street house are sparse. But we can infer that this home in Providence provided the atmo-sphere and feelings that occur in the nursery described in the story and that the Channing house in Pasadena was the basis for the positive scenes of the fictional mansion.

4. Charlotte Perkins Gilman, *The Selected Letters of Charlotte Perkins Gilman*, ed. Denise D. Knight and Jennifer S. Tuttle (Tuscaloosa: University of Alabama Press, 2009), 58.

5. The piazza at the Channing house is a featured space in the California let-ters. Always associated with beauty and delight, the spot was clearly Gilman's fa-vorite, where she could enjoy the aroma of flowers, stroll, write, and watch her daughter romp.

6. In a March 16, 1889, letter to Martha Luther, Gilman reported, "I am run-ning a 'literature class.' Some ten or twelve ladies, at five dollars a head, ten les-sons. I deal with modern literature, its causes and effects. Very successful so far." Gilman, *Selected Letters*, 51. Although she may have been using the term *modern* to mean "contemporary," it is possible to infer not only that Gilman investigated literature's experimental causes and effects in some depth but also that she was exposed to some early modern literary techniques preceding the period in which she penned "The Yellow Wall-Paper."

7. Chris Baldick, *The Concise Oxford Dictionary of Literary Terms* (New York: Oxford University Press, 1991), 213; Christopher Butler, *Early Modernism: Litera-ture, Music, and Painting in Europe, 1900–1916* (Oxford: Clarendon Press, 1994), 16.

8. Bachelard, *Poetics of Space*, 11.

9. Charlotte Perkins Gilman, "The Yellow Wall-Paper," in *Herland, The Yel-low Wall-Paper, and Selected Writings*, ed. Denise D. Knight (New York: Penguin. 1999), 167.

10. Robert Hughes, *The Shock of the New: Modern Art; Its Rise, Its Dazzling Achievement, Its Fall* (New York: Alfred A. Knopf, 1991), 113.

11. Gilman, "The Yellow Wall-Paper," 168.

12. Ibid., 169–70.

13. The coast live oak (*Quercus agrifolia*) is native to and prevalent around Pasadena. The tree has evergreen properties, so in mature specimens the branches meander to find space and water, winding and twisting away from the trunk in kinked and serpentine patterns.

14. "Being naturally moved to rejoicing by this narrow escape, I wrote *The Yellow Wall-Paper*, with its embellishments and additions, to carry out the ideal (I never had the hallucinations or objections to my mural decorations) and sent a copy to the physician who so nearly drove me mad." Charlotte Perkins Gilman, "Why I Wrote The Yellow Wall-Paper," *Forerunner* (October 1913), 271.

15. Gilman, "The Yellow Wall-Paper," 171.

16. *Cézanne and Beyond* (Philadelphia, PA: Philadelphia Museum of Art, 2009).

17. Gilman, "The Yellow Wall-Paper," 175–76, 179.

18. Peter Selz, *Mark Rothko* (New York: Museum of Modern Art, 1961), 10.

19. Gilman, "The Yellow Wall-Paper," 170. The investment of creative imagination in everyday objects hints at the Dadaist idea of the ready-made. The story's next sentence is "I remember what a kindly wink the knobs of our big, old bureau used to have, and there was one chair that always seemed like a strong friend." The "ready-made," a term coined by Marcel Duchamp in 1913, is defined by Hans Richter as a "deliberate process of 'subjectivization' of the world of objects by incorporating it as a raw material into works of art. . ." (88). Under these terms, as a large ready-made, the wallpaper itself is modernist.

20. Gilman, "The Yellow Wall-Paper," 175.

21. Gilman, *Living*, 90.

22. Gilman, "The Yellow Wall-Paper," 172.

23. Hughes, *Shock of the New*, 141.

24. Gilman, "The Yellow Wall-Paper," 171–72.

25. Barbara Maria Stafford, *Echo Objects: The Cognitive Work of Images* (Chicago: University of Chicago Press, 2007), 135.

26. Gilman, "The Yellow Wall-Paper," 171.

27. Ibid., 174.

28. Ibid., 170, 181.

29. Ibid., 170.

WORKS CITED

Bachelard, Gaston. *The Poetics of Space*. Boston: Beacon Press, 1969.

Baldick, Chris. *The Concise Oxford Dictionary of Literary Terms*. New York: Oxford University Press, 1991.

Butler, Christopher. *Early Modernism: Literature, Music, and Painting in Europe, 1900–1916*. Oxford, UK: Clarendon Press, 1994.

Cézanne and Beyond. Philadelphia, PA: Philadelphia Museum of Art, 2009.

Gilman, Charlotte Perkins. *The Living of Charlotte Perkins Gilman: An Autobiography.* 1935. New York: Arno Press, 1972.

———. Papers. Arthur and Elizabeth Schlesinger Library, Radcliffe Institute, Harvard University, Cambridge, MA.

———. *The Selected Letters of Charlotte Perkins Gilman.* Edited by Denise D. Knight and Jennifer S. Tuttle. Tuscaloosa: University of Alabama Press, 2009.

———. "Why I Wrote The Yellow Wall-Paper." *Forerunner*, October 1913.

———. "The Yellow Wall-Paper." In *Herland, The Yellow Wall-Paper, and Selected Writings*, edited by Denise D. Knight, 166–182. New York: Penguin. 1999.

———. *The Yellow Wallpaper.* Edited by Dale M. Bauer. Boston: Bedford/St. Martin's, 1998.

Hughes, Robert. *The Shock of the New: Modern Art; Its Rise, Its Dazzling Achievement, Its Fall.* New York: Alfred A. Knopf, 1991.

Richter, Hans. *Dada: Art and Anti-Art.* New York: Harry N. Abrams, 1965.

Selz, Peter. *Mark Rothko.* New York: Museum of Modern Art, 1961.

Stafford, Barbara Maria. *Echo Objects: The Cognitive Work of Images.* Chicago: University of Chicago Press, 2007.

II

Know Your Place

Limits on Women's Freedom and Power

4
"Perhaps This Was
the Opening of the Gate"

Gilman, the West, and the Free Will Problem

Brady Harrison

In "Why I Wrote The Yellow Wall-Paper" (1913), the brief coda to her most famous short story, Charlotte Perkins Gilman recounted how, after consulting with "a noted specialist in nervous diseases," she "went home and obeyed [his] directions for some three months, and came so near the borderline of utter mental ruin that [she] could see over." Then, she remarked, "using the remnants of intelligence that remained, and helped by a wise friend [Grace Ellery Channing], I cast the noted specialist's advice to the winds and went to work again—work, the normal life of every human being; work, in which is joy and growth and service, without which one is a pauper and a parasite—ultimately recovering some measure of power."[1]

Providing a sororal, political, economic, and all but profane reply to Dr. Silas Weir Mitchell and his supposed cure, Gilman also offered a culturally and historically understandable, yet perhaps too dogmatic, take on the problems of liberty and power. For Gilman, freedom for women seemed to mean the right and opportunity to work, to support oneself, and to be financially independent of men. At the same time, as we can see in *Women and Economics* (1898) and many of her other works, it also meant the ability to labor in the service of what Gilman took to be greater goods: a redefinition of the social order, the advancement of women, racial regeneration and progress, eugenics, and national progress.

Although we can certainly appreciate much of Gilman's feminist politics and economics, if we turn to *The Crux* (1911)—an exemplum of her views on gender, the economic independence of women, the lowness of some men, sexually transmitted diseases, and much more—we can argue that her notion of freedom appears troubling for at least two reasons. On the one hand, she seemed to seek a rather whole-cloth capitulation of the self to the sundry greater goods that, a priori, she deemed the right and proper goals for women. In *The Crux*, liberty appears to mean the right and opportunity to work—in the wide-open spaces of Colorado rather than the narrow, parochial spaces of the East—for the collective economic and political advancement not only of women but also of the Anglo-Saxon "race," men without sexually transmitted diseases, the American West, and the nation. Gilman seems to suggest that the individual woman—and here we will be focusing on Vivian Lane, a protagonist who, for much of the novel, seems unable to make a single decision for herself and who suffers the constant interference in her life of almost everyone she has ever known—can be said to possess freedom if she is able to serve these preordained greater goods. The author did not trouble herself with questions about whether these greater goods actually served the interests or nascent ambitions of the self.

On the other hand, as a soft determinist and a relatively sophisticated classical compatibilist in the mode of Thomas Hobbes, David Hume, and John Stuart Mill, Gilman argued that although most women, as objects and commodities, have been conditioned—or, to use the term preferred by philosophers of free will, *determined*—by forces beyond their control so as not to possess any measure of free will, they nonetheless would be better off in terms of everyday freedom if they took advantage of their predeterminedness by thinking and acting, in effect, as men think and act.[2] The author, in other words, adroitly sidestepped the free will problem and transformed Vivian and her friends from women as objects to women as petit bourgeois capitalists.

The difficulty with these two problems taken together is, as I see it, that even as Gilman argued in favor of the economic, political, and social liberty of women, she offered so narrow a standard of how a woman should be, think, and act that her solution to the lack of liberty and free will under the rule of the father is as prescriptive and oppressive as the patriarchal system she opposed.

"IS IT I, GOD, OR WHO, THAT LIFTS THIS ARM?"

Since some of the terms, theories, and debates of the philosophers of the free will problem may not be familiar to literary scholars, a brief overview seems in order. (Those familiar with the vigorous—some might even say byzantine—critical conversations on the questions of freedom and free will may wish to skip this section.) In particular, two concepts will be of central importance in our reading of *The Crux*: surface freedom and the free will problem. Although we cannot here do anything resembling justice to the long history of arguments over the meaning of such familiar yet difficult to pin down notions as *free*, *freedom*, and *free will*, we can at least offer some working definitions.

To begin, we can consider *surface freedom*, the everyday forms of freedom that—if we're lucky—many of us take for granted: the right to leave our houses when we wish, to stroll in the park, to relocate from one part of the country to another, and so on. Surface freedom, in other words, is probably what most of us would come up with if someone asked us to define *freedom*. Freedom, we might say, is "the ability to think and act as I wish"; or, put another way, we might say that freedom means "the absence of restraint or coercion." As Robert Kane, one of the leading philosophers on free will, remarks, "These everyday freedoms do seem to amount to (1) the power or ability to do what we want (and the power to have done otherwise, *if* we had wanted to) and (2) doing so without any constraints or impediments getting in our way."[3] We're free if we wish to cross state lines, buy a house in a certain neighborhood, or meet a friend for coffee and no legal, cultural, psychological, or physical impediments prevent us from acting or not acting on our desires. We're free if we wish to vote in a presidential election and no one ties us to our beds, holds us at bay with a weapon, stops all the buses, or otherwise prevents us from entering the polling station, waiting our turn, and casting our vote for the candidate of our choice.

The term *surface freedom* immediately begs any number of questions: "Surface" in comparison to what? Why use a seemingly pejorative adjective to describe the type of freedom that most of us either take for granted or long to take for granted? Isn't this the very type of freedom that matters the most? Without pushing too hard, we can pretty readily come up with all sorts of objections and caveats that complicate and undermine the concept of an unimpeded or pure freedom.

I'm free to vote, for example, if I am eighteen or older, have registered to vote, and am otherwise permitted by law to exercise the franchise. In fact, I'm not really free to vote unless other people say, in the law, that I am eligible to vote. Moreover, a person might ask, am I really free to vote for whom I wish? My family, friends, community, and country and their values certainly exert sundry influences on my decision making. The two-party system limits my choices, and I'm constantly bombarded with political advertisements and pundits trying to push me around and make up my mind for me. What about my religion or lack thereof? Aren't there any number of cultural and historical forces and traces at play in me, as the Italian Marxist Antonio Gramsci once observed, that I don't even really know about yet that work to *pre*determine how I think and therefore act? And what about my genes—who knows how they work in affecting my decisions? Then there's my unconscious, which according to Sigmund Freud is not under my control since I am, if he was right, a stranger to myself.

The list of potential factors and forces could go on and on. This brings us to the vexed question of whether we actually possess free will or just think we do.

Since at least the time of the Stoics (the early third century BCE), philosophers have wrestled with a fundamental and seemingly unanswerable problem: To what degree, if any, are our actions under our control? This, in a nutshell, is the free will problem. On the one hand, we like to think that we have freedom and free will and that we have some control over ourselves and our world, but on the other hand, we can pretty readily grasp that any number of factors and forces influence and shape our thoughts, desires, and actions. Kane explains:

> Consider that when we view ourselves as agents with free will from a personal standpoint, we think of ourselves as capable of influencing the world in various ways. Open alternatives seem to lie before us. We reason or deliberate among them and choose. We feel it is "up to us" what we choose and how we act; and this means that we could have chosen or acted otherwise—for as Aristotle succinctly put it . . . , "when acting is 'up to us,' so is not acting." This "up to us-ness" also suggests that the origins or sources of our actions lie in us and not in something else over which we have no control—whether that something else is fate or God, the laws of nature, birth or upbringing, or other humans.
>
> Historical doctrines of determinism may seem to pose a threat to either or both of these conditions for free will. If one or another form of determinism were true, it may seem that it would not be (a) "up to us" what we chose from an array of alternative possibilities, since only one alternative would be possible; and it may seem that (b) the origin or source of our choices and actions would not ultimately be "in us" but in conditions, such as the decrees of fate, the foreordaining acts of God or antecedent causes and laws, over which we had no control.[4]

For the determinists, any number of genetic, psychological, environmental, social, cultural, and spiritual factors and forces beyond our control and calculation may determine *all* our thoughts and actions.[5] If they are right, then we do not possess free will (and we may therefore not be held responsible for our thoughts and actions).[6] If at this point, as Kane believes, we are only scratching the surface of the free will problem—What do the libertarians, theologians, Stoics, Pre-Socratics, and others have to say on the subject?—then we should consider, albeit briefly, the compatibilist position, since I would place Gilman in that camp, at least at the time she was writing *The Crux*.

Kane, a libertarian and thus a philosopher in disagreement with the compatibilists, notes that "compatibilists say that indeterminism isn't required for free will; we can have all the free will (and moral responsibility) worth wanting even in a determined world."[7] According to the compatibilists, even if our thoughts and actions are predetermined by forces and factors beyond our control, this does not mean that we do not possess freedom. Rather, even if the decisions we will make and the actions we will take are already determined, as long as no one or nothing interferes with our desire or will to think and act in such a manner, we possess the only freedom worth having, in the words of Daniel Dennett (and echoed by Kane in the passage just quoted).

As Dennett remarks, "There are real threats to human freedom, but they are not metaphysical." Dennett, like Hobbes, Hume, Mill, and other classical compatibilists before him, dispenses with the free will problem—and many of the most intricate debates and arguments put forth by scores of philosophers. Instead he concentrates, like Gilman in *The Crux*, on the here and now. Anxieties over the philosophical "bugbears" that Dennett calls the Cosmic Child Whose Dolls We Are, Sphexishness, and the Disappearing Self should not distract the individual and society from focusing on such fundamentals as the dignity, desires, opportunities, and even the survival of the self: "Most people—99 percent and more, no doubt—have always been too busy staying alive and fending for themselves in difficult circumstances to have any time or taste for the question of free will. Political freedom, for many of them, has been a major concern, but metaphysical freedom has just not been worth worrying about."[8] For compatibilists like Dennett, and Gilman in *The Crux*, worrying about free will amounts to so much wasted time and energy; what really matters, as Hobbes put it, is that a person is free if he or she "finds no stop, in doing what he [or she] has the will, desire, or inclination to do," howsoever he or she may have come upon such an inclination.[9]

Although I read the author of *The Crux* as a compatibilist, we can at this point note that Gilman, perhaps like most of us, was not of a single mind on the issues of freedom and the self. As Cynthia Davis notes, "In her younger days, Charlotte had afforded greater significance to the human will: indeed, she frequently read her lecture audiences a poem by Ella Wheeler Wilcox called "Will," which praised it as a force stronger than "destiny." But the more she embraced eugenics, the more the will seemed to drop out of her equation. As she aged, she came to believe that, for some people or peoples, there was neither will nor way."[10]

Davis contends that Gilman's ideas on freedom and the self evolved: Are some individuals more free than others? Are some more wholly determined than others? Does the self matter? Should we think of the collective as more important than the self? Can we extricate the self from the collective sufficiently even to consider the self as a subject? To assert that Gilman offered a compatibilist position in *The Crux* is not to take a position on her overall career. Rather, I see her compatibilism as yet another attempt in a lifetime of thinking through the possibilities of freedom for women.

Finally, to put this wrangling among philosophers into a literary perspective, we can close this section by turning to another famous American writer's direct and deliberate dive into the free will problem. At the end of chapter 132 in Herman Melville's *Moby-Dick*, crazy old Ahab returns once more to the issues that have plagued him since the long voyage home after his first, terrible encounter with the white whale. Starbuck, seeing the old man leaning over the side of the *Pequod*, tries once more to persuade the captain to turn for home; Ahab, despite experiencing a vision of his wife and son, remains enmeshed in the free will problem: "What is it, what nameless, inscrutable, unearthly thing is it; what cozening, hidden lord and master, and cruel, remorseless emperor commands me; that against all natural lovings and longings, I so keep pushing, and crowding, and jamming myself on all the time; recklessly making me ready to do what in my own proper, natural heart, I durst not so much as dare? Is Ahab, Ahab? Is it I, God, or who, that lifts this arm?"[11]

Like Ishmael, Ahab wonders why we act as we do and why what happens to us happens, but he cannot come up with a solution to who or what moves him. Does he possess free will, does God force his every action, has everything been fated since the instant of creation for reasons and by forces he cannot even begin to fathom? He does not know, and he will not leave the problem alone; he keeps on wondering until the problem kills him. Melville, we could say, delves as deeply as any American writer into the philosophical abyss—or is it, as Dennett might put it, a self-made cesspool of useless dramatics and worry? From here we turn to Gilman's descent into the issue of surface freedom and her rather outright dismissal of the free will problem.

"SHE HAD LONGED FOR FREEDOM"

In the case of Vivian Lane, we can hardly imagine a character more susceptible to the cultural and economic forces of her place—a genteel yet suffocating New England town—*and* to the will and coercion of sundry interlopers. Although "only twenty-five—and good looking" (as Miss Josie Foote, one of the town's gossipy three maiden sisters, observes), Vivian seems younger in her inability to think and especially to act for herself.[12] On the one hand, she possesses some inchoate ambitions and desires for an education or a career, and she seems to long to break away from the stifling, parochial atmosphere of the suggestively named Bainville, Massachusetts. On the other hand, while she imagines, however vaguely, a future different from the one her parents and community expect of her, she lacks any clear sense of direction. She lacks the will to push back or away from the forces and people hemming her in, and she remains, despite her age, readily susceptible to the views, suggestions, and values of others—especially other women. Rather than being an agent possessed of a will, Vivian is subject to both macro and micro forces so far beyond her control that she seems to be a virtual cypher upon which others constantly seek to etch their opinions and exert control. No doubt Gilman wished us to understand this as precisely the plight of the young American woman at the turn of the twentieth century.

If we accept that the first enemy of the liberty of women is patriarchy and all its desires, laws, and coercive forces, we can begin to account for Vivian's hesitancy and susceptibility to the manipulations of others by examining patriarchy as Gilman concretized it in the form of Bainville and its inhabitants. As *The Crux* opens, we see the three "Foote Girls" rushing to share the latest gossip with the Lanes; as they approach "the austere home of Mr. Samuel Lane," we can already judge Vivian's parents to be humorless, rigid, and lacking in all color and spontaneity: "It was a large, uncompromising, square, white house, planted starkly in the close-cut grass. It had no porch for summer lounging, no front gate for evening dalliance, no path-bordering beds of flowers from which to pluck a hasty offering or more redundant tribute."[13]

Tim Cresswell has argued that "value and meaning are not inherent in any space or place—indeed they must be created, reproduced, and defended from heresy," and in her direct manner, Gilman wanted us to know that Vivian lives in an archly conservative, repressed, and repressive household and almost equally oppressive town.[14] When the young woman, then sixteen, intrudes on the news about Morton's expulsion from college, the full weight of repression falls upon her—yet again, we can infer. Mrs. Williams, the minister's wife, asks Vivian if she has plans to attend college, "but her questions soon led to unfortunate results," Mr. Lane immediately weighs in: "'Nonsense!' said her father. 'Stuff and nonsense, Vivian! You're not going to college.'" And in case any doubts remain about her parents' views, her mother reinforces the message: "A girl's place is at home—'till she marries." All her life Vivian has had to endure such a narrow, coercive, intellectually and emotionally violent environment, and as her parents browbeat her, the reader finds that at least some of the town shares their values: "The Foote girls now burst forth in voluble agreement with Mr. Lane."[15]

From this brief scene, we can deduce that Vivian has had little opportunity to find her own way, or even to express her own ideas, yet drawing on what rebellion and resources she possesses, and taking courage from the few more liberal elements in Bainville, she attempts to push back against her parents and the Footes: "I don't know why you're all so down on a girl's going to college. Eve Marks has gone, and Mary Spring is going—and both the Austin girls. Everybody goes now."[16] Here we see Vivian's bind most clearly: the dutiful daughter, she has been raised to obey, yet she has conflicting desires, and other young women of her class have begun to venture into the world. She has been taught to defer, to think as her parents think, and they have more or less succeeded in infantilizing what otherwise might have been an adventurous and intelligent young person. Vivian reads books on medicine and pedagogy—one of the Foote sisters calls it "pedagoggy"; was Gilman perhaps hinting at the conservative element's demagogy? Yet Vivian seems unable to take any further concrete steps, at least on her own, to break away from the dominance and values of the fathers. By now we have little doubt where Gilman stood: the rule of the fathers makes at least some young women into passive, miserable, mushy things.

If we cast Vivian's plight in terms of the free will problem, we can say that at least as far as we can tell—since the narrator usually offers glimpses into Vivian's consciousness rather than sustained passages of introspection or reflection—the protagonist's thinking has been determined by paternal and cultural forces at work in a particular place at a particular time. The conditioning she endures has reduced her thinking to mere binaries: either she can cooperate with her father's orders and vision or she can narrowly work against them by offering the alternative of college or vague notions of meaningful employment. In other words, Vivian wants what she has been habituated to want: she can either do as she is told or pursue options usually open to men (such as the ne'er-do-well object of her affections, Morton). Although the latter course may seem much more desirable, from a Gramscian point of view, Vivian wants only the little bit more that the patriarchy has already allowed in the exercise of its hegemony. Nevertheless, as a feminist and, at least at this point in her career, a compatibilist, Gilman would have had little patience for such logic: that little bit more—higher education and jobs for women—makes all the difference, even if the desire for those particular forms of advancement have been determined within the workings of patriarchal power.

The forces of normative heterosexual desire further complicate the possibility of Vivian possessing even a teaspoon's worth of free will: in addition to her incipient desires for an education and a worthwhile job, she longs for a meaningful, substantial love life: "She felt the crushing cramp and loneliness of a young mind, really stronger than those about her, yet held in dumb subjection. She could not solace herself by loving them; her father would have none of it, and her mother had small use for what she called 'sentiment.' All her life Vivian had longed for more loving, both to give and take; but no one imagined it of her, she was so quiet and repressed in manner."[17] The forces of coercion have clearly borne down on Vivian so strongly and so often that what spirit she possessed has been reduced to "dumb subjection." She cannot speak her desires, cannot act upon them—except for one kiss with Morton nine years earlier?—and her passional life seems about to wither completely.

Nevertheless, her desire for love, like her desires for an education and a job, have been largely determined by her culture and her genes. She wants what she has been conditioned to want: her parents want her to marry eventually, and she wants to be with the feckless Morton. If any measure of free will percolates in her desires, the reader would be hard-pressed to find it. Once more, however, I think that Gilman, working as a compatibilist, would not have worried about where Vivian's desires come from; what matters more is the ability of a young woman to act on her desires, howsoever determined those desires may be. For Gilman, the issues remained pretty much black and white: a smart, able, promising young person like Vivian must be allowed a wider, more challenging and rewarding life. As readers, we could hardly argue.

What Vivian needs, Gilman not too subtly suggested, is the right sort of guidance; she needs someone, in other words, to intervene in her affairs and to show her the way to a better and freer life, at least in terms of surface freedom. In her canny way, Gilman turned the preconditioning and oppression of women into an opportunity: because Vivian has been subject to the not particularly benign pressure of her parents, her community, and the greater patriarchal culture of puritanical New England, she has been made particularly susceptible to the influence of others; told repeatedly how to think and behave, she has learned to let others do most of the thinking for her. For Gilman this susceptibility became the crack in the foundation through which some light could enter: if the right person illuminates the way ahead for women like Vivian, then eventually, as they become accustomed to some everyday freedom and some freedom of thought and action, they might become valuable active contributors to society and the advancement of American civilization as well as subjects with a passion for more and more kinds of freedom that matter.

Gilman dramatized just how perilous this process can be by bringing two women into Vivian's life, each with different values and ambitions for themselves and the always beset protagonist. First we meet Adela (sometimes Adele) St. Cloud, who urges Vivian to remain loyal to Morton and who stirs in her young friend notions of romance and self-sacrifice: "Then came Mrs. St. Cloud into her life, stirring the depths of romance, of the buried past, and of the unborn future. From her she learned to face a life of utter renunciation, to be true, true to her ideals, true to her principles, true to her past, to be patient; and to wait." Playing upon both the notions of a woman's responsibility and the hackneyed conventions of romance fiction and the novel of seduction, Gilman has Adela tell her young friend that "it is the most beautiful work on earth" to shape and uplift a wastrel like Morton: "Ah, my dear, I have seen good women—young girls, like yourself—ruin a man's whole life by—well, by heartlessness;

by lack of understanding. Most young men do things they become ashamed of when they really love. And in the case of a motherless boy like this—lonely, away from his home, no good woman's influence about—what else could we expect? But you can make a new man of him. A glorious work!"[18]

We cannot really tell why Adela argues such things. She shows herself to be rather mercenary in her personal life: when one husband dies, she decides on the suitability of a replacement based largely on his income. Davis goes so far as to call her "an ultra-feminine parasite who enjoys toying with both men's and women's affections to ruinous effect."[19] Nonetheless, Adela pours non-sense into Vivian's ears, reminding her of "that hot, sweet night so long ago; the world swimming in summer moonlight and syringa sweetness; the stillness everywhere—and your first kiss!" Always susceptible to the influence of others and, as Dana Seitler argues, half in love with Adela, Vivian almost succumbs to the older woman's visions, revealing once again how little control she exerts (or knows how to exert) over her everyday freedom and how easily her life could be pushed into a punishing routine of servitude and abnegation.[20]

While Adela murmurs in one of Vivian's ears, Dr. Jane Bellair hectors in the other. Bellair, the rest of the novel makes clear, is the character who has the most—and the most positive—impact on Vivian's life and surface liberties: "And then, into the gray, flat current of her daily life, sharply across the trend of Mrs. St. Cloud's soft influence, had come a new force—Dr. Bellair."[21] However frightening and aggressive Jane may seem to Vivian, Jane also stands as Gilman's heroic progressive: seeing opportunity in the ways young women have been conditioned to allow others to do the thinking for them, she determines to save Vivian both from a life of repression and disease and from her own timidity.

Whereas Adela would have Vivian remain in Bainville and her father's house —that uncozy, stern space rife with subjugation and control—and wait for Morton to return or to summon her west, Jane all but browbeats Vivian into acting on her desires for a meaningful, fuller life of self-sufficiency. As far as Jane is concerned, Vivian must move to Colorado, a state bustling with economic and personal opportunity: "You are a grown woman, and have as much right to decide for yourself as a grown man. This isn't wicked—it is a wise move; a practical one. Do you want to grow up like the rest of the useless single women in this little social cemetery?"[22]

Adela would have Vivian marry Morton, regardless of his diseases and vices; we see her influence in Vivian's momentary vision of a life of denial: "She saw a vista of self-sacrificing devotion, forgoing much, forgiving much, but rejoicing in the companionship of a noble life, a soul rebuilt, a love that was passionately grateful." Jane, in contrast, tells her point-blank that if she marries Morton she will become ill, resulting in infertility or children born with physical and psychological challenges: "You may have any number of still-born children, year after year. And every little marred dead face would remind you that you allowed it! And they may be deformed and twisted, have all manner of terrible and loathsome afflictions, they and their children after them, if they have any." As Davis writes, "The crux of *The Crux* was Charlotte's outrage over the knowing transmission of venereal disease to unknowing women."[23] Jane, as the novel's straight-talking, no-nonsense hero, acts to save Vivian (and her potential children) from a life of anguish and instead set her on the road to a life replete with surface freedom.

In fact, Jane seizes such control over Vivian and her future that she not only bullies Vivian into action, she also takes concrete, practical steps to ensure her protégé's success. After the group of women—including Orella, Susie, Mrs. Pettigrew, and Vivian—reach Carston, Colorado, and take over the Cottonwoods boardinghouse, Vivian stagnates despite "the strange, new sense of freedom [that] grew in her heart, a feeling of lightness and hope and unfolding purpose." To keep Vivian away from Morton and tap her "natural love of children," Jane conspires to set her up in a kindergarten ("Aren't you ready to begin that little school of yours?") and finds her a beginning number of wards: "I've been making some inquiries. . . . There are six or eight among my patients that you could count on—about a dozen young ones. How many could you handle?"[24]

Jane will not take no for an answer, and once more she tries to force Vivian into action, brushing aside the young woman's anxieties over her abilities, training, and lack of formal education. Later, after Vivian rejects Morton and falls into a depression, Jane and Mrs. Pettigrew find a house for Vivian to purchase and operate as her school: "It's a first-rate little kindergarten. I've got the list of scholars all arranged for, and am going to pop the girl into it so fast she can't refuse. Not that I think she will."[25] At key moments, when Vivian seems about to succumb to the ways she was raised, or to the visions of Adela, Jane intervenes and takes advantage of the young woman's susceptibility to the influence of others and gives her a forceful shove in what she deems to be the right direction. Moreover, she taps into Vivian's undeveloped ambitions and dreams and turns them into a tangible, material reality. And, once more, who could argue? The protagonist is much better off self-employed and doing the work of the world than being burdened with the syphilitic, gonorrheal, unable Morton.

Having analyzed, however briefly, Gilman's strategy of turning subjugation into opportunity, we have now reached a critical point in our analysis: In what measure could we say that Jane's values and manipulations actually foster the protagonist's surface freedom? The answer, at least in my reading, is that Jane's feminism and emotional pressure do at first seem to result in a dramatic and

heartening enhancement of Vivian's surface freedom, yet the doctor's dedica-
tion to turning women into petite bourgeoisie while endorsing a vague form
of medically sanctioned eugenics sets Vivian on a road that reveals economic
success as possibly just another form of entrapment and suppresses any exploration (by the author, narrator, or characters) of the deeper and more difficult
matter of individual free will. Gilman, of course, would have had no sympathy for such a reading or position: we must be wooden-headed if we cannot tell that Vivian is much better off at the end of the novel than she was at
the beginning (and I am not unsympathetic to this argument). To begin this
phase of our analysis, we turn to a consideration of Jane's feminism and how
it exponentially seems to enrich Vivian's surface freedom.

Oddly, Jane's beliefs sound somewhat like Adela's, at least in terms of the
need of women to take responsibility for men, but whereas the latter hews to
romance and the old values of self-sacrifice, the former (like Gilman) takes a
no-nonsense approach to economic self-sufficiency even as she concedes that
most young women will probably want to marry young men and that the
nation needs healthy and vital children to carry forward the work of civilization. In her effort to convince the single women of Bainville to move west,
she plays upon the values they have been raised with, but she breaks them
from the realm of self-sacrifice and service solely to patriarchy and pushes
them into the realm of female economic freedom and self-sufficiency. Jane
remarks, "You folks are so strong on duty. . . . Why can't you see a real duty
[in moving to Colorado and operating a boardinghouse]? I tell you, the place
is full of men that need mothering, and sistering—good honest sweetheart-
ening and marrying, too. Come on, Rella. Do bigger work than you've ever
done yet—and, as I said, bring both these nice girls with you. What do you
say, Miss Lane?"[26] Fully realizing that most of the women—especially Susie
and Vivian, but also the somewhat older Orella—have a strong interest in
men and marriage, Jane reshapes those desires and focuses the women on men,
and their supposed responsibility toward men, in a way that not only piques
their sexual and matrimonial interests but also transforms them into modest,
money-making entrepreneurs.

Even as the women will be able indulge their desires for sweethearts and
husbands all they want, they will also be doing the hard yet rewarding work
of advancing American civilization. Jane believes (as Gilman did) not only in
the economic freedom of women but also, like Walt Whitman, in the need of
the nation to produce strong, healthy, well-educated, and independent young
people. We see this deeper set of values precisely in the directions in which Jane
gives Vivian a few timely shoves: first, Vivian must leave the stifling, crippling
social space of Bainville in order to free herself of the worst forms of patriarchal
oppression; second, once out in the expanse of the West, she must start the

kindergarten and must buy a building to house the school; and third, in the summertime she must assist the doctor in running an outdoor camp for girls.

At each step Vivian becomes more self-sufficient, self-confident, able, and economically independent; at each step she educates and inspires the young women to be like her and Jane. Everybody seems to win, especially Vivian: "She tramped the hills with the girls; picked heaping pails of wild berries, learned to cook in primitive fashion, slept as she had never slept in her life, from dark to dawn, grew brown and hungry and cheerful." From a muddling, subservient, desolate daughter and would-be partner to Morton, Vivian has transformed, under Jane's supervision, into a vibrant and happy woman enjoying a much wider, fuller, and rewarding (albeit vaguely racist and eugenic) world.[27]

The apotheosis of Vivian's transformation and surface freedom occurs in the hills and mountains of the West. Like the young Henry David Thoreau, she and her charges live the spartan, close, perceptive life of both the mind and the body, and in what may be the finest scene in the novel, Vivian comes to love not only her body but also the freedom to enjoy it and test her limits. Vivian, we could say, enjoys an exaltation of the freedom to do what she wishes, to go where she wishes, and to be whom she wishes. In other words, she enjoys an exaltation of hard-won surface freedom: "Often in the earliest dawn she would rise from the springy, odorous bed of balsam boughs and slip out alone for her morning swim. A run through the pines to a little rocky cape, with a small cave she knew, and to glide, naked, into that glass-smooth water, warmer than the sunless air, and swim out softly, silently, making hardly a ripple, turn on her back and lie there—alone with the sky—this brought peace to her heart. She felt so free from every tie to earth, so like a soul floating in space, floating there with the clean, dark water beneath her, and the clear, bright heaven above her."[28]

Vivian feels alive while immersed in nature, floating unencumbered between earth and sky. This is described in a passage that rivals the sensuality and natural imagery of Whitman's "From Pent-Up Aching Rivers," without the stark loneliness and want that permeate the observer of the energetic swimmers in the poet's "Song of Myself"; or of Kate Chopin's descriptions of Edna's first, triumphal swim in *The Awakening*, yet without the undertones of drowning and death that mark the extraordinary lyricism of the scenes at Grand Isle. The proliferation of sibilants in the descriptions of Vivian floating on the water—"glass," "smooth," "sunless," "softly," "silently," "sky," "peace," and more—evoke the sounds and sway of the water. We can feel confident that Vivian has at last passed through the gate and seized "the opportunity of a lifetime."[29] Her life could have gone so badly, so wrong, if she had married Morton, but thanks to Jane's proactive meddling, Vivian's measure of surface freedom seems to have expanded immeasurably in the open, nearly unfettered physical and social spaces of the West.

Indeed, Carston and the surrounding wilderness stand as an antithesis to Bainville and its cramped and only seemingly genial homes and culture. Although the Lanes' home embodies precisely the sort of confined, socially repressive place that Cresswell describes, Melody Graulich argues that "Gilman represents the West as a 'healing place' where women find adventure, economic independence, and work for which they are suited." Like Mary Austin, Carolyn Kirkland, Ella Higginson, and other female writers of her generation, Gilman "believed that the West offered them opportunities to live freer lives than those dictated by social conventions in more settled regions, a persistent theme in their work and lives."[30]

Unlike the houses and streets of the East, the open spaces and new towns of the West have not been overcoded with unadulterated patriarchal power and control. The space is not yet replete or oppressive; the West, as a place, has potential, and in such a relatively unsettled environment Vivian and her friends appear to thrive: whereas they enjoyed almost no surface freedom in Bainville, in and around Carston they seem to count as human beings with their own desires, bodies, and abilities. Seitler notes, "*The Crux* exemplifies a culture in uneasy transition, eschewing the vestiges of New England Puritanism for what is represented as the enlightened sexual-civic discourse of the West."[31]

At this point we can raise at least two objections to Gilman's vision of what constitutes success for a young woman. In the first instance, we might object to the strength and surety of her convictions: Gilman possessed a very clear prescriptive sense of how a young woman should think, act, and be and did not question her own value system. She had made up her mind about such matters as work, race, and eugenics, and she offered characters who embody or come to embody her beliefs. Jane *knows*, without a doubt, what is best for Vivian, but how can she be so utterly sure? Granted, the characters are not particularly rounded, and Gilman had a polemic mission—as Jill Bergman remarks, *The Crux* serves as a work of "sex education for young women."[32] Yet Gilman never really took a step back to ask whether other possibilities and other types of lives might be open to Vivian and the others from Bainville. She hinted that Vivian has a crush on Adela and Jane, but for lots of perfectly good reasons she did not push the implications or possible trajectories of these desires. Gilman had her own agenda, and readers would have to wait for later writers such as Radclyffe Hall and Djuna Barnes.

If Gilman set aside issues of alternative sexualities and genders, she also focused on work to the exclusion of other possible ways of moving forward in the world. Vivian, for example, expresses a keen interest in education and thinks at least a little about becoming a doctor, like Jane. Gilman, however, was in a rush to get her characters working and earning their own keep and so shut down any consideration of what Vivian might be losing by not going to college. Although we can certainly understand the politically motivated character and plot choices Gilman made, in the end she offered a funny vision of freedom: be free in the ways that I think are important, and let's not waste time thinking about other sorts of lives, dreams, or philosophies.

However free the women appear to be in Colorado, we can nonetheless counter Gilman's arguments and dramatizations and assert that even though Jane has good intentions, she has perhaps substituted one form of oppression for another. As Davis writes, "For the most part, [Gilman] sought her desired economic transformations within the capitalist system even while criticizing that system for its intrinsically patriarchal attitudes and practices." Davis cites a passage in Gilman's autobiography in which Gilman contends that her brand of socialism did not suit the hard-core followers of Marx: "Among the unnecessary burdens of my life is that I have been discredited by conservative persons as a Socialist, while to the orthodox Socialists themselves I was quite outside the ranks." Falling somewhere on the left, yet still willing to have women live (and, if possible, thrive) in the capitalist system, Gilman would have Vivian and the others give themselves over to a system with its own logic and imperatives—profit, growth, the exploitation of resources, and more—that perhaps once more signals the capitulation of the self to forces beyond its control.[33]

Like everyone else, the characters in *The Crux* collide with necessity, but once they have begun to enjoy a measure of economic success and independence they must, according to the pressures of the system and the logic of desire, always be rededicating themselves to their enterprises. By the logic of increase, just as Jane encouraged Vivian to buy the house and establish her kindergarten, Vivian *must* in the future take on new students and supplement her building; she *must* eventually become a manager and hire others to work for her.

The surface freedom achieved by moving from Bainville to Carston may appear to be a quantum leap in the sum of Vivian's liberty, but we might also understand it as a matter of switching masters. In Bainville Vivian was expected to follow the law of the fathers. In Carston, Vivian's (and the other women's) success seem easy enough, but the world of capital and competition may be a bit grittier and ugly than the author allowed. How much of the young woman's new strength, health, confidence, and freedom will be sacrificed to sustain and expand her business? How much will she and other women have to act like men, the dominant players in capitalism, and come to see others as objects rather than subjects? Of course, Gilman's task in writing the novel was not to ask such questions, and *The Crux* ends with marriages all around (perhaps the first ever polemic comedy about sexually transmitted diseases).

In closing, we have one more matter to consider: Why didn't Gilman, in the course of exploring the problem of surface freedom, also confront the deeper problem of free will? At first glance the answer seems obvious enough: as a soft determinist as well as a compatibilist, Gilman, I think, did not quite believe that free will exists; or if it does, it's so bruised and battered as to be negligible in the conduct of an individual's life, thoughts, and actions. Her novel suggests that women, especially young ones, have been so overcoded that they possess no measure of thought or desire of their own, or perhaps they have been so crippled by forces beyond their control that any atom of selfhood that has not been determined cannot battle those massive obscene forces.

As a matter of practical concern, Gilman did not have to worry about the free will problem: she focused on the plight of women and what might be done about it in her lifetime; she did not have time for Melvillian belly flops into the ocean-size pool of arguments and counterarguments over whether we think any thoughts or take any actions that have not been predetermined or programmed into us. I can accept this, but I think we can also understand her silence from another perspective.

Karl Marx famously wrote that "men [and women], developing their material production and their material intercourse, alter, along with this their real existence, their thinking and the products of their thinking. Life is not determined by consciousness, but consciousness by life."[34] As a hard determinist—at least in this moment of his long and shifting career—Marx suggested that we cannot think certain things at certain times; the dominant economic system tells us, in advance, what to think and how to act. If that is the case, then we could argue that the capitalism of Gilman's era prohibited, negated, or precluded her interest in exploring—indeed, her very ability to explore—the free will question. The system, as so many philosophers of ideology have argued, does not want anyone to think about problematic issues like free will; rather, the system wants folks to work at their jobs, go about their business quietly, and leave such seemingly beside-the-point questions to, perhaps, a few ne'er-do-wells hanging out at universities or a few revolutionaries hunkered down in the cafés or hinterlands of strange countries. Contrary to Dennett—and *The Crux*–era Gilman—we might then argue that for all of us, no matter what amount of surface freedom we enjoy, the question of metaphysical freedom might be precisely the issue we should be thinking about, talking about, and acting on.

NOTES

1. Charlotte Perkins Gilman, "Why I Wrote The Yellow Wall-Paper," in *The Charlotte Perkins Gilman Reader*, ed. Ann J. Lane (Charlottesville: University of Virginia Press, 1999), 19–20.

2. Since the works of Hobbes (1588–1679), Hume (1711–1776), and Mill (1806–1873) were in the intellectual air of America in the late nineteenth and early twentieth centuries, the larger debate over free will was also a topic of concern. In Herman Melville's "Bartleby, the Scrivener," for example, the narrator ponders the plight of his occasional ward and tells us that he now and then looks "a little into 'Edwards on the Will,' and 'Priestley on Necessity.'" Herman Melville, *Billy Budd, Sailor and Selected Tales*, ed. Robert Milder (New York: Oxford University Press, 1987), 31. Jonathan Edwards's *A Careful and Strict Inquiry into the Prevailing Notions of the Freedom of the Will* appeared in 1754, and Joseph Priestley's *The Doctrine of Philosophical Necessity Illustrated* was published in 1777; although we know that Melville read philosophy with some keenness, we can also imagine that if Gilman had not read Edwards or Priestley directly, she was no doubt at least familiar with some of the debates between the philosophers of the free will problem. My thanks to Robert Milder for directing me to Edwards's and Priestley's works through the excellent notes in his edition of Melville's short fiction.

3. Robert Kane, *A Contemporary Introduction to Free Will* (New York: Oxford University Press, 2005), 14.

4. Robert Kane, ed., *The Oxford Handbook of Free Will* (New York: Oxford University Press, 2002), 4–5.

5. Daniel Dennett offers one of the best summations of determinism that I have come across: "If determinism is true, then our every deed and decision is the inexorable outcome, it seems, of the sum of physical forces acting at the moment, which in turn is the inexorable outcome of the forces acting an instant before, and so on, to the beginning of time." Daniel C. Dennett, *Elbow Room: The Varieties of Free Will Worth Wanting* (Cambridge, MA: MIT Press, 1984), 1. In short, we're doomed.

6. Sam Harris leaves no doubt where he stands on the issue: "Free will *is* an illusion. Our wills are simply not of our own making. Thoughts and intentions emerge from background causes of which we are unaware and over which we exert no conscious control. We do not have the freedom we think we have." He states categorically that "seeming acts of volition merely arise spontaneously (whether caused, uncaused, or probabilistically inclined, it makes no difference) and cannot be traced to a point of origin in our conscious minds." Sam Harris, *Free Will* (New York: Free Press, 2012), 5–6. If Harris is right—and for what it's worth, I don't think he is—then he may be the bearer of good news (for at least some of us): whatever we do, we're not responsible.

7. John Martin Fischer et al., *Four Views on Freewill* (Malden, MA: Blackwell, 2007), 166.

8. Dennett, *Elbow Room*, 4, 9, 10, 13, 169. Dennett clearly takes pleasure in mocking these "bugbears." He scorns our fear that we are merely God's playthings (the Cosmic Child Whose Dolls We Are), that we are automatons "at the mercy

of brute physical causation" (Sphexishness), or that God created us but then left town, so that we are actors without meaning, beings going through motions we do not comprehend (the Disappearing Self). Dennett is, if nothing else, very witty.

9. Thomas Hobbes, *Leviathan*, ed. J. A. C. Gaskin (New York: Oxford University Press, 1996), 140. Gary Watson nicely captures at least one of the problems with the compatibilist position: "compatibilists have their own troubles explaining how human beings can be products of nature and at the same time authors of their actions, how freedom as they see it can amount to anything more than what Immanuel Kant contemptuously called 'the freedom of the turnspit.'" Gary Watson, *Agency and Answerability: Selected Essays* (New York: Clarendon Press, 2004), 197. A turnspit is a type of dog specifically bred to walk on a treadmill in order to turn a roasting spit—a fine, free life if ever there was one. Kant authored this bon mot in his *Critique of Practical Reason* (1788).

10. Cynthia J. Davis, *Charlotte Perkins Gilman: A Biography* (Stanford, CA: Stanford University Press, 2010), 300; Ella Wheeler Wilcox, "Will," In *Poetical Works of Ella Wheeler Wilcox* (Edinburgh, UK: W. P. Nimmo, Hay, and Mitchell, 1917), 129–30. For a glimpse, perhaps, of Gilman's notion of freedom and the will in her younger days, we can turn to Wilcox's sonnet:

WILL
There is no chance, no destiny, no fate,
    Can circumvent or hinder or control
    The firm resolve of a determined soul.
Gifts count for nothing; will alone is great;
All things give way before it, soon or late.
    What obstacle can stay the might force
Of the sea-seeking river in its course,
Or cause the ascending orb of day to wait?
Each well-born soul must win what it deserves.
Let the fool prate of luck. The fortunate
Is he whose earnest purpose never swerves,
Whose slightest action or inaction serves
The one great aim. Why even Death stands still,
And waits an hour sometimes for such a will.

11. Herman Melville, *Moby-Dick or, the Whale* (New York: Penguin, 1992), 592.

12. Charlotte Perkins Gilman, *The Crux*, ed. Dana Seitler (1911; repr., Durham, NC: Duke University Press, 2003), 36.

13. Ibid., 25–26.

14. Tim Cresswell, *Place: A Short Introduction* (Malden, MA: Blackwell, 2004), 9, 27. Cresswell looks back at one of his earlier works, *In Place/Out of Place: Ge-*

ography, Ideology, and Transgression (Minneapolis: University of Minnesota Press, 1996), and summarizes his intent there in a way that captures Vivian's plight even more vividly: "The purpose of [that] work was to show how place does not have meanings that are natural and obvious but ones that are created by people with more power than others to define what is and is not appropriate."

15. Gilman, *Crux*, 29. Cresswell, *Place,* 122, further argues that "various conceptions of place and place as home [play] an active role in the constitution of the normal, the natural and the appropriate and how deviation from the expected relationship between place and practice [leads] to labels of abnormality and inappropriateness." Vivian, in wishing for some other form of life than the one her parents sanction, runs the risk of being considered abnormal and inappropriate; fear of these labels—and the attendant gossip—account at least in part for how quickly and how vociferously her parents attempt to shut down her dreams. They do not want their neighbors gossiping about their daughter in the way, for example, that they talk about Morton. What makes this scene also interesting is the way in which women—Vivian's mother and the Foote sisters—serve as the agents of patriarchy. Judith Allen argues, "Gilman absorbed contemporary theories postulating 'the frontier' as a zone of freedom, democracy, and innovation, first expounded in 1893 by Frederick Jackson Turner. She represented women as holding a better sexual economic bargaining position in the demographically male-dominated West than in the female-dominated Northeast." Judith A. Allen, "Reconfiguring Vice: Charlotte Perkins Gilman, Prostitution, and Frontier Sexual Contracts," in *Charlotte Perkins Gilman: Optimist Reformer*, ed. Jill Rudd and Val Gough (Iowa City: University of Iowa Press, 1999), 176–77.

16. Gilman, *Crux*, 29.

17. Ibid., 47.

18. Ibid., 48, 108–9.

19. Davis, *Biography*, 154. I find Adela to be an interesting character, perhaps the most interesting in the novel, because she seems oddly sinister. Up front she peddles romance, but in her own affairs she focuses much more on practical matters such as money and social standing. Moreover, we learn that her gauzy coquetry while married to her first husband led to the suicide of a young male admirer, and the fate of her second husband remains a bit of a mystery, adding to the dark cloud around Mrs. St. Cloud: Is she something of a black widow, if only in terms of psychological sway? Finally, is her insistence that Vivian wait for Morton based on some sort of animosity toward either Vivian or other women in general? After all, if Vivian were to follow Adela's advice, she would certainly lead an awful life and perhaps even have a premature, painful death. Gilman did not give us much to go on, yet there are a few fascinating, unanswerable questions nonetheless.

20. Gilman, *Crux*, 109; Dana Seitler, ed., "Introduction," in *The Crux*, by

Charlotte Perkins Gilman (1911; repr., Durham, NC: Duke University Press, 2003), 15. Seitler remarks that Vivian has "a vaguely eroticized" relationship with both Adela and Dr. Jane Bellair.

21. Gilman, *Crux*, 49. Jennifer Tuttle calls Adela "the novel's patron saint of traditional gender roles" and notes that although Jane "is not the most radical example of New Womanhood, her status as a woman physician nevertheless represents a significant challenge to traditional orthodoxies of gendered behavior." Jennifer S. Tuttle, ed., "Introduction," in *The Crux*, by Charlotte Perkins Gilman (1911; repr., Newark: University of Delaware Press, 1992), 18–19.

22. Gilman, *Crux*, 60.

23. Gilman, *Crux*, 129–30; Davis, *Biography*, 303. For another of her takes on the problem of venereal disease, written in 1916, see Charlotte Perkins Gilman, "The Vintage," in *Herland, The Yellow Wall-Paper, and Selected Writings*, ed. Denise D. Knight (New York: Penguin, 1999), 297–304.

24. Gilman, *Crux*, 64, 112, 114.

25. Ibid., 151.

26. Ibid., 57.

27. Ibid., 155. "*The Crux* argues that eugenic unions are the origins of a fit and vigorous national identity." Dana Seitler, "Unnatural Selection: Mothers, Eugenic Feminism, and Charlotte Perkins Gilman's Regeneration Narratives," *American Quarterly* 55, no. 1 (2003): 72.

28. Gilman, *Crux*, 155.

29. Ibid., 57.

30. Melody Graulich, "Walking Off Society-Made Values: Did the West Liberate Women? And Which Women?" Paper presented at "Gilman Goes West," the Fifth International Conference on Charlotte Perkins Gilman, University of Montana, Missoula, June 19, 2011. My deepest thanks to Melody Graulich for such a fine plenary and for allowing me to quote from the as yet unpublished address. My thanks as well to Jennifer S. Tuttle for her wonderful coplenary, "Is Gilman a California Writer?" Finally, I wish to express my gratitude to Gary Scharnhorst for his exemplary keynote address, "Charlotte Perkins Gilman and the American West." Although I have not quoted Tuttle's or Scharnhorst's addresses directly, their remarks—and distinguished work on Gilman—have influenced this paper.

31. Seitler, "Introduction," 9.

32. Jill Bergman, "Doing It 'Man-Fashion': Gender Performance in Charlotte Perkins Gilman's *Unpunished*," in *Charlotte Perkins Gilman: New Texts, New Contexts*, ed. Jennifer S. Tuttle and Carol Farley Kessler (Columbus: Ohio State University Press, 2011), 146.

33. Davis, *Biography*, 197; Charlotte Perkins Gilman, *The Living of Charlotte Perkins Gilman: An Autobiography* (Madison: University of Wisconsin Press, 1935), 198. Perhaps, as Ishmael wryly observes, none of us can be free in this world: "Who

ain't a slave? Tell me that. Well, then, however the old sea-captains may order me about—however they may thump and punch me about, I have the satisfaction of knowing that it is all right; that everybody else is one way or another served in much the same way—either in a physical or metaphysical point of view, that is; and so the universal thump is passed round, and all hands should rub each other's shoulder-blades, and be content." Melville, *Moby-Dick*, 6.

34. Karl Marx, "The German Ideology," in *The Marx-Engels Reader*, 2nd ed., ed. Robert C. Tucker (New York: W. W. Norton, 1978), 155.

WORKS CITED

Allen, Judith A. "Reconfiguring Vice: Charlotte Perkins Gilman, Prostitution, and Frontier Sexual Contracts." In *Charlotte Perkins Gilman: Optimist Reformer*, edited by Jill Rudd and Val Gough, 173–99. Iowa City: University of Iowa Press, 1999.

Bergman, Jill. "Doing It 'Man-Fashion': Gender Performance in Charlotte Perkins Gilman's *Unpunished*." In *Charlotte Perkins Gilman: New Texts, New Contexts*, edited by Jennifer S. Tuttle and Carol Farley Kessler, 140–57. Columbus: Ohio State University Press, 2011.

Cresswell, Tim. *In Place/Out of Place: Geography, Ideology, and Transgression*. Minneapolis: University of Minnesota Press, 1996.

———. *Place: A Short Introduction*. Malden, MA: Blackwell, 2004.

Davis, Cynthia J. *Charlotte Perkins Gilman: A Biography*. Stanford, CA: Stanford University Press, 2010.

Dennett, Daniel C. *Elbow Room: The Varieties of Free Will Worth Wanting*. Cambridge, MA: MIT Press, 1984.

Fischer, John Martin, Robert Kane, Derk Pereboom, and Manuel Vargas. *Four Views on Freewill*. Malden, MA: Blackwell, 2007.

Gilman, Charlotte Perkins. *The Crux*. 1911. Edited by Dana Seitler. Durham, NC: Duke University Press, 2003.

———. *The Living of Charlotte Perkins Gilman: An Autobiography*. Madison: University of Wisconsin Press, 1935.

———. "The Vintage." In *Herland, The Yellow Wall-Paper, and Selected Writings*, edited by Denise D. Knight, 297–304. New York: Penguin, 1999.

———. "Why I Wrote The Yellow Wall-Paper." In *The Charlotte Perkins Gilman Reader*, edited by Ann J. Lane, 19–20. Charlottesville: University of Virginia Press, 1999.

Graulich, Melody. "Walking Off Society-Made Values: Did the West Liberate Women? And Which Women?" Paper presented at "Gilman Goes West," the Fifth International Conference on Charlotte Perkins Gilman, University of Montana, Missoula, June 19, 2011.

Harris, Sam. *Free Will*. New York: Free Press, 2012.

Hobbes, Thomas. *Leviathan*. Edited by J. A. C. Gaskin. New York: Oxford University Press, 1996.

Kane, Robert. *A Contemporary Introduction to Free Will*. New York: Oxford University Press, 2005.

———, ed. *The Oxford Handbook of Free Will*. New York: Oxford University Press, 2002.

Marx, Karl. "The German Ideology." In *The Marx-Engels Reader*, 2nd ed., edited by Robert C. Tucker, 146–200. New York: W. W. Norton, 1978.

Melville, Herman. *Billy Budd, Sailor and Selected Tales*. Edited by Robert Milder. New York: Oxford University Press, 1987.

———. *Moby-Dick or, the Whale*. New York: Penguin, 1992.

Seitler, Dana, ed. "Introduction." In *The Crux*, by Charlotte Perkins Gilman, 1911, 1–19. Durham, NC: Duke University Press, 2003.

———. "Unnatural Selection: Mothers, Eugenic Feminism, and Charlotte Perkins Gilman's Regeneration Narratives." *American Quarterly* 55, no. 1 (2003): 61–88.

Tuttle, Jennifer S., ed. "Introduction." In *The Crux*, by Charlotte Perkins Gilman, 1911, 11–75. Newark: University of Delaware Press, 1992.

Watson, Gary. *Agency and Answerability: Selected Essays*. New York: Clarendon Press, 2004.

Wilcox, Ella Wheeler. "Will." In *Poetical Works of Ella Wheeler Wilcox*. Edinburgh, UK: W. P. Nimmo, Hay, and Mitchell, 1917.

Charlotte Perkins Gilman's "The Giant Wistaria"

A Hieroglyph of the Female Frontier Gothic

Gary Scharnhorst

Charlotte Perkins Gilman, a socialist, a sociologist, and the "leading intellectual" in the US women's movement in the early twentieth century, first rose to public prominence as a poet and a writer of fiction during the last decade of the nineteenth. Gilman "has made a place of her own" the literary critic William Dean Howells announced, although he feared that her work was mostly appreciated by "fanatics, philanthropists, and other Dangerous Persons."[1]

Such has been the case, it seems, with two gothic tales Gilman published early in the 1890s in *New England Magazine*. The second of these stories was "The Yellow Wall-Paper," a harrowing and "macabre postpartum fantasy," which has been disinterred from the moldering pages of bound periodicals after long neglect and widely circulated.[2] The first of Gilman's works in *New England Magazine*, however—published under the name C. P. Stetson—is virtually unknown to modern readers: "The Giant Wistaria" (1891) is a largely forgotten tale remarkable for its adaptation of frontier mythology to the tradition of the female gothic, and it deserves to be resurrected in its own right.

"The Giant Wistaria" is, in its most elementary sense, a formulaic ghost story, a terrifying diptych (a work made up of two matching parts) about an unwed mother tormented by Puritan patriarchy whose spirit haunts a decaying mansion. In the first section of the story, set sometime in the late eighteenth century, the unnamed woman suffers disgrace for bearing a child upon her arrival in the wilderness of the New World. Her father physically abuses her and insists that she marry a cousin, a "coarse fellow" whose proposals she had "ever shunned." Her father also demands that she return with him to England, abandoning her child, and that she be locked in her chamber, captive to his authority until she agrees to this plan.

In the second and longer section of the story, set a century later, a young couple rents the old house and invites several friends for a visit. They consider the mansion "a *real* ghostly place" nestled in a riot of savage nature. The grounds, "once beautiful with rare trees and shrubs," have now gone to seed and become "a gloomy wilderness of tangled shade": "The old lilacs and laburnums, the spirea and syringa, nodded against the second-story windows. What garden plants survived were great ragged bushes or great shapeless beds. A huge wistaria vine covered the whole front of the house. The trunk, it was too large to call a stem, rose at the corner of the porch by the high steps, and had once climbed its pillars; but now the pillars were wrenched from their places and held rigid and helpless by the tightly wound and knotted arms."

The visitors, particularly the women, soon begin "to see bloodstains and crouching figures" in the sinister landscape, including the silhouette of a woman in the trunk of an ancient wistaria. That night, the ghost of the woman appears to two of the male visitors. The next morning, one of them reports that the "poor creature looked just like" all "those crouching, hunted figures" they had discerned the night before in the dark landscape. The other reveals that he followed the ghost into the cellar, where it rattled the chains of the drawbucket in the well. Each of them mentions a small red cross the ghost wore on a necklace of gold. The residents of the house quickly descend to the cellar, haul the mud-laden bucket to the surface of the well, and discover in it the tiny skeleton of a month-old child. The story ends as workmen find, beneath the rotting planks of the old porch and "in the strangling grasp of the roots of the giant wistaria," the bones of a woman with "a tiny scarlet cross on a thin chain of gold" around her neck.[3]

On the first reading, the story seems to be a chilling if rather transparent indictment of sexual oppression. By piecing together a number of disparate clues, the reader may guess the ending to the tale of tyranny and woe recounted in the first part. The young woman apparently escaped from her chamber, hid under the porch, drowned her baby rather than abandon it, and then starved to death rather than submit to her father's demand that she marry for the sake of propriety and return to England. As in other works of female gothicism, the protagonist is "simultaneously persecuted victim and courageous heroine." Her literary forebear is not so much Hester Prynne of Nathaniel Hawthorne's *The Scarlet Letter*, however, as the maddened slave Cassy of Harriet Beecher Stowe's *Uncle Tom's Cabin*. Lest this point seem forced or contrived, note that Gilman considered Stowe, her great-aunt, "one of the world's greatest women" and her novel "a great book" and the most popular and influential "work of fiction that was ever written."[4]

Like Cassy, the heroine of "The Giant Wistaria" kills her child rather than allowing it to suffer ostracism or persecution. In an early poem, "In Duty Bound," Gilman had alluded to childbearing as an "obligation preimposed, unsought, / Yet binding with the force of natural law." In "An Old Proverb," written some months after the "Wistaria" story, Gilman again illustrated this horror of maternity in a man-made world:

No escape under heaven! Can man treat you worse
After God has laid on you his infinite curse?
The heaviest burden of sorrow you win
Cannot weigh with the load of original sin;
No shame be too black for the cowering face
Of her who brought shame to the whole human race!
No escape under heaven!
For you feel, being human. You shrink from the pain
That each child, born a woman, must suffer again.
From the strongest of bonds hearts can feel, man can shape,
You cannot rebel, or appeal, or escape.
You must bear and endure. If the heart cannot sleep,
And the pain groweth bitter,—too bitter,—then weep!
For you feel, being human.[5]

Under the circumstances, the murder and suicide seem acts of heroic defiance that save child and mother from lives of shame. Much as Cassy haunts Simon Legree in *Uncle Tom's Cabin* until she has literally scared him to death, the ghostly presence in Gilman's story appears to exact her own measure of revenge upon her persecutors. Terrorized by men in the first part, she becomes the source of terror to men in the second.

"The Giant Wistaria" is not merely a tract in the gothic mode, however. Gilman also assimilated various elements of frontier mythology into it. Like many other American writers, she viewed the American West in paradoxical terms, as both promised land and howling wilderness. In her early allegorical poem "Nature's Answer," for example, she wrote of a man who homesteaded on the fairest spot on earth, with its "Soft hills, dark woods, smooth meadows richly green, and cool tree-shaded lakes the hills between." But a pestilence in the night swept "his paradise so fair" and "killed him there." The poem continues:

"O lovely land!" he cried, "how could I know
That death was lurking under this fair show?"
And answered Nature, merciful and stern,
"I teach by killing; let the others learn."[6]

Gilman expressed similarly ambivalent views about the American wilderness in "The Giant Wistaria." On the one hand, the mother in the story has fled the oppressive Old World for a new start in the "luxuriant" New World garden. She yearns to walk in the "green fields" of the frontier or virgin land. Elsewhere in her writings, Gilman clearly associated the westering experience with freedom and opportunity, especially for women. "As American women are given higher place—have won higher place—than any women on earth," she wrote, "so the women of the west stand higher than any in America." Or, as she wrote in her poem "In Mother-Time":

> We come to California for the sunshine and the flowers;
> Our motherhood has brought us here as one;
> For the fruit of all the ages should share the shining hours,
> With the blossoms ever-springing
> And the golden globes low swinging,
> In the sun.[7]

On the other hand, however, the mother in "The Giant Wistaria" fails to realize the freedom and independence promised in the West. Like the biblical Eve, she is banished from the garden for her sin and cursed to suffer in childbirth. The cross on the chain around her neck represents the noose or halter of orthodoxy. The grotesque wistaria that takes root in her corpse, a mere seedling in the first part of the story, even figures as a tree of knowledge, a botanical cousin to Beatrice's flowery shrub in Hawthorne's "Rappaccini's Daughter."

In her art no less than in her life, Gilman revised the traditional pattern of male flight to the geographical frontier. For the record, the story is moored autobiographically: Gilman wrote it after she left her first husband in Rhode Island and moved to Southern California, "the Garden of the Lord" with her infant daughter; that is, both the displaced author and the protagonist flee (New) England for the West.[8] Like conventional Western male heroes, it seems, women might retreat westward from the sexual battlefield, albeit with one crucial difference: Whereas Natty Bumppo and Huck Finn "light out for the territory ahead of the rest," preserving their bachelor freedom, Gilman (like the woman she portrayed in the story) headed west with a cradle in tow.[9] Obviously, mothers could not simply flee into the forest. For them, there was "no escape under heaven." They could not merely abandon their children, as the patriarch in Gilman's story proposes. At the very least, they had to arrange for alternative child care.

When she wrote the story in the winter of 1890, Gilman was (like her character) at the center of a brewing scandal, caught in a double bind: under fire as an irresponsible single mother and under pressure to return East cloaked in marital respectability.[10] "The Giant Wistaria" thus betrays the author's own predicament. Juliann Fleenor explains that female writers have often used the gothic form "to convey fear of maternity and its consequent dependent mother/infant relationship."[11] Whereas Cassy and the heroine of "The Giant Wistaria" kill their children, Gilman in 1894 dispatched her daughter to live with her former husband, the artist Charles Walter Stetson, and his second wife, the poet Grace Ellery Channing.

As an adult, Katharine Stetson Chamberlin complained that her mother had "seized the opportunity to get her freedom by shipping me East," but such a comment fails to account for Gilman's genuine regret that she had been forced to relinquish custody of her child. Gilman wrote later in her autobiography, "There were years, years, when I could never see a mother and child together without crying." Gilman desperately wished to be free of the burdensome routine of motherhood, to be sure, but she purchased her freedom at a terrible price: a wrenching and permanent physical separation from her daughter, a premeditated and "guilt-producing form of death" that she had anticipated and symbolically described in "The Giant Wistaria."[12]

Unfortunately, this all too tidy biographical analysis of Gilman's tale may tend to obscure some of its startling formal characteristics as a literary text. Leslie Fiedler reminds us that gothicism is an avant-garde literary movement, a protest or "rebellion of the imagination" against fiction of the commonplace.[13] An ambiguous, half-told tale disrupted by silences and ellipses, "The Giant Wistaria" is a type of open-ended riddle rather than a closed authorial monologue, an alternative fiction that reaches across the frontier of expression. The text responds to problems of authority by declaring its own indeterminacy.

The story consists almost entirely of dialogue. Events are narrated by several distinct voices, none of them predominant—a cacophony of language akin to Mikhail Bakhtin's notion of heteroglossia.[14] The decentralizing, centrifugal forces tearing at the discourse—Gilman's refusal to employ a single perspective or intelligence that can be trusted to observe and explain—compels the reader to sift through the fragments of debris and puzzle over a sequence of episodes. These parts, by any method of addition, yield no simple sum or symmetrical whole. Gilman's tale resolves no causation, repairs no rifts in the mosaic of the wistaria vine grown from an innocuous sprig. The past has become a Gordian knot, a monstrous tangle of events that can never be straightened.

The narrative is, perhaps, all the more terrifying for the questions it leaves dangling.

Who really kills the child? The heroine seems the most likely candidate, but her despotic father had earlier wished aloud that his pregnant daughter would be cleanly drowned than live to this end.[15] Does the heroine really hide under the porch and starve to death, or is she murdered (again, by her father?)

and her body secreted beneath the loose boards? And who fathered her child? Might the heroine have been the victim of incest, given her father's insistence on abandoning the infant and returning immediately to England? None of these questions can be definitively answered on the basis of what we are told in the story, although we might reasonably expect some or all of them to be answered in a traditionally unified authorial monologue. Like other female gothicists such as Mary Shelley, Gilman amplified the terror her story evokes by refusing to resolve it.

Nor are these the only gaps or "places of indeterminacy" in the text.[16] For example, the heroine (the conventional designation never seemed less appropriate) is never directly described. Her presence is signified in the first part of the story by two brief comments; from the beginning, it seems, she is virtually a disembodied voice. Her father quickly silences her, significantly, by striking her across the mouth. As a ghost in the second part of the story, she does not speak at all. When addressed "rather fiercely" by one of the men, "she [doesn't] seem to notice." Instead, her eerie presence is reported secondhand by the visitors to the mansion who see her in the nightmare landscape. The deceptions author(iz)ed by patriarchy are underscored when one of the weekend visitors, a reporter for a New York newspaper, declares upon his arrival that "if we don't find a real ghost, you may be very sure I shall make one. It's too good an opportunity to lose!" After the ghost appears, he proposes to "put it in the Sunday edition!"[17]

Without the dialogue available in the first part of the story, however, the journalist in "The Giant Wistaria" can neither raise the salient issue of sexual oppression nor pose questions about the identities of the murderer and the victim. Blind to the intimations of sexual and maternal terror in the wilderness, he trivializes the mystery by writing a spooky little story for the Sunday supplement about rattling chains and bumps in the night.

In retrospect, then, "The Giant Wistaria" is an experiment in the female frontier gothic worthy of the author of "The Yellow Wall-Paper," a tale Gilman completed only five months later. Both stories oppose sexual stereotypes and extend the frontiers of female identity. The heroine of the first no less than the narrator of the second is confined in a prison of language, represented by a turret room and an attic nursery, respectively. Neither woman is permitted to describe her predicament as a victim of patriarchy; indeed, the first woman disappears from the story, at least in a corporeal sense, after speaking a total of three sentences, and the second writes a clandestine epistolary tale, an absolutely forbidden discourse. Rather than submit to the demands of male authority, each woman devises a set of signs that defy patriarchal control. Paula Treichler observes that by the close of "The Yellow Wall-Paper" the narrator has changed "the terms in which women are represented in language" and extended "the conditions under which women will speak."[18]

"The Giant Wistaria" is a tale with similar implications. The doltish men who visit the haunted mansion initially ridicule the women for seeing ghosts. One of the men imagines "a woman picking huckleberries," a benign form of domestic drudgery, whereas one of the women perceives "a crouching, hunted figure." Another man cracks wise when his wife discerns in the trunk of the wistaria a "writhing body—cringing—beseeching!"[19] The narrative's young mother has become, it seems, a natural hieroglyph in the hallucinatory wilderness or liminal frontier.

Much as the narrator of "The Yellow Wall-Paper" reads "sprawling outlines" of her predicament in the pattern on the walls of her attic prison, the female visitors in "The Giant Wistaria" detect the intimations of sexual horror in the retrograde garden. Each of them respects the indeterminacy inscribed by the foreboding hieroglyphics of the landscape. "I'm convinced there is a story, if we could only find it," one of them declares—a far cry from the male reporter's avowed intention to tell a story even if he cannot find one.[20]

"The Giant Wistaria" is, of course, the story as one of the female characters might have written it, not the authoritative half-truth of the journalist. The implied author of the narrative understands that the land is cursed—not by the blood of bondsmen or the victims of genocidal war (the dark figures in the landscape are neither supplicant slaves nor crouching Indians) but by the tears of anguished women on the most ancient of frontiers, the interstice defining the status and distinguishing the roles of men and women in patriarchal society. Gilman wrote in her poem "Nature's Answer" that a young maid once

found such work as brainless slaves might do,
By day and night, long labor, never through;
Such pain—no language can her pain reveal.[21]

Like the young woman in this poem, like the narrator of "The Yellow Wall-Paper," and even like the author in her autobiography, the heroine of "The Giant Wistaria" devises a language to express ineffable pain—in her case, a hieroglyphic of a natural symbol. Ironically, her tale has been mostly unread for nearly a century now—the same length of time that elapsed between the heroine's death and her revelation in the shadows and twisted vines. Eerily, the story seems to have anticipated its reception.

NOTES

1. Carl N. Degler, ed., "Introduction," in *Women and Economics: A Study of the Economic Relation between Men and Women as a Factor in Social Evolution*, by Charlotte Perkins Gilman (1898; repr. New York: Harper & Row, 1966), viii;

W. D. Howells, "Life and Letters," *Harper's Weekly*, January 25, 1896; Howells, "The New Poetry," *North American Review*, May 1899.

2. Ellen Moers, *Literary Women: The Great Writers* (Garden City, NY: Doubleday, 1977), 148.

3. C. P. Stetson, "The Giant Wistaria," *New England*, June 1891, 482, 483, 485.

4. Moers, *Literary Women*, 139; Charlotte Perkins Gilman, "Comment and Review," *Forerunner*, July 1911, 196–97; Charlotte Perkins Gilman, "Social Darwinism," *American Journal of Sociology* 12 (March 1907): 173.

5. Charlotte Perkins Gilman, *In This Our World* (Boston: Small, Maynard, 1898), 34, 137–38.

6. Ibid., 3.

7. Stetson, "Giant Wistaria," 480–85; Charlotte Perkins Gilman, "Woman Suffrage and the West," *Kansas Suffrage Reveille*, June 1897; Gilman, *In This Our World*, 146.

8. Gilman, *In This Our World*, 145.

9. Mark Twain, *Adventures of Huckleberry Finn* (New York: Webster 1885), 366.

10. Charlotte Perkins Gilman, diary, vol. 29, March 11, 1890, Charlotte Perkins Gilman Papers, Arthur and Elizabeth Schlesinger Library, Radcliffe Institute, Harvard University, Cambridge, MA.

11. Juliann Fleenor, ed., "The Gothic Prism: Charlotte Perkins Gilman's Gothic Stories and Her Autobiography," in *The Female Gothic* (Montreal, Canada: Eden Press, 1983), 227.

12. Mary A. Hill, *Charlotte Perkins Gilman: The Making of a Radical Feminist, 1860–1896* (Philadelphia, PA: Temple University Press, 1980), 232, 234; Charlotte Perkins Gilman, *The Living of Charlotte Perkins Gilman: An Autobiography* (New York: Appleton-Century, 1935), 163–64.

13. Leslie Fiedler, *Love and Death in the American Novel* (New York: Dell, 1966), 122.

14. Mikhail Bakhtin, *The Dialogic Imagination*, ed. Michael Holquist, trans. Caryl Emerson (Austin: University of Texas Press, 1981).

15. Stetson, "Giant Wistaria," 480.

16. Wolfgang Iser, "Indeterminacy and the Reader's Response in Prose Fiction," in *Prospecting: From Reader Response to Literary Anthropology* (Baltimore: Johns Hopkins University Press, 1989), 3–30.

17. Stetson, "Giant Wistaria," 484.

18. Paula Treichler, "Escaping the Sentence: Diagnosis and Discourse in 'The Yellow Wallpaper,'" in *Feminist Issues in Literary Scholarship*, ed. Shari Benstock (Bloomington: Indiana University Press, 1987), 75.

19. Stetson, "Giant Wistaria," 482.

20. Ibid.

21. Gilman, *In This Our World*, 4.

WORKS CITED

Bakhtin, Mikhail. *The Dialogic Imagination.* Edited by Michael Holquist. Translated by Caryl Emerson and Michael Holquist. Austin: University of Texas Press, 1981.

Degler, Carl N., ed. "Introduction." In *Women and Economics: A Study of the Economic Relation between Men and Women as a Factor in Social Evolution,* by Charlotte Perkins Gilman, 1898, vi–xxxv. New York: Harper & Row, 1966.

Fiedler, Leslie. *Love and Death in the American Novel.* New York: Dell, 1966.

Fleenor, Juliann, ed. *The Female Gothic.* Montreal, Canada: Eden Press, 1983.

Gilman, Charlotte Perkins. "Comment and Review." *Forerunner,* July 1911.

———. *In This Our World.* Boston: Small, Maynard, 1898.

———. *The Living of Charlotte Perkins Gilman: An Autobiography.* New York: Appleton-Century, 1935.

———. Papers. Arthur and Elizabeth Schlesinger Library, Radcliffe Institute, Harvard University, Cambridge, MA.

———. "Social Darwinism." *American Journal of Sociology,* March 1907.

———. "Woman Suffrage and the West." *Kansas Suffrage Reveille,* June 1897.

Hill, Mary A. *Charlotte Perkins Gilman: The Making of a Radical Feminist, 1860–1896.* Philadelphia, PA: Temple University Press, 1980.

Howells, William Dean. "Life and Letters." *Harper's Weekly,* January 25, 1896.

———. "The New Poetry." *North American Review,* May 1899.

Moers, Ellen. *Literary Women: The Great Writers.* Garden City, NY: Doubleday, 1977.

Stetson, C. P. "The Giant Wistaria." *New England Magazine,* June 1891.

Treichler, Paula. "Escaping the Sentence: Diagnosis and Discourse in 'The Yellow Wallpaper.'" In *Feminist Issues in Literary Scholarship,* edited by Shari Benstock, 62–78. Bloomington: Indiana University Press, 1987.

Twain, Mark. *Adventures of Huckleberry Finn.* New York: Webster 1885.

III

Reclaiming and Redefining a "Woman's Place"

6

"A Crazy Quilt of a Paper"

Theorizing the Place of the Periodical in Charlotte Perkins Gilman's *Forerunner* Fiction

Sari Edelstein

In a 1915 issue of the *Forerunner*, Charlotte Perkins Gilman published an editorial entitled "Are Love Affairs News?" For Gilman, the answer was a resolute no. She observed, "The papers of Chicago are again filling columns, even pages, with the miscellaneous, and to most people, offensive, love affairs of one man. Our newspapers make loud outcry about their business being to publish 'news,' and retain the right of sole decision as to what is news and what isn't. This sort of story is not 'news.'" The question of what constituted news preoccupied Gilman, who was deeply committed to the necessity for a reliable press; in her words, "We have no social function today more important than The Press. The very essence of human life, i.e. social life, is in the power of intercommunication."[1] As Gilman saw it, the authority to determine what the public reads and knows is a major political power, a responsibility not to be taken lightly or misused.

Deeply committed to journalism's potential as a vehicle for social reform, Gilman was concerned with preserving the periodical as a space devoted to public affairs, not love affairs. I have argued elsewhere that Gilman's most celebrated story, "The Yellow Wall-Paper," stages her earliest critique of mainstream newspaper culture in its portrayal of the narrator's fraught relationship with the maddening wallpaper in her room.[2] This fictional scenario protests women's entrapment by the media's invasive techniques and criticizes the aesthetic as well as the social problems that Gilman attributed to sensationalism.

Beyond "The Yellow Wall-Paper," Gilman's engagement with the press became even more explicit; many of her stories and poems register her artistic, personal, and political opposition to mainstream journalism. In poems such as "The Yellow Reporter" and "Hyenas" she criticized intrusive male reporters and libelous papers and lamented the failure of newspapers to deliver the truth. She bemoaned the proliferation of women's magazines, such as the *Ladies' Home Journal*, which she saw as diminishing rather than expanding women's lives. Shelley Fisher Fishkin notes, "Gilman knew that many women were accustomed to allowing their own agendas to be set by publications that felt that freckle removal was a problem worthy of serious attention."[3] In the face of consumerist propaganda and unchecked sensationalism, Gilman retained her faith in the importance of the periodical, and her concerns about the deficiencies of the mainstream press ultimately compelled her to found her own magazine.

Written entirely by Gilman herself, the *Forerunner* was published monthly from 1909 until 1916. Sold for ten cents an issue, or a dollar for an annual subscription, the *Forerunner* never exceeded more than fifteen hundred subscribers.[4] In her efforts to salvage the civic function of the press, she exerted scrupulous control over all of the content, which ranged from political essays to short stories, poetry, and serialized novels. She even wrote the advertisements herself until eventually cutting advertising out entirely. With domestic scandals making headlines in daily newspapers, Gilman saw the *Forerunner* as compensating for the shortcomings of mainstream periodical culture; for her it was a bastion of serious and timely ideas about culture and politics that counteracted the messages disseminated by the dominant culture. The *Forerunner* aimed to transform women into active, informed citizens rather than mere consumers and housewives. Indeed, Gilman's periodical jettisoned the standard agenda of the women's magazine and instead featured essays on suffrage and socialism.

In this chapter I consider the *Forerunner* not merely as the venue for Gilman's short fiction but also as a crucial context for its interpretation. That is, her *Forerunner* fiction should be understood as embedded within and circulating through the periodical that Gilman founded, edited, and wrote herself for seven years. In emphasizing their status within the *Forerunner*, I posit that the stories reveal the influence that Gilman attributed to periodical culture as a tool for remapping the world. She understood the profound power of the media to direct readers and to transform public and private relationships, and she harnessed this power to upset, rather than affirm, existing social geographies. Her *Forerunner* fiction, including "Their House," "Dr. Clair's Place," and "When I Was a Witch" disrupt women's alignment with the domestic sphere and unsettle the entrenched divisions between male and female concerns. As a periodical, the *Forerunner* wielded a kind of portable power, domestic in its invasiveness of the middle-class home yet also public in its distribution of the political content that corresponded to these ideological goals. If, as Tim Cresswell writes, "particular orderings of things in the world have a socio-geographical basis," then we might read the *Forerunner* as a tool for dis-ordering society to reveal the constructed nature of both gender and place.[5]

The *Forerunner*'s pages revealed Gilman's commitment to what might be called an ethos of displacement. The journal repeatedly featured articles about turning kitchen duties into wage labor and making mothering a communal project—in other words, strategies for transforming the home into a public space and for bringing public aims into domestic space.[6] According to Cress-well, "The notion that everything 'has its place' and that things can be 'in-place' or 'out-of-place' is deeply ingrained in the way we think and act," and the mainstream media regularly reinforces these spatial laws, linking gender deviance to transgressions of place."[7] *Ladies' Home Journal* and *Good House-keeping*, with their prescriptive domestic lessons, not to mention their very titles, are prime examples of the mainstream media's investment in affirming normative spatial arrangements. In contrast, Gilman embraced the opportu-nity to disturb normative geographies; indeed, "out of place" is precisely where she wants to put her readers. The *Forerunner* stories aimed to unsettle women, to move them from the domestic to the public, from the interior to the exte-rior world, and ultimately from complacence to engagement.

The "place of women" was one of Gilman's ongoing concerns. On January 21, 1891, she gave a lecture at the Los Angeles Women's Club entitled "Our Place Today" in which she sought to jolt her audience into action: "What is a woman's place? By the side of man! . . . It is your city as much as theirs. How much do you know about it? How much do you know of the city gov-ernment, the city business, the city sin? . . . If the city government does not properly attend to the city drainage and your home is invaded by disease— is not that your business?"[8]

The domestic and the public, according to Gilman, are not inherently sepa-rate spheres, and women cannot commit to one without making an invest-ment in the other. As she pointed out, the "city drainage" determines whether "your home is invaded by disease." According to Gilman, women have a re-sponsibility, even an obligation, to know about their communities and to take an interest in public affairs, and she used the *Forerunner* to encourage women to expand the scope of their concerns, utilizing fiction to dramatize the posi-tive communal and individual rewards that result from focusing their ener-gies beyond their designated roles and social locations.[9]

WOMEN OUT OF PLACE

It is not incidental that Gilman's 1915 story "Dr. Clair's Place" begins with two women becoming acquainted on a train. The story celebrates female mobility and indeed sees it as integral to female friendship. One of the women is in a deep depression, and the narrator urges her to visit "Dr. Clair's Place," where her own depression was successfully treated. Of her new acquaintance, the narrator observes, "There was no air of tragedy about her. She was merely dead, or practically so."[10] So deeply does the narrator believe in the benefits of Dr. Clair's treatment that she pays the other woman's fare to make the trip. This serendipitous encounter on a train ends up saving the woman's life, affirming the benefits of female solidarity.

The story of a sanitarium for neurasthenic women, "Dr. Clair's Place" is an explicit critique of and alternative to S. Weir Mitchell's infamous rest cure. Far from being isolated or confined to bed rest, the women who spend time at Dr. Clair's Place, known as the Hill, weave baskets, exercise outdoors, and are encouraged to read; education and physical exertion are the key components of treatment. The story's title refers both to Dr. Clair's Place as a physical location and to Dr. Clair's unconventional place in society as a female doctor. Indeed, she has a man's first name, Willy, and has kept her maiden name but is also married with children, suggesting the beneficial results of disregarding gender mores.

Similarly, the Hill's verdant physical setting suggests the advantages of blending masculine and feminine attributes. "From year to year, the famousness of the place increased, and its income also, she built and improved; and now it was the most wonderful combination of peaceful, silent wilderness and blossoming fertility." Gilman's emphasis of the "wonderful combination" of "silent wilderness" and blossoms suggests the benefits of fusing masculine and feminine qualities and indicates that Dr. Clair's method is in keeping with nature rather than resisting it. Indeed, whereas nonconformity to spatial order is often associated with dirt, chaos, or horror, the women's disregard for normative geographies has regenerative, healthy consequences. The narrator observes, "I can tell you a boarding-place that is as beautiful, as healthful, as exquisitely clean and comfortable, and as reasonable as hers in price, is pretty popular." Dr. Clair so scrupulously and thoughtfully manages her retreat that women are actually reluctant to leave after successful treatment.[11]

Spending time at the Hill enables women to find their places. Once they are no longer spatially or psychologically limited by gender conventions, the visitors to Dr. Clair's Place experience themselves as more expansive and alive. The narrator benefits from a month of what she calls "physical enlargement."[12] The story encouraged the *Forerunner* readers to restore themselves by finding solace and strength in the outdoors. More than simply an indictment of Weir Mitchell's stringent, infantilizing rest-cure regimen, "Dr. Clair's Place" is a blueprint for self-renewal and actualization and a call for women to venture beyond the confines of the domestic realm.

Another *Forerunner* story, published in 1912, "Their House" similarly celebrates a woman who opts out of her assigned place in the home and in the social world more generally. Unlike "Dr. Clair's Place," this story begins with the description of a traditional home with a traditional patriarchal distribution of labor and property: "Mr. Waterson's house was small, owing to the smallness of his income, but it was clean, most violently and meticulously clean, owing to the proficiency of Mrs. Waterson as a housekeeper."[13] It is notable that the house is described solely as "Mr. Waterson's," indicating that his wife has no property or claim to their real estate. His small income determines the size of their house, indicating that perhaps he is not the best businessman, and the fact that the house is "violently and meticulously clean" implies that Mrs. Waterson's energy might be better utilized in other tasks. In other words, the assigned gender roles in this house are not creating optimal living conditions or material benefits for either husband or wife. Although they are both cramped by the size of the house and by the terms of their marriage, they lack the resources—financial or otherwise—to make a change.

When Mr. Waterson receives a rare opportunity to join a scientific expedition, which will allow him to grow and discover the world, quite literally, Mrs. Waterson agrees to run his dry goods store on her own. It turns out, "to her sincere surprise," that Mrs. Waterson finds running the business "more congenial than that of forever recooking similar food and reclearing the same rooms, clothes and dishes." Her husband's absence enables her to move beyond the parameters that had formerly confined her, giving her the space to expand herself and to improve both of their lives. After a few months, she consults with an efficiency expert, enlarges the dry goods store into a department store, opens a laundry, and purchases a hotel. "Her natural energies had now for the first time room for full action."[14] Just as in "Dr. Clair's Place," Gilman redefines "natural," suggesting that women's natures are far more expansive and active than mainstream gender ideology allows. So successful are Mrs. Waterson's business establishments that she sells their home, purchases a vacant lot, and builds a large new house. She simply needed "room" to exercise her full range of talents; as soon as she had that space, she was able to excel in the real estate business and as an entrepreneur.

When Mr. Waterson returns four years later, he is dazzled by her successes. Despite the fact the he begins the story "thoroughly imbued with the conviction that woman's place is the home," he eventually realizes and delights in his wife's entrepreneurial talents. While the mainstream media were insisting that women belong in the home, Gilman suggested that conventional gender roles are actually "unnatural" and that the Watersons' marriage was endangered by a blind adherence to such constructed norms. The story's final sentence—"This is Our House, John!"—epitomizes its message that collective ownership and shared responsibility improve marriage and society.[15]

"Dr. Clair's Place" and "Their House" resist the naturalized assumptions about gendered spaces with which women are indoctrinated and aim to de-familiarize the messages of mainstream culture. Aleta Cane writes, "In every one of the short stories in the *Forerunner*, Gilman questions the absolute truths that were preached from the pulpit and reiterated in the popular media, such as films and magazines like the *Ladies' Home Journal*, and that governed so many women's lives."[16] In other words, the *Forerunner* was a vehicle for thwarting the messages of more powerful media outlets and urging women to unlearn the so-called truths about gender that pervaded the culture.

Through seemingly simple stories of women "out of place," the stories re-map the possibilities for women's lives and suggest new ways of being oriented in the world. Sara Ahmed explains, "Orientations shape not only how we inhabit space, but how we apprehend this world of shared inhabitance. . . . Inhabiting spaces 'decides' what comes into view. . . . When we follow specific lines, some things become reachable and others remain or even become out of reach."[17] Gilman's stories highlight the way certain orientations, directions, and normative routes obstruct women, and instead they endorse veering off course and out of place.

Gilman was well aware of how unprofitable, and even unpalatable, these ideas were. She established the *Forerunner*, what she called a "special medium," precisely because she wanted to circulate content that was unwelcome in and critical of the established periodicals of the day. She wrote, "The difficulties of reaching the public with any charges against the press are extreme; because that press is the chief medium of communication. It has to be done, for the most, in minor publications, such as leaflets and pamphlets . . . and in the meantime the offender still has the ear of the public, and a range of power open to none of the others."[18] The press's monopoly on public opinion can be subverted only through "minor publications," and even then, the press maintains its position of social dominance.

For the remainder of this chapter I want to consider how one *Forerunner* story in particular links the role of the press to the critique of normative gender geographies and celebrates displacement as the basis for reform. Although it seems to be a whimsical tale without much explicit political critique, "When I Was a Witch" concerns a woman who wants to disorient, invert, and restructure society, and it also addresses the mainstream press's outsized role in shaping the lives of its readers. The first-person narrator recounts a brief supernatural episode in her life, which she refers to as the "time of witching."[19] As a witch, the narrator suddenly finds herself endowed with the power to euthanize animals, improve public services, and enact a range of sometimes bizarre wish fulfillments through the sheer exertion of her will.

The story begins when the narrator, who lives in an apartment in New York City, heads up to the roof of her building to cool off from "a sultry and thunderous evening." Frustrated with urban life, the crowds, the "mendacious" newspapers, and the spectacle of fashion and status, she notes, "I was in a state of simmering rage—hot enough, even without the weather and the furnace." Shortly after going up to the roof, she sees a carriage driver whipping a tired horse and suddenly "wishes that every person who strikes or otherwise hurts a horse unnecessarily, shall feel the pain intended—and the horse not feel it!" Upon noticing the success of her wish, she proceeds to wish that all urban pets would be "comfortably dead," since she sees them "leading unnatural lives of enforced celibacy, cut off from sunlight, fresh air, the use of their limbs."[20]

Significantly, the witch is most troubled by the fact that the animals are out of place, "cut off from sunlight [and] fresh air," and her frustration with their "unnatural lives" resonates with the unnatural lives of women in many of her stories." Like urban pets, women are supposedly in the right place in the home, limited in "the use of their limbs," but she denaturalizes the notion of house pets just as she destabilizes the association of women with domestic work.

Delighted with her newfound powers, the narrator improves the food business, public transportation, and corporate culture in general. In accordance with Gilman's socialist leanings, the witch contemplates exploited workers and class inequality: "I bethought me of the remote stockholders, of the more immediate directors, of the painfully prominent officials and insolent employees—and got to work." Through exerting her powers as a witch, she is able to incite a "conscientious revival all over the country"; "in mills and mints and railroads, things began to mend" and a "wave of humane feeling" swept the city.[21]

DISPLACING GENRES

Gilman's use of the witch in this story, and the supernatural in general in her work, is generically as well culturally significant. The *Forerunner*, like most mass-media periodicals, contained multiple genres, mixing news and fantasy, the gothic and the comic—refusing to adhere consistently to generic limits and conventions. Like places, genres enable certain conditions while prohibiting others. Genre conventions limit the kinds of stories that can be told, and we might read Gilman's generic restlessness as a signal of her desire to reimagine women's roles and the world itself, as a grasping for physical and intellectual space, and as a longing for new narrative possibilities.

"When I Was a Witch" epitomizes the critical appropriation and mixing of genres that characterized her career. Given the story's use of a witch as the protagonist and the fact that it takes place on Halloween, "When I Was a Witch" initially seems generically aligned with Gilman's gothic fictions, such as "The Giant Wistaria," "The Rocking Chair," or even "The Yellow Wall-Paper." According to Carol Davison, female gothic fiction typically "centers its lens on a young woman's rite of passage into womanhood and her ambivalent relationship to contemporary domestic ideology, especially the joint institutions of marriage and motherhood."[22] Yet even though "When I Was a Witch" is certainly interested in gender norms, the story offers a surprising reversal of female gothic conventions. Rather than highlighting the horrors of marriage and domestic space, Gilman focused on the shortcomings of public spaces, including subways, mills, railroads, and even the public sphere of journalistic discourse. These are hardly the tropes or devices that one associates with the female gothic, which tends to address women's fears of entrapment within the female body and the domestic sphere. Indeed, given that the female gothic is often interested in domestic confinement, it seems particularly striking that the protagonist of "When I Was a Witch" is remarkably mobile. The story begins on the roof of her apartment building, and it later follows her onto a streetcar as she goes to her office. The house, that classic gothic symbol, is utterly absent.

Thus it might be useful then to consider this story in terms of what Janet Beer and Avril Horner call the "parodic gothic." This term applies to "stories in which the idea of the supernatural is used not only to question the values at the heart of American culture and civilization, but also to draw attention to the politics of representation and narration."[23] In "When I Was a Witch," Gilman gestured toward the gothic but redirected her female protagonist's attention from the self to society, and in so doing she exposed the gendered assumptions on which the genre depends. Indeed, we might read the story's invocation of the gothic as a meditation on the inadequacies of life *outside the home.* In other words, the fact that the story commences on the roof, rather than in the oppressive interior, suggests an orientation above and outside the domestic. The story seems to suggest that women might have (or even *should* have) anxieties about what goes on beyond their own psychic and interior space. Just as "The Yellow Wall-Paper" anticipated and rejected Virginia Woolf's injunction that a woman simply needs a "room of one's own," this story suggests that women ought to have a stake in public spaces and should be troubled by inefficiencies and inequalities beyond the home. It was not the home that needed improvement, cleanliness, or efficiency, as the women's magazines suggested; rather, the *Forerunner* urged women to treat cities as home and to consider their houses as inherently public and political.

Gilman's decision to characterize this protagonist as a witch clearly signals her embrace of women who spurn gender norms and social conventions in general, and the characterization would have had significant contemporary resonances, most notably with L. Frank Baum's publication of *The Wizard of Oz* in 1900. According to Marion Gibson, "By 1900 witches had become liberal metaphors for political dissent and female self-empowerment, pointing the way to a future where traditional delusions were comical and obsolete."[24] The resurgence of interest in witches at the turn of the twentieth century made sense in light of the rise of the New Woman, a figure who overturned many of the prevailing assumptions about gender.

Consequently, since the figure of the witch was pervading popular culture at this time, it offered a clear cautionary, even disciplinary, representation of independent womanhood. Indeed, a 1909 book by Oliver Madox Hueffer called *Witches and Their Craft* went so far as to link witches to suffragists. According to Linda McDowell, "Women who did not conform or keep to their place were constructed as wicked or fallen, forcing them to reconsider their decision to participate in the public sphere."[25] Gilman appropriated this association of witches with new womanhood and suggested the social good that witches, or unconventional and powerful women, can do. Her civically engaged witch is not wicked; rather, she is able to see wickedness in the existing social conventions and inequalities. And in telling her own story, the witch assumes narrative authority; no longer the object of ridicule or anxiety, Gilman's witch undoes and even mocks a persistent stereotype about nonnormative women.

Just as Gilman parodied the gothic, she also gestured toward realism without upholding the conventions of the genre. With its commitment to objectivity, realism was closely aligned with the values and practices of mainstream journalism and the male-dominated literary establishment. In his classic study of American realism, Michael Davitt Bell notes that William Dean Howells's "notion of objectivity in fiction . . . functions to associate realism, once again, with 'real' pursuits, 'men's activities.'"[26] Heavily influenced by journalistic techniques and often written by former newspapermen, realist fiction purported to represent the truth accurately and without slant. By using a witch as a protagonist, Gilman was refusing to participate in the realist mode, an insufficient form for representing her visions of a more just civilization.

Although its New York City setting and its interest in urban problems invoke the realist tradition, the story takes a supernatural turn that is fundamentally incompatible with the genre's commitment to documenting a stable and recognizable reality. Realism cannot disorient readers; it can merely reflect a visible and accepted version of reality back to its readers, often constructing and stabilizing a world that is actually chaotic. Gilman wanted to undermine reality and to upset the belief that social truths are natural and unchangeable. By emphasizing the outrageous and the unrealistic, Gilman jars her readers into new and unexpected ways of thinking about the world.

"THE MERE PRINTING OF TRUTH"

In conjunction with her refusal to align herself with realism, Gilman dispar-aged mainstream journalism, another discourse that was offering a version of the world masquerading as fact. Indeed, the story begins and ends with the narrator's complaints about "mendacious" and "salacious" newspapers, which serve as the object of the witch's final and most efficacious reform. After all her other reforms have been enacted, the story offers an explicit denuncia-tion of daily newspapers for their failure to deliver accurate, unbiased infor-mation. The witch seeks to ameliorate the corruption of the press through a color-coding scheme: "All intentional lies, in editorial, news, or any other column . . . [appeared] Scarlet. All malicious matter . . . Crimson. All careless or ignorant mistakes . . . Pink. All for direct self-interest of owner . . . Dark green. All mere bait—to sell the paper . . . Bright green. All advertising, pri-mary or secondary . . . Brown. All sensational and salacious matter . . . Yellow. All hired hypocrisy . . . Purple. Good fun, instruction, and entertainment . . . Blue. True and necessary news and honest editorials . . . Ordinary print."[27]

The goal of this system of color coding is to make visible the disproportion-ate amount of untruthful and insubstantial material circulating in the main-stream press. The newspaper's content—the advertising, the hypocrisy, the sensationalism—presents itself as trustworthy and objective, but the witch's system illuminates the failure of the newspapers to actually offer any "true and necessary news." The newspaper, it seems, must be parsed, deciphered, and organized by a responsible woman.

After enacting the color-coding scheme, the witch explains, "There was such a change in all kinds of business, following the mere printing of truth in the newspapers. It began to appear as if we had lived in a sort of delirium—not really knowing the facts about anything. As soon as we really knew the facts, we began to behave very differently, of course."[28] The description of the previous mode of existence as a "sort of delirium" makes explicit the connection be-tween social and journalistic convention: Journalism determines our behavior and our experience of reality. The "mere printing of truth" frees citizens from mental confusion and enables them to live more clearly, more deliberately.

We might read the witch's influence on newspapers as a supernatural brand of editorial power, a testament to the fact that representation itself is a kind of magic that can effect change in the real world. Reflecting on the newly color-coded paper, the witch remarks, "You never saw such a crazy quilt of a paper."[29] By describing the newspaper as a "crazy quilt," she suggests that her powers have served not only to visually encode the newspaper but also to do-mesticate it. Indeed, by using the language of domesticity to describe the most public of documents, she converts the newspaper into a household object, conventionally the product of women's labor. Read this way, it seems that one of the witch's powers is her ability to unsettle seemingly entrenched divisions, including those between public and private, life and death, supernatural and actual, and fact and fancy, revealing their permeable and constructed nature.

More than a "crazy quilt," the color-coding system also turns the newspaper into a map. Whereas the newspaper readers were once lost in a miasma of pseudonews, the witch locates figurative pitfalls and land mines and indicates the best routes for the readers, distinguishing reliable, "honest" news from "mere bait." Just as Gilman decried the infiltration of love affairs into the daily newspaper in her *Forerunner* editorial, so too does this story suggest that social change relies on the reorganization of periodicals. By color-coding the newspaper, the witch illuminates the causal relationship between social dysfunction and journalistic corruption.

Given the witch's success in ameliorating so many social ills, it would seem that the story serves as a fantasy about the possibilities for female influence in the public arena. However, "When I Was a Witch" ends on a strange, sobering note. At the conclusion of the story, the witch attempts to enlighten and unite women and realizes the limits of what she calls her "black magic." She explains, "I wished—with all my strength—that women, all women, might realize Womanhood at last . . . that they might see their duty as human beings, and come right out into full life and work and happiness! I stopped, breathless, with shining eyes. I waited, trembling, for things to happen. Nothing happened."[30]

The witch's magic cannot unite women or make them cognizant of their unrealized potential. Why did Gilman choose this cynical ending for her comical story? Why *can't* the witch use her supernatural powers to awaken women to their full capacities as human beings? One explanation is that when the witch contemplates the untapped potential of women, her "heart swelled with something that was far from anger."[31] Whereas all her other reforms are born of anger, this final wish stems from something else: a genuine concern for women's humanity and a desire for solidarity. According to this story, the goals of feminism cannot be achieved merely through magic, nor can anger alone effect social change. Feminist critics have long considered the expression of anger fundamental to social protest and a potent source of creative energy, but Gilman's story suggests that anger alone is insufficient. Rather, true social change must emerge from positive action.

Although Gilman claimed to always write for a purpose, her work often delivers more than a single intended message.[32] According to the witch's own color scheme, "When I Was a Witch" would clearly be coded blue, signifying "good fun, instruction, and entertainment," but the story exceeds this categorization. In its ingenious revision of gothic and realist conventions and its astute criticisms of public life, the story operates as a thought experiment on social change. If, as the witch realizes, the majority of women are "blind, chained, untaught, in a treadmill," then it is only through enlightenment and education that the situation can be remedied.[33] These are precisely the offerings of the *Forerunner*, which provided what Gilman called a "clear, consistent view of human life and how to live it."[34] Her stories enjoin readers to privately consider how they might improve society if they were granted supernatural powers for a day, and then it allows those readers to magically join a like-minded community. She ascribes to journalism the capacity to unite women in what Nancy Fraser has called a "counterpublic sphere," a space "where members of subordinated groups invent and circulate counter-discourses to formulate oppositional interpretations of their interests and needs."[35] Thus the *Forerunner* is the vehicle that can achieve what the witch cannot: an effective, enduring route to awakening women to their intellectual abilities and political potential.

Periodicals and newspapers exert an almost supernatural power to shape individuals and societies. With her *Forerunner* fiction, Gilman exploited that power, uncoupling women from kitchens and motherhood and instead locating them in business and nature, urban planning and medicine. While the male-dominated, "salacious" newspapers failed to fulfill their public duty and inundated women with messages about marriage, motherhood, and consumerism, the *Forerunner* enabled female readers to, as Gilman put it, "see their duty as human beings, and come right out into full life and work and happiness," the very hope of the witch in the story. These stories offer readers a new set of coordinates and directions for modern life, celebrating rather than denigrating women's failure to stay in their proper places. Just like the witch, Gilman offered her readers a purified periodical as a map to guide them away from the sensational and prescriptive and toward the "true and necessary."

NOTES

1. Charlotte Perkins Gilman, "Are Love Affairs News?" *Forerunner*, November–December 1915: 301, 336.

2. Sari Edelstein, "Charlotte Perkins Gilman and the Yellow Newspaper," *Legacy* 24, no. 1 (2007): 72–92.

3. Shelley Fisher Fishkin, *Feminist Engagements: Forays into American Literature and Culture* (New York: Macmillan, 2009), 34.

4. Aleta Cane, "The Heroine of Her Own Story: Subversion of Traditional Periodical Marriage Tropes in the Short Fiction of Charlotte Perkins Gilman's *Forerunner*," in *"The Only Efficient Instrument": American Women Writers and the Periodical, 1837–1916*, ed. Susan Alves and Aleta Cane (Boston: Northeastern University Press, 2001), 97.

5. Tim Cresswell, *Place: A Short Introduction* (Oxford, UK: Wiley-Blackwell, 2004), 2.

6. "Gilman repeatedly advocated reforms such as children's day-care and kitchenless houses to release women from domestic duties and to allow them to pursue the professions for which they were most suited." Charlotte J. Rich, ed., "Introduction," in *What Diantha Did*, by Charlotte Perkins Gilman (1910; repr., Durham, NC: Duke University Press, 2005), 6.

7. Tim Cresswell, "Weeds, Plagues, and Bodily Secretions: A Geographical Interpretation of Metaphors of Displacement," *Annals of the Association of American Geographers* 87, no. 2 (1997): 334.

8. Charlotte Perkins Gilman, "Our Place Today," in *Charlotte Perkins Gilman: A Non-Fiction Reader*, ed. Larry Ceplair (New York: Columbia University Press, 1991), 59–60.

9. See, e.g., Charlotte Perkins Gilman, "The Unnatural Mother," *Forerunner*, November 1916. Gilman undermined the assumption that a woman's first priority must be her family; instead, she described a woman who puts her community before her own children, saving numerous lives rather than focusing only on her own loved ones.

10. Charlotte Perkins Gilman, "Dr. Clair's Place," *Forerunner*, June 1915, 141–45.

11. Ibid.

12. Ibid.

13. Charlotte Perkins Gilman, "Their House," *Forerunner*, December 1912.

14. Ibid., 312, 313.

15. Ibid., 309.

16. Cane, "Heroine," 112.

17. Sara Ahmed, *Queer Phenomenology: Orientations, Objects, Others* (Durham, NC: Duke University Press, 2006), 3, 14.

18. Charlotte Perkins Gilman, "Newspapers and Democracy," *Forerunner*, November 1916, 301.

19. Charlotte Perkins Gilman, "When I Was a Witch," *Forerunner*, May 1910, 1.

20. Ibid., 1, 2. One observer has noted, "Gilman's advocacy of euthanasia . . . placed her at the forefront of the humane movement." Catherine Golden, "Marking Her Territory: Feline Behavior in 'The Yellow Wall-Paper,'" *American Literary Realism* 40, no. 1 (2007): 16.

21. Gilman, "Witch," 3, 4.

22. Carol Margaret Davison, "Haunted House/Haunted Heroine: Female Gothic Closets in 'The Yellow Wallpaper,'" *Women's Studies* 33 (2004): 48.

23. Janet Beer and Avril Horner, "'This Isn't Exactly a Ghost Story': Edith Wharton and Parodic Gothic," *Journal of American Studies* 37, no. 2 (August 2003): 270.

24. Marion Gibson, "Retelling Salem Stories: Gender Politics and Witches in American Culture," *European Journal of American Culture* 25, no. 2 (2006): 90.

25. Linda McDowell, *Gender, Identity, and Place: Understanding Feminist Geographies* (Minneapolis: University of Minnesota Press, 1999), 149.

26. Michael Davitt Bell, *The Problem of American Realism: Studies in the Cultural History of a Literary Idea* (Chicago: University of Chicago Press, 1993), 30.

27. Gilman, "Witch," 5–6.

28. Ibid., 6.

29. Ibid.

30. Ibid.

31. Ibid.

32. Gilman, *The Living of Charlotte Perkins Gilman*, 121.

33. Gilman, "Witch," 6.

34. Gilman, "As to Purpose," *Forerunner*, November 1909, n.d.

35. Nancy Fraser, "Rethinking the Public Sphere: A Contribution to the Critique of Actually Existing Democracy," *Social Text* 25/26 (1990): 67.

WORKS CITED

Ahmed, Sara. *Queer Phenomenology: Orientations, Objects, Others.* Durham, NC: Duke University Press, 2006.

Beer, Janet, and Avril Horner. "'This Isn't Exactly a Ghost Story': Edith Wharton and Parodic Gothic." *Journal of American Studies* 37, no. 2 (August 2003): 269–85.

Bell, Michael Davitt. *The Problem of American Realism: Studies in the Cultural History of a Literary Idea.* Chicago: University of Chicago Press, 1993.

Cane, Aleta. "The Heroine of Her Own Story: Subversion of Traditional Periodical Marriage Tropes in the Short Fiction of Charlotte Perkins Gilman's *Forerunner.*" In *"The Only Efficient Instrument": American Women Writers and the Periodical, 1837–916*, edited by Susan Alves and Aleta Cane, 85–112. Boston: Northeastern University Press, 2001.

Cresswell, Tim. *Place: A Short Introduction.* Oxford, UK: Wiley-Blackwell, 2004.

———. "Weeds, Plagues, and Bodily Secretions: A Geographical Interpretation of Metaphors of Displacement." *Annals of the Association of American Geographers* 87, no. 2 (1997): 330–45.

Davison, Carol Margaret. "Haunted House/Haunted Heroine: Female Gothic Closets in 'The Yellow Wallpaper.'" *Women's Studies* 33 (2004): 47–75.

Edelstein, Sari. "Charlotte Perkins Gilman and the Yellow Newspaper." *Legacy* 24, no. 1 (2007): 72–92.

Fishkin, Shelley Fisher. *Feminist Engagements: Forays into American Literature and Culture.* New York: Macmillan, 2009.

Fraser, Nancy. "Rethinking the Public Sphere: A Contribution to the Critique of Actually Existing Democracy." *Social Text* 25/26 (1990): 56–80.

Gibson, Marion. "Retelling Salem Stories: Gender Politics and Witches in American Culture." *European Journal of American Culture* 25, no. 2 (2006): 85–107.

Gilman, Charlotte Perkins. "Are Love Affairs News?" *Forerunner*, November–December 1915.

———. "Dr. Clair's Place," *Forerunner*, June 1915.

———. *The Living of Charlotte Perkins Gilman*. New York: Appleton-Century, 1935.

———. "Newspapers and Democracy." *Forerunner*, November 1916.

———. "Our Place Today." In *Charlotte Perkins Gilman: A Non-Fiction Reader*, edited by Larry Ceplair, 53–61. New York: Columbia University Press, 1991.

———. "Their House." *Forerunner*, December 1912.

———. "The Unnatural Mother." *Forerunner*, November 1916.

———. "When I Was a Witch." *Forerunner*, May 1910.

Golden, Catherine. "Marking Her Territory: Feline Behavior in 'The Yellow Wall-Paper.'" *American Literary Realism* 40, no. 1 (2007): 16.

McDowell, Linda. *Gender, Identity, and Place: Understanding Feminist Geographies*. Minneapolis: University of Minnesota Press, 1999.

Rich, Charlotte J., ed. "Introduction." In *What Diantha Did*, by Charlotte Perkins Gilman, 1910, 1–23. Durham, NC: Duke University Press, 2005.

7

The Power of the Postal Service in Gilman's "Turned"

Exposing Adultery and Empowering Women to Find a Meaningful Place

Catherine J. Golden

Except for the infamous yellow wallpaper, material artifacts have rarely been the focus of Gilman scholarship. To develop plot and characterization, Charlotte Perkins Gilman incorporated many revealing material objects in her fiction, including newspapers in "When I Was a Witch" (1910), furniture in "The Rocking Chair" (1893) and "The Chair of English" (1913), and letters in "Turned" (1911); the latter are the focus of this analysis. In her short story "Turned," published in the *Forerunner*, Gilman used letters to infiltrate domestic space, inviting critics to read the story from the lens of place (a concept from human geography). Tim Cresswell defines *place* as "a meaningful location" as well as "a way of understanding the world."[1] Incorporating postal history, material culture studies, triangular desire, and the spatial concept of place, this chapter illuminates how the mail, in exposing adultery, empowers two women—an educated white female and her untutored foreign domestic—who together find a meaningful place in a gendered world.

Our age relies on e-mails, texts, and tweets, the hallmarks of computer-mediated communication. We still depend on the post office for aspects of our daily living; Gilman's "Turned," however, returns readers to a time when people communicated primarily by letter. In the early twentieth century, telegrams and telephones were available but expensive. Sending a letter was the most affordable way to communicate with professional associates, friends, and loved ones who lived at a distance and to stay in touch with family members and friends while traveling for business or pleasure. Gilman herself was an avid letter writer.[2] She understood that an address in a familiar handwriting or typeface, as in "Turned," spoke to the receiver before she or he even opened the envelope.

Letters are common plot devices in nineteenth-century fiction and narrative painting. Letters declare undying love; think only of Captain Wentworth's missive to Anne Elliot at the close of Jane Austen's *Persuasion* (1818): "You pierce my soul. I am half agony, half hope. Tell me not that I am too late, that such precious feelings are gone for ever."[3] Letters announce the death of a relative and the receipt of an inheritance as well as unending love. In Charlotte Brontë's *Jane Eyre* (1847), for example, Jane receives a letter informing her of the death of her uncle, who leaves her a fortune of 20,000 pounds.

Letters also serve a range of functions in works by two Victorian authors that Gilman admired: George Eliot and Charles Dickens.[4] Letter writing becomes a vehicle for Reverend Edward Casaubon to propose marriage to Dorothea Brooke in *Middlemarch* (1872); in turn, Dorothea accepts his offer in a letter. Dickens uses letter writing and handwriting daringly throughout *Bleak House* (1853), such as to enlighten Lady Dedlock that her former lover (and father of her illegitimate daughter) is still alive (she recognizes his distinctive handwriting on legal documents) and later to fuel slander when Lady Dedlock's French maid, Mademoiselle Hortense, posts dozens of anonymous letters blaming Lady Dedlock for a murder that Hortense herself has committed. In Eliot's fiction a letter thus grants its receiver a significant place, whereas in Dickens's fiction it aims to displace.

In Victorian narrative painting, letters infiltrate the home to reveal a woman's clandestine past and punish her. Augustus Egg plants such a letter to inform a distraught husband of his wife's betrayal in his triptych of marital infidelity entitled *Past and Present* (1858). In the first of three panels (see figure 7.1), the cuckolded husband sits at the dining room table in shock, holding the letter that informs him of his wife's indiscretion. The erring wife—who has been peeling an apple, a symbol of temptation—lies prostrate at her husband's feet, begging forgiveness. The couple's daughters, at the left side of the picture, are building a house of playing cards, symbolizing the fragility of their family. The house of cards balances precariously on top of a book with the name HONORÉ DE BALZAC blazed on its spine; Egg thus associates the wife's adultery with racy French novels with infidelity plots like Balzac's own *Cousin Bette* (1846) and Gustave Flaubert's *Madame Bovary* (1856).

The second and third panels of *Past and Present* show the effects of the wife's infidelity on her two children, her husband, her bastard child, and herself. In the second canvas the couple's daughters are staring at the moon, and in the third panel the outcast wife gazes upon this very same moon from her precarious berth by the polluted Thames where she nurses her dying illegiti-

Figure 7.1. Augustus Leopold Egg, *Past and Present*, No. 1, 1858, ©Tate, London, 2015

mate child. Egg appended a fictional diary quotation to the triptych when he exhibited the painting at the Royal Academy in 1858; it reads in part: "so his poor children have now lost both parents." From this note, which intensifies the painting's function as a morality tale, we know that the betrayed husband is now dead—presumably of a broken heart—and the fallen wife is treated as one dead.[5]

Egg was not the only painter to employ the device of an incriminating letter in a painting that resembles a cautionary tale. Richard Redgrave uses a letter in his depiction of an unwed young woman's fall in *The Outcast* (1851) (see figure 7.2). In this painting the situation is clear without the letter, leading George Landow to conclude, "The device of an incriminating letter, which Augustus Egg employed in *Past and Present (I)*, seems a bit unnecessary here since the daughter holds her illegitimate child in her arms—clear enough evidence that she's a fallen woman!"[6] Might the inclusion of the letter that conveys the daughter's sad history underscore the righteousness of the father's wrath? The viewer has no doubt why the father is so determined to punish his fallen daughter, despite her pleading and that of another daughter who kneels at his back and begs him to repent. At the left of the picture, a con-

Figure 7.2. Richard Redgrave, *The Outcast*, 1851, courtesy of the Royal Academy of Arts, London

cerned mother comforts her son, who buries his head in his arms in grief, as well as a younger daughter. However, the focus of the painting is the right side of the picture, where the daughter stands apart from her family. An open letter lies on the floor. The angry patriarch glares at his fallen daughter, positioned at the threshold of the open doorway in the dark of night. The fallen woman swaddles her child with her shawl and looks beseechingly at her stern father, but the aged patriarch is unyielding. He points his finger to go, banishing his outcast daughter and her child to the cold, dark, snowy outdoors.

Aspects of these narrative paintings of fallen women surface with a twist in "Turned," in which Gilman used letters for a feminist purpose. Gilman engineered an epistolary mix-up to reveal not a wife's adultery, but a husband's. At the turn of the twentieth century, adultery was "a subject genteel folk avoided talking about, except to denounce the women who engaged in it," Ann Lane notes.[7] The epistolary mix-up introduces adultery in a "genteel" way, opening Marion's eyes to her husband's affair with their Swedish live-in domestic, Gerta Petersen. The lens of place as Cresswell's "way of understanding" illuminates how Marion arguably finds her home threatened by the attachment her husband has formed with their now-pregnant servant as well as her initial exclusionary reaction to banish pregnant Gerta from the Marroners' home, which would render the servant placeless. Ultimately, however, mixed-up letters—objects of material culture that entered the home on a daily basis—disrupt the dynamics of the time-honored romantic triangle to expose and denounce an adulterous husband. His two love interests transform from passive objects of desire to active characters who leave home, find a new place, and gain strong identities apart from him.

To recap the plot of "Turned": Gilman centers her story on "two women and a man. One woman was a wife: loving, trusting, affectionate. One was a servant: loving, trusting, affectionate—a young girl, an exile, a dependent; grateful for any kindness; untrained, uneducated, childish." The two women are Marion Marroner, an educated woman with a PhD who served on a college faculty before her marriage, and Gerta Petersen, an untutored, too trusting, pregnant eighteen-year-old Swedish domestic residing in their home. The man is Mr. Marroner (Gilman never reveals his first name), who is traveling abroad on business; he is largely absent throughout most of the story. Public and private spheres intersect when two letters from Mr. Marroner arrive in the same late mail delivery, one addressed to his wife and the other to Gerta, to whom he often sends a "picture postcard." Opening an envelope in a familiar type addressed to her, Marion Marroner finds a letter from her husband that is clearly not intended for her; the letters have inadvertently been put in the wrong envelopes. At once Marion discerns the identity of Gerta's previously unknown seducer.[8]

The letters also explain the story's opening scene, which focuses on two weeping women, each in a different location in the Marroner home: in a luxurious bedroom, Marion sobs despite "her dignity, her self-control, her pride"; in a poorly furnished attic, fallen Gerta unabashedly "wept for two." Initially Marion feels sympathy for Gerta, "a tall, rosy-cheeked baby; rich womanhood without, helpless infancy within"; she treats her kindly and resolves "'to see her through this safely . . . and then get her back to Sweden somehow with her baby.'" However, the mood of the story changes with the arrival of the mixed-up letters. Marion at first turns against Gerta, her rival object of desire in the story's sexual triangle, but then changes her mind and turns against the traditional notions of marriage and the home, both of which Gilman radically critiqued in her theoretical works, fiction, and poetry. The epistolary mix-up becomes a means to empower both Mr. Marroner's betrayed wife and his mistress, who together transcend helplessness and achieve happiness.[9]

These two mixed-up letters are among many that Mr. Marroner sends home during his prolonged business trip and that Gerta receives from her home in Sweden (Marion is surprised that this letter for Gerta is *not* from Sweden). Gilman was writing decades after the reduction of national and international postal rates in the 1870s and 1880s made letter writing affordable to most

Americans and to people from countries in the Universal Postal Union. As literacy rates began to rise in the 1840s and 1850s and more people began to write letters, postage rates dropped. In 1883, two cents became the uniform rate for all mail weighing up to one-half ounce in the United States, regardless of the distance.[10]

On July 1, 1875, the General Postal Union was founded. This specialized agency, which quickly became the Universal Postal Union, brought great reductions in overseas postage among member nations; the United States and Sweden, Gerta's homeland, were two of the first of the twenty-two nations in the Universal Postal Union. By 1911, when Gilman published her story, the postal service was an established way to stay in touch with loved ones as well as a vehicle for intimacy within courtship and marriage. One could travel abroad for business, as in Mr. Marroner's case, or relocate for work, as in Gerta Petersen's, with the confidence that one could keep in contact with family and friends whom one might not see for months, years, or ever again.[11]

Along with the increase in letters in the nineteenth century arose a greater market for letter-writing manuals. Such manuals, in ready circulation during the early twentieth century, provided advice on practical topics, like applying for a job and advertising a job, and sensitive matters, such as how to convey news of bereavement, break off an engagement, or declare one's true love and affection. For example, *Webster's Ready-Made Love Letters* offered model romantic missives to help a gentleman succeed at "matrimony, or at keeping bright the little golden circlet that is at once its token and its pledge."[12] *Webster's* favored letters as the means by which to preserve the glowing love a gentleman professed and offered along with the wedding ring. The "golden circlet" was not only a keepsake; it was a promise of devotion.

Mr. Marroner's epistolary habits before the mix-up connote conjugal affection in an era when people proposed, renewed affection, and broke off engagements by mail. In accordance with popular advice manuals, Gilman established Mr. Marroner as a model husband who recognizes the importance of writing to his absent beloved. Going abroad for one month that expands into seven months, Mr. Marroner "wrote to his wife, long, loving, frequent letters, deeply regretting the delay." His letters could have come directly from *Perfect Etiquette: Or, How to Behave in Society,* which advises that a letter of love "is controlled altogether by the heart, and the feelings of that vital part is the best criterion to go by." Anticipating his return home in three weeks, Mr. Marroner tells his wife, "'And you will be looking so lovely, with that eager light in your eyes and the changing flush I know so well—and love so well! My dear wife! We shall have to have a new honeymoon—other moons come every month, why shouldn't the mellifluous kind?'" The rhetoric of this passage emphasizes the heart and the feelings. Writing at a time when letter writing was an indicator of character, Gilman constructed a missive that seems motivated "altogether by the heart." Mr. Marroner compliments his wife's looks. He remarks on her "flush" of desire and his anticipation of "honeymoon" intimacy after a long absence, rekindling their newlywed joy when he first offered her the "golden circlet." Moreover, his loving letters are long, which is significant in an age when inconstancy and brevity were hot topics in letter-writing manuals and a love letter's length served as a barometer of affection.[13]

Period letter-writing manuals like *The Wide World Letter Writer: Letters with Answers* focus on how the very sight of a letter could move the receiver to kiss the treasured letter in lieu of the absent beloved, as Marion does in "Turned." David Henkin notes, "Handwritten letters bore the trace of physical contact and not simply the recognizable imprimatur of individual identity." An extant letter from a Civil War soldier to his loving wife articulates how handwriting provided a link to a loved one's physical presence: "'There is something in the exchange of letters that ranks next to the greeting of palm to palm. When I receive one of your letters the sheet seems to contain more than you were writing; it is something which has been touched by your hand, which has caught a pulse of your feeling, and which represents more than the words can possibly say.'"[14]

Edward Bulwer-Lytton, in his 1832 novel *Eugene Aram*, even suggests that the sight of familiar handwriting may be more pleasurable than a meeting between lovers: for example, when the postman hands Madeline Lester a letter from her suitor, she responds to Aram's handwriting: "'Happy blush—bright smile! Ah! no meeting ever gives the delight that a letter can inspire in the short absences of a first love.'"[15] Is this "blush," as Bulwer-Lytton describes it, akin to the "flush" of intimacy that Mr. Marroner eagerly anticipates in his wife's loving welcome?

Reading "Turned" in the context of these epistolary examples from Victorian life and fiction, we are not surprised that Marion rejoices upon seeing a letter from her long-absent, beloved husband: "One letter for her—her husband's letter. She knew the postmark, the stamp, the kind of typewriting. She impulsively kissed it in the dim hall. No one would suspect Mrs. Marroner of kissing her husband's letters—but she did, often." Marion reacts "impulsively" with joy simply because the letter "has been touched by [her husband's] hand." Yet, as Gilman's qualifier, "No one would suspect Mrs. Marroner of kissing her husband's letters," indicates, we do not "suspect" her of caressing this treasured love object with her lips because she is a "Boston-bred" woman who prides herself in maintaining "dignity" and "self-control." Gilman has told us that Marion is not easily given to emotion, but a "mass of emotion" aptly describes her in the opening weeping scene as well as when she caresses her husband's letter in private.[16]

In this intimate epistolary scene, readers are voyeurs who glimpse Gilman's "Boston-bred" professor savoring not only the "kind of typewriting" but also the postmark and stamp on an envelope that bears the trace of her husband's "touch." Observing Marion Marroner, we glimpse how love letters in early twentieth-century American culture were treasured objects that allowed one to "speak to those we love or esteem" or "converse with them by letter," according to the rhetoric of letter-writing manuals.[17]

Recall, however, that two letters arrive in the late mail that fateful day in "Turned." One is addressed to "Gerta, and not from Sweden. It looked precisely like her [Marion's] own." The visual resemblance between the two letters strikes Marion as "a little odd, but Mr. Marroner had several times sent messages and cards to the girl," whom he pejoratively refers to as "'little Gerta'" and "'the child.'" The letter whose envelope Marion kisses in expectation of delight and takes to her room to read alone contains a fifty-dollar bill and the following advice: "'My poor child, . . . You must bear it bravely, little girl. I shall be home soon, and will take care of you, of course. I hope there is not immediate anxiety. . . . Here is money, in case you need it. . . . If you have to go, be sure to leave your address at my office.'"[18]

The language of this passage and Marion's response to the letter also invite rhetorical analysis. Mr. Marroner's patronizing reference to Gerta as his "little girl" famously recalls the paternalistic rhetoric of Dr. John in "The Yellow Wall-Paper," who calls the nameless narrator his "little girl" and his "blessed little goose" and insists that his wife rest in a yellow wallpapered nursery-prison. Marion observes that the typing of the letter is "not unusual," but the letter "was unsigned, which was unusual. It enclosed an American bill—fifty dollars. It did not seem in the least like any letter she had ever had from her husband, or any letter she could imagine him writing. But a strange, cold feeling was creeping over her, like a flood rising around a house."[19]

Marion perceives that she is drowning in a swell of emotion that floods her like Alice in Wonderland when she finds herself sinking in a pool of her own tears. Moreover, Gilman has taken pains to note that this letter is unsigned, probably knowing very well that etiquette books caution, "Never send a letter without your signature, for anonymous epistles are the invention of knaves and fools."[20] In this scene Mr. Marroner's untrustworthiness is eerily "creeping" over his betrayed wife in "Yellow Wall-Paper"–like fashion, and his treachery easily grants Mr. Marroner the status of being among the "knaves and fools."

Marion instructs Gerta to open the letter addressed to her and states brusquely, "'Do you not see? Your letter was put in my envelope, and my letter was put in your envelope. Now we understand it.'" Marion then dismisses Gerta: "'Go and pack your trunk. . . . You will leave my house tonight.'"[21] The possessive "my" in Marion Marroner's command displaces Gerta from where she lives:

the house is Marion's only, and Gerta no longer has a place in it. This is the very response Mr. Marroner coldly anticipated when he tucked in the fifty-dollar bill and said, "If you have to go, be sure to leave your address at my office." Marion is thus originally positioned in the stance of the outraged patriarch in Egg's and Redgrave's narrative paintings of fallen women as well as in nineteenth-century literature.

In Elizabeth Gaskell's "Lizzie Leigh" (1855), for example, Mr. Leigh, upon receiving his own letter returned from his daughter Lizzie's former mistress in Manchester, learns "that Lizzie had left her service some time—and why." Gaskell allowed her knowing readers to fill in the blank. The patriarch denies his fallen daughter a place in his home, declaring, "henceforth they would have no daughter; that she should be as one dead."[22] Marion Marroner also recalls the distressed patriarch in Egg's *Past and Present (I)*: the deceived husband holds in his left hand the incriminating letter that contains evidence of his wife's adultery. With his left foot, the betrayed husband stamps on a miniature portrait of his wife's lover, and the incriminating letter exposes an unfaithful wife, who clutches her hands in prayer and begs for forgiveness, which will not come. Marion's rejection of the young, pregnant, unmarried Gerta perhaps most closely matches the subject matter of Redgrave's *The Outcast*, particularly in Redgrave's depiction of an unyielding patriarch who sends his erring fallen daughter and grandchild out into a snowy, friendless night. This is the same unyielding, compassionless stance temporarily granted to Marion Marroner. Giving Gerta packing orders and a month's wage, Marion "had no shadow of pity for those anguished eyes, those tears which she heard drop on the floor."[23]

Ideas explored by Cresswell inform our reading of this scene. Gerta's "anguished eyes" speak to her disconnection from her homeland and her new home; she has suddenly lost her place in the hierarchy of the Marroner household. "Gerta had literally thrown herself at [Marion's] feet and begged her with streaming tears not to turn her away. She would admit nothing, explain nothing, but frantically promised to work for Mrs. Marroner as long as she lived—if only she would keep her." Gilman, like Gaskell, chose to leave the details of the affair blank. Gerta's main concern is that that Marion not "turn her away." As an immigrant, Gerta is already living out of place, although Marion has helped her to "feel so much at home in this new land."[24] The fear of homelessness compounds Gerta's dislocation from her place of origin, so we can understand why she grows hysterical and desperate. From the vantage point of place, Gerta is trying to hold onto "a clear place in a social hierarchy that was beginning to dissolve."[25] Gerta offers to indenture herself to the Marroners or become a slave so as not to lose her new home, her place.

Although the home is the site of male sexual transgression, Marion is not just an innocent victim in this story. Her home is also a place of social and ethnic segregation, reflecting Gilman's nativist tendency, evident in much of white America at the time Gilman wrote the story.[26] The opening paragraphs show us Gerta residing in an "uncarpeted, thin-curtained, poorly finished chamber on the top floor" of Marion's home; this undesirable location within the home contrasts sharply to Marion's own "soft-carpeted, thick-curtained, richly furnished chamber" with a "wide, soft bed." The carefully chosen adjectives in the opening sentences of the first and fourth paragraphs invite a rhetorical comparison and critique from today's vantage point of an enlightened awareness about immigrant populations. Racial and ethnic oppression undeniably remains a potent issue today, and when Gilman was writing, Americans were experiencing a similar moral panic over the large influx of refugees (or "exiles," as Gerta is called) into the melting pot of America. Marion describes Gerta condescendingly and reveals a xenophobic attitude: Marion "had grown to love the patient, sweet-natured child, in spite of her dullness." She calls her an "ignorant child" and tries "to educate her somewhat."[27]

Yet the lens of place also allows us to sympathize with Marion. Given the epistolary mix-up, home is no longer Marion's domestic haven but a site of sexual transgression and abuse. Marion loves her husband before her recognition of his betrayal—she even puts aside her "Boston-bred" dignity to kiss his letters. Worse, it is clear that Mr. Marroner has been unfaithful to her in her own home: "He had done this thing under the same roof with her—his wife." Arguably, "having no babies of her own," Marion feels vulnerable because of the attachment her unfaithful husband has formed with their domestic servant, who is now carrying his child, a privilege she has been denied. Marion has longed for a child, which is revealed in her response to Gerta's unwed motherhood: "'How they [babies] do come where they are not wanted—and don't come where they are wanted! Mrs. Marroner . . . almost envied Gerta.'"[28]

Cresswell explains that rejection, racism, and bigotry often arise when "'our place' is threatened and others have to be excluded."[29] Marion is arguably responding like someone who believes that her place—literally and metaphorically— is in danger. If we view Marion's initial banishment of Gerta as her wish to preserve her marriage rather than to kick out a now unwelcome immigrant, then we might also read her rejection of Gerta as a way to dispel the perceived threat of the younger woman whose fertility mocks her own childlessness.

Marion quickly reflects upon her "sentence of instant banishment." Rising above her own hurt, she decides not to send the unfortunate young woman out into the night alone, like Redgrave's depiction in *The Outcast*. Rather, Marion achieves a new way of understanding: "As the older, wiser woman forced herself to understand and extenuate the girl's misdeed and foresee her ruined future, a new feeling rose in her heart, strong, clear, and overmastering:

a sense of measureless condemnation for the man who had done this thing." The "older, wiser" Marion intuitively knows that Gerta is not a true rival for her husband's affection; indeed, "he had fairly forgotten Gerta and all that. Her name aroused in him a sense of rage. She had come between him and his wife. She had taken his wife from him. That was the way he felt." Mr. Marroner blames his victim for his own misdeed. However, Marion knows that Gerta is the victim of her husband, rhetorically reduced to "he," a generic pronoun, and "the man who had done this thing."[30]

"Naming is power," Yi-Fu Tuan notes, "the creative power to call something into being, to render the invisible visible." Marion, in turning her husband into "the man," renders him nearly invisible. Mr. Marroner's position is suddenly akin to the defeated patriarch in Gilman's poem "An Obstacle" (1890) in which a clever woman defeats "Prejudice" when she has a "sudden inspiration" and "walked directly through him / As if he wasn't there!" With an equally "sudden inspiration," Marion casts off her husband's name and takes back her maiden name, Wheeling, rendering her marriage invisible, too. Calling herself "into being," Marion Wheeling gains rhetorical power by renaming herself. Martha Cutter's analysis of Mrs. McPherson's transformation in Gilman's short story "The Widow's Might" (1911) also applies to Marion Wheeling's own transformation: she "makes the transition from a good domestic saint to an independent woman with a voice of her own."[31]

Marion gains compassion as well as strength of purpose, a "voice of her own," and maternal tenderness: "Perhaps having no babies of her own made her love the big child the more, though the years between them were but fifteen." Does a maternal instinct toward innocent Gerta trigger Marion's change of heart as she recognizes this out-of-wedlock pregnancy as "'the sin of man against woman. . . . The offense is against womanhood. Against motherhood. Against—the child'? Gerta, in Marion's view, "ought, of course, to have resisted temptation; but Marion is wise enough to know how difficult temptation can be to recognize when it comes in the guise of friendship and from a source one does not suspect." Marion also wisely recognizes the politics of social class within the hierarchy of their home: "Where obedience was due, how could [Gerta] refuse?" In contrast, her husband, who is in a position to command obedience, "could fully foresee and measure the consequences of his act. He appreciated to the full the innocence, the ignorance, the grateful affection, the habitual docility, of which he deliberately took advantage." Thus, rather than view Gerta as her rival in the sexual triangle, Marion aligns herself with her husband's cast-off mistress.[32]

Literary constructions of the sexual triangle, dating back centuries, take a range of forms. René Girard explores how a "mediator" in a sexual triangle may actually fuel romance; in this case, the third member, or mediator, has no amorous designs but "is there, above the line, radiating toward both the subject and the object." Eve Sedgwick alternately explores how the sexual triangle facilitates male homosocial desire in Victorian fiction, asserting that male-male desire can find expression only through a nonexistent desire for a woman. Heterosexual triangles in nineteenth- and early twentieth-century fiction typically consist of one man choosing between two women as love interests or one woman choosing between two male lovers. The woman or man who assumes the upper point of the triangle typically has the ability to choose between two potential suitors at the base points and thus largely determines the romantic outcome. Phyllis Susan Dee asserts that the female-based sexual triangle with the woman at the upper point choosing between two men at the base point can allow women to exercise authority: "Though at times the women in these novels are passive objects of masculine desire, they resist and revise their roles as objects, assume the active position of desiring subject, and struggle to escape the male-initiated bonds of sexual desire." Romance more typically ends happily when a male occupies the upper point of the triangle, as we witness in a work by one of Gilman's favorite authors, Dickens's *David Copperfield* (1850)—but not in "Turned."[33]

Gilman proposed a daring variation on all these paradigms that has a powerful feminist spin. Gilman boldly twisted the sexual triangle and the patriarchal icon of the incriminating letter solely to punish the sender. The two-timing husband's letters serve as a vehicle to denounce Mr. Marroner and exclude him from the sexual triangle altogether. Gilman has allowed one of the two base points on the triangle—typically not the position of choice—to achieve female agency, but not to find another partner as Dee describes. Rather, Marion rejects her former place in the patriarchal home and relocates with Gerta. Living under her maiden name of Wheeling, she returns to the university town where she lived before her marriage. With her new name to empower her, Marion resists being an object of Mr. Marroner's sexual desire in order to help herself and Gerta "to escape the male-initiated bonds of sexual desire."[34]

In Gilman's variation, akin to Girard's model of mediation in a romantic triangle, the man becomes a nonexistent choice for both women, whose outcome is sisterhood, although arguably a tinge of same-sex desire rears its head in the closing paragraphs, where Gerta's "blue, adoring eyes fixed on her friend—not upon him [Mr. Marroner]." Even if these "adoring eyes" hint at same-sex desire—a point those interested in queering Gilman might readily explore—both women escape the now poisoned home together. Indeed, Gilman's presentation of the home as a source of economic and sexual oppression (which which she called the *sexuo-economic* condition in her 1898 feminist treatise *Women and Economics*) powerfully anticipated the work of today's

feminist geographers like Gillian Rose, who views the home as a place of neglect and abuse in a chapter entitled "No Place for Women."[35]

The sexual triangle in "Turned" becomes a means to interrogate the un-
equal dynamics of gender under patriarchy and to allow Marion and Gerta to
find not only a new place to live but also a new way of thinking. In the final
paragraphs, before her departure from her former home, Marion leaves a letter with her lawyer cousin to be delivered to her husband in person. The letter simply reads, "'I have gone. I will care for Gerta. Good-bye. Marion.' That
was all. There was no date, no address, no postmark, nothing but that." Unlike the letters Mr. Marroner posts from abroad, hers leaves no tangible traces
for her husband to caress with his eyes or clues to help him find her. The letter reads concisely, almost brusquely, which contrasts to the long love letters
Mr. Marroner sends his wife before the epistolary mix-up. It takes "detectives"
and "careful and prolonged work" over two seasons to find Miss Wheeling.
Entering her parlor, Mr. Marroner becomes nostalgic; he recalls, "All their
years of happiness . . . the exquisite beginnings; the days of eager longing before she was really his; the deep, still beauty of her love." He chauvinistically
assumes, "Surely she would forgive him—she must forgive him." But "the
woman who had been his wife" does not forgive her husband as he fervently
anticipates. The use of the past perfect tense ("had been") signals that the
role of wife is no longer viable for Marion Wheeling. Marion stands alongside Gerta, "a tall Madonna, bearing a baby in her arms." Gerta possesses "a
new intelligence," and "her blue, adoring eyes [are] fixed on her friend—not
upon him." We still detect a xenophobic attitude in the story, however: the
once ignorant Gerta, under Marion's care, has become a majestic, "intelligent"
Madonna seemingly overnight.[36]

From the lenses of material culture and place, the epistolary mix-up in
"Turned" becomes a feminist tool within the sexual triangle. Mr. Marroner's
love child functions as a "bulwark" between Mr. Marroner and his two objects
of desire, who have both transformed for the better. Mr. Marroner's traditional
home in "Turned" is no longer a tenable place for Marion Wheeling, Gerta
Petersen, or the child they appear to be jointly raising—a situation foretell-
ing of alternative families today. The story ends with the forceful words of
Marion Wheeling, who tells her former husband firmly but "quietly": "'What
have you to say to us?'"[37]

"Us" includes two women, Marion and Gerta, and excludes Mr. Marroner,
whom they banish from the romantic triangle. Moreover, the plural "us" unites
two women who previously occupied separate floors of a home—one location
"soft-carpeted" and the other location "uncarpeted," one "thick-curtained" and
the other "thin-curtained," one area "richly furnished" and the other "poorly
furnished." Gerta now has "a new intelligence in her face" as well as a new

place. Mr. Marroner, rather, is rendered "dumb": "He looked from one to the other dumbly."[38] A mix-up of mail ultimately prompts two passive objects of the same man's desire to unite and transform into empowered women who reject the domestic sphere and find a meaningful place.

NOTES

1. Tim Cresswell, *Place: A Short Introduction* (Oxford, UK: Blackwell, 2008), 7, 11.

2. Charlotte Perkins Gilman, *The Selected Letters of Charlotte Perkins Gilman*, ed. Denise D. Knight and Jennifer S. Tuttle (Tuscaloosa: University of Alabama Press, 2009). Gilman's letters offer insight into her theories as well as her relationships and personal demons. The editors, both noted Gilman scholars, have arranged the letters according to significant life events and the important people with whom Gilman corresponded.

3. Jane Austen, *Persuasion*, ed. Gillian Beer (1818; repr., London: Penguin, 2003), 222.

4. Gary Scharnhorst and Denise D. Knight, "Charlotte Perkins Gilman's Library: A Reconstruction," *Resources for American Literary Study* 23, no. 2 (1997): 181–219. The authors list eight of Dickens's novels and four of Eliot's novels as well as a book of Eliot's poems in their itinerary of what works Gilman read or owned.

5. The note reads "August the 4th: Have just heard that B has been dead more than a fortnight, so his poor children have now lost both parents. I hear she was seen on Friday last near the Strand, evidently without a place to lay her head—What a fall hers has been!" For a fuller discussion of the Egg triptych, see Catherine J. Golden, *Posting It: The Victorian Revolution in Letter Writing* (Gainesville: University Press of Florida, 2009), 188–91. This source also includes a black-and-white reproduction of the first panel.

6. George Landow, ed. "*The Outcast* by Richard Redgrave, RA. 1851," Victorian Web, January 11, 2015, http://www.victorianweb.org/painting/redgrave/paintings/4.html.

7. Anne J. Lane, ed., "The Fictional World of Charlotte Perkins Gilman," in *The Charlotte Perkins Gilman Reader* (Charlottesville: University Press of Virginia, 1980), xxii.

8. Charlotte Perkins Gilman, "Turned," in *The Charlotte Perkins Gilman Reader*, ed. Ann J. Lane (Charlottesville: University Press of Virginia, 1999), 89, 93.

9. Ibid., 87, 88, 90.

10. Frank Staff, *The Penny Post, 1680–1918* (Cambridge, UK: Lutterworth Press, 1992), 125.

11. David Henkin, *The Postal Age: The Emergence of Modern Communications*

in Nineteenth-Century America (Chicago: University of Chicago Press, 2006), 34–36; Golden, *Posting It,* 197.

12. *Webster's Ready-Made Love Letters* (New York: De Witt, 1873), 9. Advice on letter writing sometimes appeared in etiquette books that gave counsel on courtship, health, and homemaking.

13. Gilman, "Turned," 89; *Perfect Etiquette: Or How to Behave in Society* (New York: Hurst, n.d.), 47; see also Golden, *Posting It,* 215–22.

14. Henkin, *Postal Age,* 55–56.

15. Edward Bulwer-Lytton, *Eugene Aram* (New York: Harper, 1832), 61.

16. Gilman, "Turned," 87, 90; Henkin, *Postal Age,* 55.

17. Rev. T. Cooke, *The Universal Letter Writer: Or, New Art of Polite Correspondence* (London: Milner, ca. 1850), vi.

18. Gilman, "Turned," 89, 91.

19. Charlotte Perkins Gilman, "The Yellow Wall-Paper," in *The Charlotte Perkins Gilman Reader,* ed. Ann J. Lane (Charlottesville: University Press of Virginia, 1999), 6, 11; Gilman, "Turned," 91.

20. *Perfect Etiquette,* 48.

21. Gilman, "Turned," 92.

22. Elizabeth Gaskell, "Lizzie Leigh," in *Nineteenth-Century Stories by Women: An Anthology,* ed. Glennis Stephenson (Peterborough, Canada: Broadview Press, 1993), 254.

23. Gilman, "Turned," 93.

24. Cresswell, *Place,* 110–19; Gilman, "Turned," 89, 90.

25. Cresswell, *Place,* 111.

26. For a discussion of Gilman's racism and ethnocentrism, see Catherine J. Golden and Joanna Schneider Zangrando, *The Mixed Legacy of Charlotte Perkins Gilman* (Newark: University of Delaware Press, 2000), 11–22.

27. Gilman, "Turned," 87, 88, 89, 93.

28. Ibid., 87, 89, 90, 93.

29. Cresswell, *Place,* 11.

30. Gilman, "Turned," 92, 93, 95.

31. Yu-Fi Tuan, "Language and the Making of Place: A Narrative Descriptive Approach," *Annals of the Association of American Geographers* 81, no. 4 (1991): 688; Charlotte Perkins Gilman, "An Obstacle," in *The Yellow Wall-Paper: A Sourcebook and Critical Edition,* edited by Catherine J. Golden (New York: Routledge, 2004), 41–42; Martha Cutter, *Unruly Tongue: Identity and Voice in American Women's Writing, 1850–1930* (Jackson: University Press of Mississippi, 1999), 126.

32. Gilman, "Turned," 89, 93, 94.

33. René Girard, *Desire, Deceit, and the Novel: Self and Other in Literary Structure* (Baltimore, MD: Johns Hopkins University Press, 1976), 2; Eve Sedgwick, *Between Men: English Literature and Male Homosocial Desire* (New York: Colum-

bia University Press, 1985), 16, 21–27; Phyllis Susan Dee, "Female Sexuality and Triangular Desire in *Vanity Fair* and *The Mill on the Floss*," *Papers on Language & Literature* 35, no. 4 (1999): 392. The female in the position of choice may also remain torn between two inadequate objects of desire; George Eliot, another author Gilman admired, demonstrates this paradigm in *The Mill on the Floss* (1860), which was included in Gilman's select library; again, however, this was not Gilman's purpose for the sexual triangle in "Turned."

34. Dee, "Female Sexuality," 392.

35. Gilman, "Turned," 97; Gillian Rose, *Feminism and Geography: The Limits of Geographical Knowledge Polity* (Cambridge, UK: Cambridge University Press, 1993), 41–61.

36. Gilman, "Turned," 95–97.

37. Ibid., 97. Gilman and Grace Ellery Channing, her close friend who married Walter Stetson after he and Gilman divorced, also functioned as comothers for Gilman's daughter, Katharine Beecher Stetson.

38. Ibid.

WORKS CITED

Austen, Jane. *Persuasion*. 1818. Edited by Gillian Beer. London: Penguin, 2003.

Brontë, Charlotte. *Jane Eyre*. 1847. Edited by Richard J. Dunn. New York: W. W. Norton, 2001.

Bulwer-Lytton, Edward. *Eugene Aram*. New York: Harper, 1832.

Cooke, Rev. T. *The Universal Letter Writer: Or, New Art of Polite Correspondence*. London: Milner, ca. 1850.

Cresswell, Tim. *Place: A Short Introduction*. Oxford, UK: Blackwell, 2008.

Cutter, Martha. *Unruly Tongue: Identity and Voice in American Women's Writing, 1850–1930*. Jackson: University Press of Mississippi, 1999.

Dee, Phyllis Susan. "Female Sexuality and Triangular Desire in *Vanity Fair* and *The Mill on the Floss*." *Papers on Language & Literature* 35, no. 4 (1999): 391–416.

Dickens, Charles. *Bleak House*. 1853. London: Chapman & Hall, 1892.

———. *David Copperfield*. 1850. Edited by Jerome H. Buckley. Illustrated by Hablot Knight Browne. New York: W. W. Norton, 1990.

Eliot, George. *Middlemarch*. 1872. Reprint. Ed. W. J. Harvey. New York: Penguin, 1976.

———. *The Mill on the Floss*. 1860. Edited by Gordon S. Haight. Oxford, UK: Oxford University Press, 1980.

Gaskell, Elizabeth. "Lizzie Leigh." In *Nineteenth-Century Stories by Women: An Anthology*, edited by Glennis Stephenson, 249–83. Peterborough, Canada: Broadview Press, 1993.

Gilman, Charlotte Perkins. "An Obstacle." In *The Yellow Wall-Paper: A Source-*

book and Critical Edition, edited by Catherine J. Golden, 41–42. New York: Routledge, 2004.

———. *The Selected Letters of Charlotte Perkins Gilman*. Edited by Denise D. Knight and Jennifer S. Tuttle. Tuscaloosa: University of Alabama Press, 2009.

———. "Turned." In *The Charlotte Perkins Gilman Reader*, edited by Ann J. Lane, 87–97. Charlottesville: University Press of Virginia, 1999.

———. "The Yellow Wall-Paper." In *The Charlotte Perkins Gilman Reader*, edited by Ann J. Lane, 3–20. Charlottesville: University Press of Virginia, 1999.

Girard, René. *Desire, Deceit, and the Novel: Self and Other in Literary Structure*. Baltimore, MD: Johns Hopkins University Press, 1976.

Golden, Catherine J. *Posting It: The Victorian Revolution in Letter Writing*. Gainesville: University Press of Florida, 2009.

Golden, Catherine J., and Joanna Schneider Zangrando. *The Mixed Legacy of Charlotte Perkins Gilman*. Newark: University of Delaware Press, 2000.

Henkin, David. *The Postal Age: The Emergence of Modern Communications in Nineteenth-Century America*. Chicago: University of Chicago Press, 2006.

Landow, George, ed. "*The Outcast* by Richard Redgrave, RA. 1851." Victorian Web, January 11, 2015. http://www.victorianweb.org/painting/redgrave/paintings/4.html.

Lane, Ann J., ed. "The Fictional World of Charlotte Perkins Gilman." In *The Charlotte Perkins Gilman Reader*, ix–xliii. Charlottesville: University Press of Virginia, 1980.

Perfect Etiquette: Or How to Behave in Society. New York: Hurst, n.d.

Rose, Gillian. *Feminism and Geography: The Limits of Geographical Knowledge Polity*. Cambridge, UK: Cambridge University Press, 1993.

Scharnhorst, Gary, and Denise D. Knight. "Charlotte Perkins Gilman's Library: A Reconstruction." *Resources for American Literary Study* 23, no. 2 (1997): 181–219.

Sedgwick, Eve. *Between Men: English Literature and Male Homosocial Desire*. New York: Columbia University Press, 1985.

Staff, Frank. *The Penny Post, 1680–1918*. Cambridge, UK: Lutterworth Press, 1992.

Tuan, Yu-Fi. "Language and the Making of Place: A Narrative Descriptive Approach." *Annals of the Association of American Geographers* 81, no. 4 (1991): 684–96.

Webster's Ready-Made Love Letters. New York: De Witt, 1873.

The Wide World Letter Writer: Letters with Answers. London: Milner, n.d.

8
Eavesdropping with Charlotte Perkins Gilman

Fiction, Transcription, and the Ethics of Interior Design

Peter Betjemann

> "I never could see why people are so fierce about listening. It doesn't say in the Bible, 'Thou shalt not listen.' I looked, with a concordance."
> Charlotte Perkins Gilman, *Benigna Machiavelli* (1914)

Charlotte Perkins Gilman avowed a theory of fiction that emphasized didacticism over what she described as the novelistic complexities of "individual character"; in her lifetime, Cynthia Davis tells us, Gilman's "literary friends accused her of trading aesthetics for homiletics."[1] Given this, what are we to make of the sudden convolutions of character that *do* appear in the very last paragraphs of many of her novels? Such a dramatic twist can seem to derail the social argument that the rest of the novel builds.

In *Benigna Machiavelli* (1914), for example, the teenage protagonist spends the entire novel honing her ability to cleverly manage events for the benefit of women's economic autonomy, freedom to travel, and liberation from the confinements of domestic labor. But at the very end of the novel she "began to think" about her marital prospects with a cousin she has only just met, whose "nice name" (he is called, strikingly, "Home") turns our sense of Benigna's independent future on its head.[2]

In *The Crux* (1911), an abstinence novel designed to warn young women about the irreversible dangers of contracting syphilis and gonorrhea, the final section of the final chapter mounts a transformative ending that has all the marks of Shakespearean comedy. Rather than reinforcing the novel's hard-driven lessons about the immutability of lifestyle and sexual choices, the conclusion announces that "all is forgiven" while presenting a marital engagement between a man who is a "relic . . . of the once Wild West" (Mr. Skee has "grown up in a playground of sixteen states and territories") and a watchful and scrupulous New England grandmother who has escorted a group of young women to Colorado precisely to protect them from the seductions of men who, like her husband-to-be, can boast of a "long and checkered career."[3]

But the best example is the surprise ending of *Herland* (1915). Readers have long wondered why the shrewd and ever cautious women of Herland would send Terry Nicholson—the novel's scheming, lying, and, indeed, criminal individualist—back to the United States on the basis of nothing more than his promise not to reveal the location of their country. As in *Benigna Machiavelli* and *The Crux*, the last sentence ("with which agreement we at last left Herland") reposes its trust in customs and conditions that the rest of the novel has taught us to doubt.[4]

Each of the examples I have offered might be individually explained. *Benigna Machiavelli* is easily read as an autobiographical text, and Benigna MacAvelly's ultimate attraction to her Scottish cousin Home MacAvelly thus echoes Charlotte Perkins Gilman's marriage to her cousin Houghton Gilman. In *The Crux* the grandmother is well past childbearing age and thus not vulnerable in the same ways as young women, for the novel stresses the dangers of sexually transmitted diseases to reproductive health. So too, the bizarre decision by the women of Herland is vaguely justified by their appeal to Terry as a "gentleman," a category that they believe his prideful sense of masculine honor will cause him to respect.[5]

But what really interests me here is that, first, Gilman has asked us to do so much work rationalizing the conclusions, and, second, a certain shred of justificatory logic applies not to each case but to all the cases. For in each text Gilman yoked the unbelievable final paragraphs to an apparently counterbalancing trust in the power of language to reliably name, promise, or describe. This is most obvious in *Herland*, since the very untrustworthiness of the ending turns on the potency accorded to Terry's vow. A similar pattern, wherein the language of an unreliable character suddenly becomes convincing, appears in *The Crux*. Throughout the novel Mr. Skee speaks in a kind of colorfully evasive, riddling vernacular, saying much but revealing little; his iconoclastic life isolates him where "no one could speak his language." When he reveals his engagement, however, his speech becomes straight and to the point. The final character to speak in the novel, Mr. Skee brings it to a rhetorically grand summation: "namely, and to wit," he announces after working up to the confession, "I am engaged to be married to that Peerless Lady, Mrs. Servilla Pettigrew."[6]

By ending the novel with a gesture of reliable naming—even as the text pulls the rug out from under the expectations it has established for its readers—Gilman anticipated the two-step pattern that appears in the last two sentences of *Benigna Machiavelli*. There Benigna justifies her sudden attraction to a domestic life on the basis that in this marriage to her cousin she will retain her last name and its signification of her Machiavellian self: "His name was MacAvelly, too!" Benigna realizes. "And I had thought I never could keep it."[7]

The drama of these cases is this: at the moment Gilman forces readers to confront a sudden shift in narrative, moral, and social circumstances, she also presents a short bit of speech (Terry's promise, Mr. Skee's announcement, Benigna's last name) as an accurate and viable record. Individuals may be fickle, the endings of these novels suggest, but certain designations or speech acts cannot be gainsaid. One of Gilman's very first published stories, "The Unexpected" (1890), establishes just this pattern for her oeuvre: moving toward a sudden revelation (the unexpected occurrence promised in the title), the story suggests that it thereby proves the "French proverb" that "it is the unexpected which happens."[8] Weaving together the uncertainty of circumstances and the certainty of the proverb, Gilman seems to have imagined fiction as a medium that could maneuver the contingencies of human affairs into a revelation about the evidentiary accuracy of a few words.

I am interested in this pattern, in general, because it offers a focal point for what has been a dominant line of scholarly discussion about Gilman's fiction. The collective body of criticism on *Herland* (1915)—the only novel to receive sustained attention—places the elusive qualities of the narrative (exemplified, e.g., by the flashing glimpses readers are afforded of Ellador, Celis, and Alima darting through the trees) in dialogue with the novel's prescriptive and even authoritarian qualities (exemplified, e.g., by its depiction of a racially purified, deeroticized society in which clarity trumps contingency).[9]

Similarly, interpretations of "The Yellow Wall-Paper" from every perspective must negotiate the tensions between the obvious social purpose of the story and the notorious unreadability of the central text, the wallpaper itself, that the story presents. Barbara Hochman's essay on the text *as* a study in nineteenth-century reading practices illustrates the case by showing how Gilman was responding both to the didactic tradition in American letters, a tradition she identified with her father's reference book *The Best Reading*, and to the popularity of "reading for escape"—a mode amenable to plots that were as "flamboyant, inconsistent, or outrageous" as the wallpaper's design.[10] Conclusive speech acts of the kind I have identified (i.e., conceived in relation to unreliable narratives) thus appear less eccentric than central to the very textures of Gilman's fiction, as several decades of critical inquiry on her best-known texts have taught us to see that work.

I am particularly interested in this pattern because it can be tracked outside Gilman's best-known works and, I will argue, because it can be extended into the realms of physical place and space. The remainder of this essay details how Gilman frequently invented characters whose clever maneuvering in complex architectural and decorative environments allows them to acquire accurate recordings, transcriptions, dictations, and similarly summative texts. Those recordings, some of them on actual phonographic cylinders and others in notebooks, typically expose patriarchal privilege and, most important for my purposes, operate much like the endings of the novels I have explored—for just as Gilman opposes an act of clear naming to the sudden collapse of narrative continuity, she also opposes an acquired recording to an architectural, decorative, and domestic environment that often disables clear communication or disturbs an individual's secure sense of place and self.

Surveying her oeuvre chronologically, the rest of this chapter considers how and why Gilman's reformist politics centered so consistently on fictional individuals whose good listening and accurate recording offer something of a stay against a built environment that (like human character itself, as revealed in the inexplicable endings of *Benigna Machiavelli*, *The Crux*, and *Herland*) is anything but univocal or socially, ethically, and politically stable. That the built environment *should* be honest and stable was a presumption of Gilman's era, in ways I will explain, and so the ultimate implications of my argument involve Gilman's attitudes toward the design theory of her day. In inventing protagonists whose transcriptions and records bring honesty to homes and their furnishings—rather than finding honesty intrinsically and already lodged in certain kinds of things—Gilman endorsed early twentieth-century visions of architectural and decorative authenticity only to the degree that she saw such authenticity as requiring actualization, vigilance, and activity. To put all of this most briefly: Gilman demands that we stay on our toes—or, to use a metaphor that will appear more apt, that we keep our ears open. True speech and accurate language appear as carefully achieved virtues in worlds, both narrative and material, that offer less intrinsic stability than we might expect.

GILMAN, THE ARTS AND CRAFTS MOVEMENT, AND THE LANGUAGE OF THINGS

I begin with chairs, which feature in several of Gilman's works, and in Gilman's era, as central furnishings in dramas of honesty and authenticity. Gustav Stickley's Morris chair (see figure 8.1) is perhaps the most iconic piece of the age. For Stickley, whose magazine the *Craftsman* (1901–1916) ran at the same time as Gilman's magazine the *Forerunner* (1909–1916) and expressed a similarly progressive agenda, such solid pieces were designed to ensure the healthy stability of the interior. Once placed, a chair like this could not easily be relocated. Believing that "nothing so much disturbs the much-desired home atmosphere as to make frequent changes in the disposition of the furniture," Stickley equated "a favorite chair moved to another place" with the lightsomeness of Victorian bric-a-brac.[11]

Even more pointedly, Stickley believed that sincerity and honesty were embedded in the very structure of such pieces. Near the bottom of the front legs, notice where a joint cut into the lower apron travels clear through the leg;

No. 369
RECLINING CHAIR, SPRING SEAT
CUSHION
SHEEPSKIN, VELOUR OR COTTON
VELVET $34.50
CRAFTSMAN CANVAS   27.50
HEIGHT OF BACK FROM FLOOR
40 in.
HEIGHT OF SEAT FROM FLOOR
15 in.
SIZE OF SEAT 23 in. WIDE,
27 in. DEEP

Figure 8.1. Gustav Stickley's Morris chair (*Catalogue of Craftsman Furnishings Made by Gustav Stickley*, Eastwood, NY, 1909, p. 47)

the same detail appears on the top of the armrest, near the front, where the leg projects through the armrest. This joint, known as a *through tenon* (distinct from a *blind tenon*, in which the joint is invisibly housed in the wood), makes the structure of the piece visible and thus, as Stickley framed it, countered the dissimulation of applied period details. The peculiar finish that Stickley gave to all his pieces—at least until impending bankruptcy caused him to reinvent his style near the end of his career—constituted another aspect of their presumed stability, sincerity, and truthfulness. Rather than applying stain to the surface of the wood, Stickley fumed his oak furniture with extremely concentrated ammonia vapor. Ammonia, he discovered in a horse stall, reacts with the natural tannins in oak, deepening its color while preserving the subtleties of the wood grain. Like the through tenon, ammonia fuming represented style not applied to but drawn from the structure of the piece. Fuming, Stickley wrote, "might be compared to the experiences and trials of an individual," for it "discloses unsuspected qualities of beauty previously lying concealed within [the wood's] heart."[12]

The correlation proposed here, between the character-building trials of individuals and the beauty-revealing process of ammonia fuming, typifies Stickley's conviction that the authenticity of his style of furnishings, known as Craftsman, was directly comparable to the honesty that could be expected of people. His theories about the "influence of material form over mental mood" proposed that rectilinear and unornamented furniture (or rather, furniture in which the only ornament "appears to proceed from within outward") would promote a corresponding uprightness and sincerity among the individuals who lived with it. Stickley earnestly believed that square and stable furniture made square and stable people and that seeing the tenon poking through the post would encourage early twentieth-century citizens ("busy workers," he noticed, who were "troubled about many things") to a correlative truthfulness.[13]

Gilman, like all Americans of her age, knew Stickley's work and the tenets of the movement, the American Arts and Crafts, for which he was the major spokesman. Indeed, in 1904 Gilman published a critique of the "magpie instinct" for collecting bric-a-brac in Stickley's magazine the *Craftsman* and in 1914 wrote a story ("His Record," considered below) that centers on his Craftsman architecture.[14] The material environment of Herland clearly suggests Arts and Crafts aesthetics, as well as the movement's emphasis on how form follows function as its organic result: the furnishings in Herland are "strong, strong, simple in structure, and comfortable in use; also, incidentally, beautiful."[15] Dressed in tunics and robes for ease of movement and the effective practice of their trades, the citizens of Herland call to mind the romanticized vision of medieval artisans' guilds popularized by the Arts and Crafts movement; one well-known crafts utopia, Elbert Hubbard's Roycroft community (founded in 1895), in fact prescribed just such tunics and robes as the ideal dress.

But perhaps the most important point of comparison between Gilman and the Arts and Crafts movement concerns not the details she incorporated into certain works but the trajectory of her fiction itself. For the stories Gilman wrote in the early 1890s, just before the appearance of the American Arts and Crafts style, reveal that Gilman was driven by the same concerns about honesty and sincerity as those who gave birth to the decorative reform effort. When Stickley developed his Craftsman style around 1898, he turned away from an established career as a period furniture manufacturer who counted the Waldorf-Astoria Hotel among his clients. In doing so, Stickley was reacting not just against the mass-market availability of the imitation styles that he was producing, but also against what many critics saw as the overall illegibility of the nineteenth-century interior environment.

As exemplified by Owen Jones's *Grammar of Ornament* (1856), the nineteenth century classified thousands of decorative details by their historical and geographical origins; whether tagged as colonial, Chippendale, Moorish, or Persian, the crowded spaces preferred by the Victorians could seem not just overstuffed but specifically Babylonish, composed as they were of furnishings and bric-a-brac from dozens of traditions. The pressure of this kind of decorative environment drove Stickley's commitment to honest, identifiable, and structural design, and the same pressure is easily visible in such works of fiction as Gilman's "The Yellow Wall-Paper" (1892), "Through This" (1893), and "The Rocking-Chair" (1893). The first two stories present straightforward examples of how illegible or overcomplicated environments threaten the viability of human communication itself. Notoriously, the pattern in the yellow wall-paper cannot be accurately described or named even by a narrator who understands the "principles of design," creating a kind of decorative Gordian knot that is mirrored in "Through This." The latter story, a narrative of an exhausted wife and mother, opens at dawn with a prismatic burst of rapidly changing colors on the wall in the narrator's bedroom, proceeds to describe the excruciatingly minor decorative details of domestic economy ("I wonder if torchon would look better, or Hamburg?"), and concludes—the crucial fact, for my purposes—with fatigue so profound that the narrator's ability to "write a letter" has been entirely sapped. As in "The Yellow Wall-Paper," where the narrator's ability to "write a word" is disabled not just by the rest cure but also by the indecipherable pattern, "Through This" yokes the intricacy of the interior environment to the collapse of effective written expression.[16]

"The Rocking-Chair" offers a more sustained, though more subtle, example and represents Gilman's first use of a chair in particular as the epicenter of the drama of legibility, honesty, and communicative sincerity that defined the decorative culture of the age. The story involves a pair of roommates—Hal and the narrator, Maurice—who inquire about leasing an apartment largely because they are so charmed with a young woman they see rocking at one of the windows. Although the chair is "still rocking gently" when they enter but the woman is nowhere to be found, the friends take the apartment in the hope that she will reappear. She does not, however, except in ghostly glimpses and in the evidence afforded by the chair, which they find still in motion whenever they enter the room. The narrator learns something of the "great brass-bound" rocking chair from the landlady:

> "Is it old?" I pursued.
> "Very old," she answered briefly.
> "But I thought rocking-chairs were a modern American invention?" said I.
> She looked at me apathetically.
> "It is Spanish," she said, "Spanish oak, Spanish leather, Spanish brass, Spanish—." I did not catch the last word, and she left the room without another.[17]

The narrator's presumption is correct. Rocking chairs are thought to have originated in the seventeenth-century American colonies. But the landlady's correction of what she sees as a mistaken label (a "modern American invention") is the keynote of the passage, which presents two additional ways in which representation fails: the landlady's apathetic involvement in the conversation gives up little information about the chair's history, and the uncaught word concludes the conversation with an incomplete list. In fact, the communicative lacunae here actually strike the keynote of the whole story, which chronicles how the young men lose their trust in dialogue and in their ability to deal honestly with one another. They are newspapermen by trade, so they should be able to accurately gather and relay facts. But each believes that the other is conducting a secret relationship with the young woman. Each complains that he has never "had speech of her" and laments that he has passed "no word" with her, even while the other must have "seen her day after day—talked with her."[18] Each repeatedly charges that the other must be lying.

The ghostly love triangle in "The Rocking-Chair" makes this a compelling story to read for its revelations about same-sex intimacy: the "three-cornered cut" inflicted on the narrator's "more than brother" by the chair's leg seems to mark the chaos visited on the men's relationship once the young woman enters the picture.[19] (Bizarrely, Hal is bludgeoned to death by the massive rocking chair at the end of the story.) The plot seems to parallel Gilman's own devastation when Martha Luther, most likely her first lover, began to contemplate marriage. Rocking chairs in general suggest the comforts of home: a mother nursing, a tired worker resting, a grandfather or grandmother ruminating. The divisive ghost-woman and the murderous rocking chair thus disrupt a number of domestic fantasies of intimacy. For my purposes, the story is most interesting for challenging these fantasies by depicting rhetorical breaks, epitomized by the broken communicative links between Hal and Maurice, between Maurice and the landlady, and even between the material components of the chair itself ("Spanish leather, Spanish brass, Spanish—"). Failures of authentic and complete discourse threaten the idealized appeal, iconically embodied in a rocking chair, of home sweet home.

Like "The Yellow Wall-Paper" and "Through This," "The Rocking-Chair" does not offer an alternative to the conditions it depicts. Yet although this triad of decorative stories from the early 1890s reveals the potential mendacity of interior furnishings, by 1914 Gilman—working parallel to Stickley and the Arts and Crafts movement and undoubtedly influenced by their calls for sincerity, legibility, and honesty in interior space—had created an astonishingly consistent string of characters whose careful listening and recording appear as explicit alternatives to the communicative fissures of Victorian design and domesticity.

Consider the story "Fulfilment" (1914), a kind of companion piece to "The Rocking-Chair." "Fulfilment" opens at a hotel, with two sisters rocking and conversing. One of the two, Elsie, has a "soul affinity to rocking-chairs"; the story makes clear that she has sacrificed her independence, her sense of possibility, and her physical fitness to a conventional role as mother and wife. The other sister, Irma, has led a self-made life in California, accepting children into a boarding school she has built in the foothills. Irma has no affection for rocking chairs, even though she is rocking at the outset of the story. Instead, "her air and her garments suggested other seats: desk-chairs, parlor-chairs, and no chairs at all."[20]

Most of the moralizing story consists of the dialogue between the women, in which Irma presents a vivid narrative of her life in the hope of convincing her patronizing sister (who has never cared to hear about the details of that life) not to view her unconventional choices as a sad and lesser alternative to raising a biological family of her own. Again, as in the earlier story, the rocking chair marks a communicative limit. Elsie's "soul affinity" to rocking chairs signifies the entire package of her indifference to her sister's life story and the breakdown in their intimacy, at least until Irma's insistence on narrating her history forces Elsie to stop seeing her as "poor Irma." But if the rocking chair thus reveals what it also does in "The Rocking-Chair"—that is, the underbelly of domestic idealizations, in the form of discursive elisions and communicative lacunae—"Fulfilment" features a curious third character whose behavior could not be more unlike Elsie's initial indifference to her sister's narrative. For a "deep, broad, accurate, [and] relentless" novelist eavesdrops on the entire conversation from a "hard little sofa" positioned behind the blinds of a nearby window. As he listens, he begins transcribing the "invaluable material" that he hears. He falls in love with Irma and, the last paragraph of the story hints, plans to follow her back to California.[21]

Although we learn little more about the novelist than what I have related, he represents the moral center of the tale. His intense appreciation of Irma's story contrasts with Elsie's apathy, just as his seat, the hard sofa, differs notably from her rocking chair. Moreover, the novelist's bit part forces us to reflect on our own reading of "Fulfilment" itself. Calling the novelist "conscienceless" and "unprincipled" because he collects other people's words, Gilman scripted the piece to call such assignations into question: set against Elsie's passive and therefore poor listening, the novelist's deep response to what he hears appears anything but conscienceless, and his accurate transcriptions must be seen as principled stands that differ from the projections and a priori assumptions of Elsie's interlocutor.[22] As in the story of 1893, the rocking chair again appears as the false promise of domestic intimacy and loving communication, but in this case Gilman offered a truer and more respectful practice of careful listening and transcribing.

Crucially, for my purposes, that practice is exemplified both by the character of the novelist in the story and by the work required of us as readers, who must see through the narrative red herrings of the story's own depiction of the novelist's immorality. To put this another way: the untrustworthiness of the material environment is mirrored by the untrustworthiness of the narrative environment—and just as in the endings of the novels analyzed at the beginning of this chapter, Gilman aimed to relocate our confidence to a short, accurate, and summative text recorded, in this case, by the figure lurking on a hard sofa behind the window blinds. The apparently incidental inclusion of the minor character is thus precisely the point, for in a story about false projections and poor listening, he stands for the "relentless" quality of narrative brevity itself.

THE CHAIR OF ENGLISH: MATERIAL CULTURE AND TRANSCRIPTION IN GILMAN'S LATE FICTION

I would not be tempted to make too much of the novelist's behavior in "Fulfilment," nor of the communicative indolence signified by the rocking chair, if a similar pattern did not recur throughout the fiction Gilman wrote after 1910. In this period Gilman urged both her characters and her readers to listen through walls, to hear through the limits of conventional domesticity or patriarchal privilege, by using architecture and décor as conduits for truthful words and accurate transcriptions. Indeed, these conduits are often more literally tubelike than the window and blinds through which the novelist records Irma's story.

"Mrs. Beazley's Deeds" (1911) centers on a woman oppressed by a husband who forces her to sign over her familial property to him, sells the property, and then banks the profits in her name to protect it from his creditors. Her subjugation is marked at the outset of the story with a familiar image: "she vibrated nervously in [a] wooden rocker." But she is also shown "listening at a stove-pipe hole" that connects her living room to the mercantile shop where her husband conducts his business. Through this tube, she learns certain specifics of his dealings (when he discovers the hole, he claims to have "always wondered at them intuitions of yours"), and by the end of the story, with the encouragement and material aid of a "woman lawyer" who has boarded with the Beazleys, Mrs. Beazley has used the legal fact of the assets being in her name to reclaim those assets and turn Mr. Beazley outdoors. In this story, authority over space and over verbal and written language are tightly intertwined: Mrs. Beazley recovers her property, including the home she grew up in, by learning specifics through the stovepipe hole and then using that knowledge to insist upon the letter of the law. Mr. Beazley may protest to the local justice that sheltering assets in his wife's name constitutes a common "matter of business," but the story as a whole establishes that careful listening and properly recorded "deeds"—meaning both legal documents and actions—trump the conventions of patriarchal authority.[23]

Benigna Machiavelli, published three years after "Mrs. Beazley's Deeds," presents the same architectural conduit. Benigna listens to her father's maltreatment of her mother through a stovepipe hole in the attic, and here the record of what she learns appears not after the fact (as when Mrs. Beazley invokes her documented legal rights) but right away: Benigna "used to sit by the floor and take down [what she heard] in shorthand." Benigna MacAvelly figures in a number of ways as Gilman's most adept transcriber, combining her stenographic skills with a private cipher to create a comprehensive, multivolume "record of things Father did."[24] Such comprehensive listening and recording enables Benigna to invent and implement a complex plan that tricks her father into moving to Scotland and her mother into taking a long holiday on a New York farm; while they are gone, Benigna establishes an enormously successful boardinghouse business that saves the struggling family from Mr. MacAvelly's conviction that he knows best and from Mrs. MacAvelly's capitulation to all her husband's decisions.

But the most interesting aspect of *Benigna Machiavelli*, in terms of practices of transcription, involves the appeal to careful reading (not just passive recording) that is also visible in "Fulfilment." In this chapter's epigraph, Benigna describes a combination of covert listening and a meticulous reader's interpretation: when she invokes the Bible as justification for eavesdropping ("It doesn't say in the Bible, 'Thou shalt not listen'"), she also explains that she has checked the entire text with a concordance. Similarly, Benigna's explication of her cipher draws as much attention to her voracious reading practices as to her writing: "I learned about substitution codes from [Edgar Allan Poe's] 'The Gold Bug,'" she explains, "and in some other books, too."[25] At these moments Gilman has linked the image of Benigna at the stovepipe hole, listening and recording, with the image of Benigna at her texts, whether the Bible, its concordance, "The Gold Bug," or the "other books" she invokes.

Like "Fulfilment," *Benigna Machiavelli* connects listening with reading, the ethical empowerment of transcribing with a similarly thorough and comprehensive approach to written material. Gilman's eavesdroppers, hearing through the invidiously gendered power structures of the domestic interior, thus model a practice that very much applies to us, as readers of her (or any) texts. These eavesdroppers also appear in their own right not as passive transcribers of the voice but as vigorous interpreters, arrangers, and exegetists. In this Gilman transformed the Arts and Crafts model even as she inherited its emphasis on the honesty required of the interior. Stickley and other Arts and Crafts artisans offered Americans material things in which honesty and sincerity were said to be intrinsic. Gilman absorbed the era's excitement about the ethics of space but presumed a much more active role for individuals: truth, for Gilman, was channeled through space rather inherently lodged in it.

"The Chair of English" (1913) offers a kind of case study in Gilman's reaction to the philosophy and decorative style associated with the Arts and Crafts movement. On the face of it, the story's title refers not to a material object but to a department head in English, an unscrupulous administrator who attempts to convince a woman, Mona Beale, that her husband, a professor of physics, is having an affair with the wife of the university president; the chairman, Dr. Manchester, hopes that the revelation will cause the Beales to accept an offer made to Mr. Beale by a different college, thus opening up that faculty position for a relative of Dr. Manchester's. English appears to be a fallen discipline in the story. Affecting certain hesitancies, the chairman's rhetorical slipperiness correlates with his profession: his "scholarly articles of exquisite diction" have made him a "practiced expert in the use of words" who uses his training, in laying out the false case to Mrs. Beale, for misdirection and subterfuge.[26]

The title "The Chair of English" is a pun, however, since it also refers to the physical place where trustworthy English *is* available: a "big lounging chair that stretched comfortable arms against the background of a richly embroidered tall Japanese screen." This setting evokes the Arts and Crafts style quite clearly, and not just because a large lounging chair with broad arms would have called to mind Stickley's iconic Morris chair for any American in 1913— the year in which Stickley reached the zenith of his visibility, running a restaurant, a club, a farm school, the magazine, and an eleven-story corporate building and showrooms on Fifth Avenue. The inclusion of the Japanese screen as a background for the chair pointedly suggests the Arts and Crafts movement. Article after article in the *Craftsman* focused on how Japanese design could be integrated with what one such essay described as the "coming American style" of Arts and Crafts furnishings; a piece in 1911 focused in particular on Japanese screens for the American home.[27]

In "The Chair of English" the Stickleyesque chair next to the Japanese screen is first occupied by the mendacious Dr. Manchester. But as soon as Dr. Manchester leaves, Mrs. Beale immediately telephones Dr. Gates, a "'real doctor'" (i.e., a medical one) whose advice she trusts. Seating him in the "same big chair by the golden storks and lilies," she queries him about the account of the affair and finds that he possesses certain evidence of Dr. Manchester's dissimulation; Gilman's identification of Dr. Gates's medical degree as more "real" than Dr. Manchester's academic one is the keynote of a scene that aims to discredit all the language associated with the departmental chairman. Mrs. Beale in fact then reveals that a dictograph—a recording device using a phonographic cylinder—has been concealed behind the Japanese screen. In a final showdown in a lawyer's office, Mrs. Beale uses the recording to force the supposed "master of English" to admit his falsehoods and drives him from his departmental position.[28] By the end of the story, we recognize the "Chair of English" not as the deposed Dr. Manchester but as the physical item—big, solid, structural, and clearly tied to the Arts and Crafts aesthetics—where English is held to a higher standard of recorded veracity and where spoken words cannot be disavowed.

As we uncover the pun in the title throughout the course of reading the story, we perform the same operation as Mrs. Beale herself, replacing literary slipperiness (represented by the "extremely learned" departmental chairman of English) with true speech (acquired in a "chair of English" stylistically associated with honesty).[29] That basic pattern, whereby literary prevarication or uncertainty appears to be stabilized by recorded or otherwise summative speech, is the one I mean to have drawn out in the opening paragraphs of this chapter and to have tied to the promotion of more honest interior space in the first two decades of the twentieth century.

But just as Gilman's other works require the ability to correctly read the stories one picks up—whether through stovepipe holes or in the written form of fiction itself—"The Chair of English" presents the chair and the screen not as intrinsically suggestive of honesty but as its context and conduit. In relying on the dictograph, Mrs. Beale indeed beats Dr. Manchester at his own game of rhetorical manipulation. She defeats him, that is, not because he has been moved to speak honestly—the formula about more ethical material surroundings articulated by Stickley—but because she has lured him into making certain absolute and therefore actionable statements, and because she and the lawyer summon Dr. Manchester to the lawyer's office by pretending to subpoena him in a suit of divorce supposedly initiated by Mrs. Beale. The chair and screen position Dr. Manchester correctly for the better operation of the secret device and the consequent empowerment, through the shrewd use of the recording, of Mrs. Beale's rhetorical authority.

While Gilman was writing "The Chair of English," dictographs were very much in the news, and in a way that suited her own skepticism about the salvific force that the Arts and Crafts movement accorded to the intrinsic honesty of material things themselves. When it originally appeared in 1907, the dictograph was conceived not as a recording device but as a two-way instrument for intraoffice communication: a transmitter could be placed in each of several departments, all of which were connected back to a master station in the office of an executive or a foreman. Yet within two years the dictograph had been adapted to clandestine recording. By 1911 dictographic evidence had been introduced in two major, widely reported criminal cases (one of which placed Clarence Darrow on trial for witness tampering), and the device's manufacturer had begun selling a Detective Dictograph to the public.[30]

Touting the smaller transmitter that could be concealed, for example, in the hanging finial of a light in a corporate conference room (so that an executive could eavesdrop on his employees), the Dictograph Manufacturing Company offered instructions with every unit for hiding the cord under carpets or in the cracks of moldings and floors. If the instructions weren't sufficient, eavesdroppers were invited to call the company's Detective Service Department for situation-specific advice about channeling, drilling, and perforating the furniture. One might, for instance, route the wires through a "hollowed table leg" situated directly over a "tiny hole" in the floor. Sensational journalism described dictographs concealed "in walls, under sofa[s] and chair[s], in [a] chandelier, behind a desk, [or] beside a window."[31]

In a general way, the emphasis on recording overheard speech in the era of the dictograph (1907–1919) applies to many of Gilman's novels, all but one of which were written in the same period. Benigna Machiavelli's reams of notebooks, for instance, anticipate the "careful and accurate account of all we told them" kept by the women of *Herland*. Exemplifying Gilman's conviction that transcription demands good reading as much as correct recording, this account is sifted into "a sort of skeleton chart, on which the things we said and the things we palpably avoided saying were all set down and studied."[32]

In more particularly architectural ways, however, Gilman seems to have absorbed dictographic examples of furniture as all-hearing and the house itself as a swiss cheese network of holes, raceways, channels, and tracks for receivers and wires. Even before one of the characters in *The Crux* actually drills a hole in the floor of Dr. Hale's house, for instance, that structure is heavily perforated: it includes a laundry chute, an enormous dumbwaiter, a special elevator for firewood, and a profusion of what the novel calls "mysterious inner holes."[33] One of the dramas of *The Crux* involves the fact that Dr. Hale, a male physician, has so much access to information: his house, in addition to being so porous, has a kind of open-door policy and is frequented by the townspeople. Yet, even so, he essentially refuses to protect the health of Vivian Lane by revealing to her that her suitor has syphilis. His house thus appears as a potent resource that, unlike the stovepipe holes used by Mrs. Beazley and Benigna or the dictograph concealed by Mrs. Beale, does not fulfill its potential as a way of hearing through men's deceptions of women. Fortunately for Vivian, Dr. Bellair, a female physician whose very name connotes open and permeable space (a point that has been made in relation to her association with the open landscape of the West but not in relation to architecture and interior space), knows what to do with the information that she also spies out, collects by telephone, and overhears.

Such surveillance networks might be understood as an admonitory version of the Arts and Crafts aim of promoting honesty in and through the home.

Porous acoustic spaces demand that individuals attend to the accuracy of their words, even as they (like, I have argued, Gilman's fictional characters) relocate the stimulus for such honesty from things themselves to the listeners who hear through things. The most sustained example of this appears in the novel *Unpunished*, completed in 1929 but published posthumously. *Unpunished* presents the husband-and-wife detective team themselves in terms of dictography: Jim has "a memory like a dictograph," whereas Bess, a stenographer, records what he recalls "straight, in sequence," and with perfect accuracy.[34]

Moreover, the house in which the murder of Wade Vaughn occurs appears as porous as Dr. Hale's home in *The Crux*, with the differences that here the channels between the rooms are more specifically auditory and here an individual who lives in the house does not fail to make the most of them. A speaking tube connects Jacqueline Warner's room with the upstairs kitchen. A second device, which she discovers by accident, allows her to listen in on at least two different rooms in the house and to make shorthand recordings of what she hears; this contrivance, tuned in by making adjustments on the base, bears a striking similarity to the so-called master station of the original corporate dictograph, through which the operator could communicate with various departments by pressing different buttons on the base. The master station is clearly visible on the executive's desk, with the buttons linked to employees—invariably including a stenographer—elsewhere (see figure 8.2).

In *Unpunished*, Jacqueline Warner is both the executive operator of the master station and the stenographer, a powerful double position that allows her to record Wade Vaughn's operations as a tyrant and a blackmailer and thus, ultimately, to reveal his turpitude at the inquest for his murder. Through Warner's listening and transcribing, Vaughn's despotically patrilineal powers are publicly exposed: by the terms of his father-in-law's will, the members of the family receive certain money in trust only if they maintain absolute obedience to Vaughn. Our sympathy, and that of the public, settles not on the murder victim but on the five individuals who for good reason attacked the heartless tormentor of his family and community.

But what *Unpunished* demands of its readers, who listen in on the story of patrilineal authority, appears most clearly when Bess Hunt, the detective and stenographer, explains to her husband how she has discovered yet another acoustic conduit in the house:

> "I've made a clear plan of the house, a regular blueprint, see? Here's that side door, the little square entry with the doors into his room and the dining room and coat closet at the back end. Here's a china closet opening from the dining room, with a small sink in it. Over the slide used to be a slide into Vaughn's office, as if that was the dining room

Figure 8.2. The dictograph's master station (Cover of *The Dictograph—Turner Telephone System*, New York: General Acoustic, 1912)

once. It was all papered over on that side . . . on the closet side the slide was boarded up [with] a chunk of plank . . . [but] with a knife blade the whole thing comes out!"

"What made you think of trying?"

"My conscientious use of a dust cloth, Jim. I was dusting the frame of that picture and I happened to notice a sort of streak in the paper below it, close under the edge, hardly visible, a long level crack."

"Well, paper does crack sometimes, Bess."

"Yes, I know it does, and this looked all right except that it was so straight. So I measured the distance and found it was at the top of that slide. Then I poked about a bit and out came the plank, and I saw daylight. . . ."

"How about hearing?"

" . . . regular sounding board, that thin slide, plus the crack."[35]

The revelation of the acoustic crack between the china closet and Vaughn's office, a "regular sounding board," begs readers to pay special attention to our own hearing of the novel. First, Bess's description of her "blueprint" actually confuses the reader's ear: the floor plan is very tough to imagine, not least because the passage alliterates so many *c* and *s* sounds, blending the whole mixture of "side" and "slide," "coat closet" and "china closet," into a bewildering description of space. Second, the passage describes speech conveyed not just between rooms but through Gilman's oeuvre itself: the long horizontal streak on the wallpaper has an obvious textual antecedent. In both ways—presenting a difficult-to-read description and quoting her own best-known fictional work—Gilman has forced the reader to become an interpreter. Like whoever listens at the crack, like Jacqueline Warner in her upstairs room, like Benigna Machiavelli, like Mrs. Beazley, and like Mona Beale, the readers of this passage must listen actively through architectural space, piecing together what we can of the house's floor plan and perhaps overhearing, as if through a dictograph, a distant source of these words in a text at the opposite end of Gilman's career, "The Yellow Wall-Paper." In that sense the statement in this passage that "paper does crack" may present a double meaning, referring to the paper pages of books as well as to the wallpaper in the Vaughn house. Words in Gilman's corpus are like the spaces presented: acoustically porous, subject to cracking and piecing together, and demanding that we listen with close attention to the sounding boards of her fiction.

Gilman's most radical fictional paradigm thus offers architecture not as a utopian blueprint (a claim that has been made about texts like *Herland* and *Moving the Mountain*), but as a network of cracks, conduits, and channels that must be actualized by clever protagonists and engaged readers.[36] If Gilman occasionally described objects of Stickleyesque clarity and intention, like the furniture in Herland, her more nuanced position presented interior space as permeable and traced the dynamics by which social reform flows from the ability to hear the truth over—and through—material surroundings.

Nevertheless, the short story "His Record" (1914), with which I will conclude, reveals as clearly as anything in Gilman's corpus how her notions of architectural honesty did flow from the specific design principles of the Arts and Crafts movement, even as Gilman adapted those principles to emphasize agentive and active listening-in. "His Record" concerns a young man, Jim Henry, hired as a general aide-de-camp for Polly Marshall and her three children, who are summering on a Maine island. Polly hires Jim because a family friend describes his impeccable record; he has "taken charge of this" and "managed that," all "alone and single-handed." But Jim proves to be lazy and shiftless, a circumstance that causes Polly's aged Aunt Selina, traveling with the family, to recruit other relatives (Polly's half brother, George, and his daughter Georgina) to come to the island. The question of where to house George and Georgina has already been handled by Aunt Selina:

> "I've ordered one of those little Craftsman set-up and take-down houses," pursued the old lady. "It'll be a good thing to have here anyway. George can put it up—he'll love to. They're coming Thursday."
>
> Mrs. Marshall took it as sweetly and bravely as she usually met life.
>
> "How dear of you, Aunt Selina, to give us a house!" she said with a little squeal of delight. "I always wanted one of those Craftsman's . . ."
>
> Certain furnishings and fittings came too, to the delighted admiration of the whole family.[37]

The reference here is to Stickley's style rather than to the actual products of his company, since the Craftsman architectural department sold only the plans for such houses, not the kits themselves. But the passage remains an explicit reference to the Arts and Crafts movement. Indeed, the very popularity of kit homes known as Craftsman (the Sears and Alladin companies manufactured tens of thousands of such structures) marks the widespread appeal of Stickley's enterprise in Gilman's America.

More important, Aunt Selina's choice makes the essential associations visible throughout Gilman's oeuvre: Craftsman style connotes greater honesty, but that honesty must be proved and shepherded by a protagonist whose activities of listening and recording drive the story's development. Once the house arrives, Aunt Selina reveals that she has been keeping a careful log of everyone's activities. Reading from the log at the end of the story, she details the days on which one of the children teased another, the days on which the daughter behaved splendidly, and, most important, the entire history of Jim Henry's laziness around camp. Confronted with his actual record, not the false one that gets him the job, Jim declares that he has "behaved like a chump" and will reform.[38] The moral of "His Record" is overdrawn and the story is not one of Gilman's best. But a matter of plot exemplifies her triangulation of honest things, eavesdropping protagonists, and accurate records. George and Georgina are originally said to have been summoned to take over Jim Henry's duties. In the event, however, they appear useful primarily because George enjoys working on the Craftsman house alongside a local builder. This circumstance is immediately followed by Aunt Selina's revelation of the record and Jim's apparent reformation, which, if trustworthy, renders George and Georgina's presence no longer necessary. More than the day-to-day help of the relatives, then, the house precipitates the necessary changes.

Stickley published dozens of moralizing tales about architecture and décor in the *Craftsman* and would have loved this subtlety in the plot; it stresses the ethical centrality of a structure, and its associated furnishings, in his own peculiarly ethical decorative style. But the potential of physical things must be made good, must be held to account, by the vigorous listening and correct documenting modeled, in this case, by Aunt Selina. A common account of Gilman's work—promoted in part by Gilman herself—identifies her fiction as primarily a pass-through, a conduit for her vision of a materially better world. In much of her fiction, I see the case the other way around: the material world instead appears as a conduit for her fundamentally narrative imagination. What matters, in this way of looking at Gilman's career, is the stuff of the author's calling: the active reading, writing, and transcribing that the built environment makes possible.

NOTES

1. Cynthia J. Davis, *Charlotte Perkins Gilman: A Biography* (Stanford, CA: Stanford University Press, 2010), 295.

2. Charlotte Perkins Gilman, *Benigna Machiavelli*, ed. Sasha Newborn (1914; repr., Santa Barbara, CA: Bandanna Books, 2013), 177.

3. Charlotte Perkins Gilman, *The Crux*, ed. Dana Seitler (1911; repr., Durham, NC: Duke University Press, 2003), 80, 170.

4. Charlotte Perkins Gilman, *Herland*, in *Herland, The Yellow Wall-Paper, and Selected Writings*, ed. Denise Knight (New York: Penguin, 1999), 143.

5. Ibid.

6. Gilman, *Crux*, 170–71.

7. Gilman, *Benigna*, 178.

8. Gilman, "The Unexpected," In *Herland, The Yellow Wall-Paper, and Selected Writings*, ed. Denise Knight (New York: Penguin, 1999), 147.

9. Critics who emphasize the elusive qualities of *Herland* generally link its open-ended qualities with its feminist politics, either identifying such openness as an alternative to patriarchal authority or arguing that such openness pushes readers into an evaluative, critically reflective stance. See, e.g., Jean-Jacques Weber, "Educating the Reader: Narrative Technique and Evaluation in Charlotte Perkins Gilman's *Herland*," in *The Language and Literature Reader*, ed. Ronald Carter and Peter Stockwell (London: Routledge, 2008), 177–86; Laura Donaldson, "The Eve of De-struction: Charlotte Perkins Gilman and the Feminist Re-creation of Paradise," *Women's Studies* 16 (1989): 373–87; and Christopher Wilson, "Charlotte Perkins Gilman's Steady Burghers: The Terrain of *Herland*," *Women's Studies* 12 (1986): 271–92. Critics who emphasize the authoritative qualities of the text tend to describe the ways in which the novel ironically reinforces conservative thinking about gender roles and about racial diversity. See, e.g., Kathleen Margaret Lant, "The

Rape of the Text: Charlotte Perkins Gilman's Violation of *Herland*," *Tulsa Studies in Women's Literature* 9, no. 2 (1990): 291–308; and Thomas Galt Peyser, "Reproducing Utopia: Charlotte Perkins Gilman and *Herland*," *Studies in American Fiction* 20, no. 1 (1992): 1–16. A number of critics place the interplay of the novel's elusive and authoritative modes at the center of their analysis. See, e.g., Susan Gubar, "*She* and *Herland*: Feminism as Fantasy," in *Coordinates: Placing Science Fiction and Fantasy*, ed. George Slusser, Eric Rabkin, and Robert Scholes (Carbondale: Southern Illinois University Press, 1983), 139–49; Chris Ferns, "Rewriting Male Myths: Herland and the Utopian Tradition," in *A Very Different Story: Studies in the Fiction of Charlotte Perkins Gilman*, ed. Val Gough and Jill Rudd (Liverpool, UK: University Press, 1999), 24–37; and Val Gough, "Lesbians and Virgins: The New Motherhood in *Herland*," in *Anticipations: Essays on Early Science Fiction and Its Precursors*, ed. David Seed (Syracuse, NY: Syracuse University Press, 1995), 195–215.

10. Barbara Hochman, "The Reading Habit and 'The Yellow Wallpaper,'" *American Literature* 74, no. 1 (2002): 89, 92.

11. "The Living Room: Its Many Uses and Its Possibilities for Comfort and Beauty," *Craftsman*, October 1905. The article cited here appeared anonymously, a frequent occurrence in the *Craftsman*. In this chapter I identify the ideas contained in the anonymous articles with Stickley himself because the magazine served so clearly as a forum for his ideas and because, in most cases, we can reasonably presume that Stickley was in fact the author. However, I do not name Stickley in the citations unless the piece actually appeared under his name.

12. "Structure and Ornament in the Craftsman Workshops," *Craftsman*, January 1904. I have written at length elsewhere about the literary context of these ideas (but without addressing Gilman); see Peter Betjemann, *Talking Shop: The Language of Craft in an Age of Consumption* (Charlottesville: University of Virginia Press, 2011), 142–93.

13. "Structure and Ornament"; Gustav Stickley, "Thoughts Occasioned by an Anniversary: A Plea for a Democratic Art," *Craftsman*, October 1904.

14. Charlotte Perkins Gilman, "Domestic Art," *Craftsman*, February 1904.

15. Gilman, *Herland*, 29.

16. Charlotte Perkins Gilman, "The Yellow Wall-Paper," in *Herland, The Yellow Wall-Paper, and Selected Writings*, ed. Denise Knight (New York: Penguin, 1999), 168, 172; Charlotte Perkins Gilman, "Through This," in *Herland, The Yellow Wall-Paper, and Selected Writings*, ed. Denise Knight (New York: Penguin, 1999), 195, 196.

17. Charlotte Perkins Gilman, "The Rocking-Chair," in *Herland, The Yellow Wall-Paper, and Selected Writings*, ed Denise Knight (New York: Penguin, 1999), 183, 189.

18. Ibid., 190.

19. Ibid., 190, 191.

20. Charlotte Perkins Gilman, "Fulfilment," *Forerunner*, March 1914, 57.

21. Ibid., 57, 58.

22. Ibid., 57, 61.

23. Charlotte Perkins Gilman, "Mrs. Beazley's Deeds," in *Herland, The Yellow Wall-Paper, and Selected Writings*, ed. Denise Knight (New York: Penguin, 1999), 207, 208, 209, 218, 219.

24. Gilman, *Benigna*, 82, 100, 102.

25. Ibid., 82, 102.

26. Charlotte Perkins Gilman, "The Chair of English," in *Herland, The Yellow Wall-Paper, and Selected Writings*, ed. Denise Knight (New York: Penguin, 1999), 256.

27. Ibid., 255; "Japanese Architecture and Its Relation to the Coming American Style," *Craftsman*, May 1906; "Japanese Screens for the American Home," *Craftsman*, October 1911.

28. Gilman, "Chair of English," 257, 261.

29. Ibid., 261.

30. Kathryn W. Kemp, "'The Dictograph Hears All': An Example of Surveillance Technology in the Progressive Era," *Journal of the Gilded Age and Progressive Era* 6, no. 4 (2007): 416–17.

31. French Strother, "What the Dictograph Is," *World's Work*, 1912; Edward Lyell Fox, "Eavesdropping by Science," *Popular Electricity*, June 1912.

32. Gilman, *Herland*, 81.

33. Gilman, *Crux*, 74.

34. Charlotte Perkins Gilman, *Unpunished*, ed. Catherine J. Golden and Denise Knight (New York: Feminist Press, 1997), 6, 24.

35. Ibid., 65–66.

36. For the utopian basis of Gilman's architectural imagination, see Polly Wynn Allen, *Building Domestic Liberty: Charlotte Perkins Gilman's Architectural Feminism* (Amherst: University of Massachusetts Press, 1988), 83–102.

37. Charlotte Perkins Gilman, "His Record," *Forerunner*, November 1914, 281, 283–84.

38. Ibid., 285.

WORKS CITED

Allen, Polly Wynn. *Building Domestic Liberty: Charlotte Perkins Gilman's Architectural Feminism*. Amherst: University of Massachusetts Press, 1988.

Betjemann, Peter. *Talking Shop: The Language of Craft in an Age of Consumption*. Charlottesville: University of Virginia Press, 2011.

Davis, Cynthia J. *Charlotte Perkins Gilman: A Biography*. Stanford, CA: Stanford University Press, 2010.

Donaldson, Laura. "The Eve of De-struction: Charlotte Perkins Gilman and the Feminist Re-creation of Paradise." *Women's Studies* 16 (1989): 373–87.

Ferns, Chris. "Rewriting Male Myths: Herland and the Utopian Tradition." In *A Very Different Story: Studies in the Fiction of Charlotte Perkins Gilman*, edited by Val Gough and Jill Rudd, 24–37. Liverpool, UK: University Press, 1999.

Fox, Edward Lyell. "Eavesdropping by Science." *Popular Electricity*, June 1912.

Gilman, Charlotte Perkins. *Benigna Machiavelli*. 1914. Edited by Sasha Newborn. Santa Barbara, CA: Bandanna Books, 2013.

———. "The Chair of English." In *Herland, The Yellow Wall-Paper, and Selected Writings*, edited by Denise Knight, 255–62. New York: Penguin, 1999.

———. *The Crux*. 1911. Edited by Dana Seitler. Durham, NC: Duke University Press, 2003.

———. "Domestic Art." *Craftsman*, February 1904.

———. "Fulfilment." *Forerunner*, March 1914.

———. *Herland*. In *Herland, The Yellow Wall-Paper, and Selected Writings*, edited by Denise Knight, 3–143. New York: Penguin, 1999.

———. "His Record." *Forerunner*, November 1914.

———. "Mrs. Beazley's Deeds." In *Herland, The Yellow Wall-Paper, and Selected Writings*, edited by Denise Knight, 207–20. New York: Penguin, 1999.

———. "The Rocking-Chair." In *Herland, The Yellow Wall-Paper, and Selected Writings*, edited by Denise Knight, 183–93. New York: Penguin, 1999.

———. "Through This." In *Herland, The Yellow Wall-Paper, and Selected Writings*, edited by Denise Knight, 194–97. New York: Penguin, 1999.

———. "The Unexpected." In *Herland, The Yellow Wall-Paper, and Selected Writings*, edited by Denise Knight, 147–53. New York: Penguin, 1999.

———. *Unpunished*. Edited by Catherine J. Golden and Denise Knight. New York: Feminist Press, 1997.

———. "The Yellow Wall-Paper." In *Herland, The Yellow Wall-Paper, and Selected Writings*, edited by Denise Knight, 166–82. New York: Penguin, 1999.

Gough, Val. "Lesbians and Virgins: The New Motherhood in *Herland*." In *Anticipations: Essays on Early Science Fiction and Its Precursors*, edited by David Seed, 195–215. Syracuse, NY: Syracuse University Press, 1995.

Gubar, Susan. "*She* and *Herland*: Feminism as Fantasy." In *Coordinates: Placing Science Fiction and Fantasy*, edited by George Slusser, Eric Rabkin, and Robert Scholes, 139–49. Carbondale: Southern Illinois University Press, 1983.

Hochman, Barbara. "The Reading Habit and 'The Yellow Wallpaper.'" *American Literature* 74, no. 1 (2002): 89–110.

"Japanese Architecture and Its Relation to the Coming American Style." *Craftsman*, May 1906.

"Japanese Screens for the American Home." *Craftsman*, October 1911.

Kemp, Kathryn W. "'The Dictograph Hears All': An Example of Surveillance

Technology in the Progressive Era." *Journal of the Gilded Age and Progressive Era* 6, no. 4 (2007): 409–30.

Lant, Kathleen Margaret. "The Rape of the Text: Charlotte Perkins Gilman's Violation of *Herland*." *Tulsa Studies in Women's Literature* 9, no. 2 (1990): 291–308.

"The Living Room: Its Many Uses and Its Possibilities for Comfort and Beauty." *Craftsman*, October 1905.

Peyser, Thomas Galt. "Reproducing Utopia: Charlotte Perkins Gilman and *Herland*." *Studies in American Fiction* 20, no. 1 (1992): 1–16.

Stickley, Gustav. "Thoughts Occasioned by an Anniversary: A Plea for a Democratic Art." *Craftsman*, October 1904.

Strother, French. "What the Dictograph Is." *World's Work*, May 1912.

"Structure and Ornament in the Craftsman Workshops." *Craftsman*, January 1904.

Weber, Jean-Jacques. "Educating the Reader: Narrative Technique and Evaluation in Charlotte Perkins Gilman's *Herland*." In *The Language and Literature Reader*, edited by Ronald Carter and Peter Stockwell, 177–86. London: Routledge, 2008.

Wilson, Christopher. "Charlotte Perkins Gilman's Steady Burghers: The Terrain of *Herland*." *Women's Studies* 12 (1986): 271–92.

9
Recovering the Work of Charlotte Perkins Gilman; or, Reading Gilman in Rome

Jennifer S. Tuttle

Io sono una donna che non è a sua disposizione. (I am not a woman at your disposal.)

Rosy Bindi

In 2010 I delivered the keynote address at a conference observing Charlotte Perkins Gilman's 150th birthday.[1] The audience, intent and passionate and including many participants from beyond academia, filled every seat and spilled out into the aisles. People came seeking an outlet for their anger at women's myriad forms of oppression and voiced their demands for social change. Organized by Cristina Giorcelli, Laura Moschini, and Anna Scacchi, the event was held not in Gilman's home country of the United States but at the University of Rome III in Rome, Italy, with the theme "Donna e Polis: Charlotte Perkins Gilman Oggi" ("Women and Polis: Charlotte Perkins Gilman Today").

Having attended many previous Gilman conferences, I had come to expect that such an event would be vibrant and compelling, but never have I experienced such an electric, vital, and engaged audience as I did in Italy near the end of the Silvio Berlusconi era. As the conference organizers themselves explained, "It is particularly timely and appropriate to reconsider Gilman's analysis of the social dynamics of power, gender, and sexuality today in Italy, given the . . . stereotyped representation of women in Italian culture and their virtual nonexistence in political and economic institutions." The organizers documented an upsurge of outrage and activism among feminists from all walks of life and across the professional and academic spectrum, all of which was evident at the Rome conference. In explaining their rationale for holding the event, Giorcelli, Moschini, and Scacchi asserted the value of Gilman's work "for Italian young women today" notwithstanding the "'flaws' of her white middle-class perspective"; they also noted explicitly that the conference was

Figure 9.1. Anna Scacchi's Italian translation of
Gilman's works, *La terra delle donne* (*The Land of
Women*); used by permission of Donzelli Press

meant to provide a platform to launch "Anna Scacchi's new translation of *Her-land*, 'The Yellow Wall-Paper' and a selection of short stories" (see figure 9.1).

Although this event exemplified the confluence of sexual and literary politics that has been a hallmark of feminist criticism since the field took shape in the 1960s "as part of the international women's movement," according to Elaine Showalter, the organizers' overt link to the publication of Scacchi's Italian edition of Gilman's writing signals that *recovery*—retrieving writers and their work from obscurity, republishing out-of-print texts, and issuing editions of unpublished or so-called private writing—is the bedrock of politically engaged literary praxis. In the United States, notes Catherine Golden, the advent of Gilman studies occurred as part of an early second-wave "frenzy to publish 'lost' and 'neglected' works by U.S. women writers": "scholars felt an urgency to bring more of Gilman's work back into print." Like literary criticism in general, the scholarship of recovery is clearly shaped by the demands of its context. Golden writes, "The pressing issues of any given historical moment have influenced how an evolving community of feminist critics" interprets Gilman's writing; acts of recovery are similarly shaped by the social, sexual, cultural, political, and historical forces in which the scholarly community does its work.[2] Indeed, the "urgency" of recovery to which Golden refers was everywhere evident in Rome in 2010, fueling Scacchi's recent volume and the Italian translations that preceded it—for what is the translation of primary sources if not recovery for a new context and a new readership?

In this chapter I argue that recovery in Gilman studies is inextricable from the politics of its time: it offers us a window into the concerns of successive generations of feminist scholars and publishers, but it also represents a vital form of feminist activism. Theorizing recovery work in this way requires more than self-reflection on the part of Gilman scholars; it also demands a global perspective in order to account for translation projects like Scacchi's, which enact the activism of recovery in non-Anglophone milieux. This analysis therefore hinges on the theme of place, broadly defined as both cultural context and geographical orientation. I begin by considering Gilman's published texts, specifically the three most prominent works recovered during the second wave of the US women's movement: *Women and Economics*, "The Yellow Wall-Paper," and *Herland*. No less significant is the recovery of her unpublished writing; I focus particularly on her correspondence, taking as a case in point the recently discovered letter she sent to her physician, S. Weir Mitchell. But while both of these categories are necessary for a thorough study of recovery work, they are not sufficient: Gilman's growing popularity in Italy (and elsewhere abroad) demands a more capacious definition of recovery and a transnational, hemispheric, even global framework for theorizing such scholarship. In this essay, therefore, I consider the printing and reprinting of Gilman's writing as well as the translation of her work for global audiences.

When Gilman died in 1935, most of her writing was out of print. In a 1934 letter to Zona Gale, she expressed the hope that her "scrappy, imperfect, desperately earnest work" might be republished.[3] She wanted her work recovered; more than that, she believed it could still change the world for the better, for she well knew that many of the problems she addressed had not yet been solved. Despite the great strides global women's movements have made to secure the equality of the sexes, some of those problems remain unsolved to this day. At the very foundation of Gilman's social philosophy was the simple notion that women are people—that their femaleness is secondary to their basic humanity. "So utterly has the status of woman been accepted as a sexual one," she wrote in *Women and Economics*, "that it has remained for the women's movement of the nineteenth century to devote much contention to the claim that women are persons! That women are persons as well as females,— an unheard of proposition!"[4]

Eighty years after Gilman's death, the fact that women are above all human beings who deserve to be taken seriously is not yet universally recognized—an appalling circumstance indeed. Certainly, were she alive today, Gilman would have championed the Italian parliamentarian Rosy Bindi, who in 2009 was disparaged on national television by then Prime Minister Silvio Berlusconi with the intentionally ironic comment that she was "more beautiful than . . . intelligent." Bindi was the only woman "on a stage full of men," and she famously retorted, "I am not a woman at your disposal."[5] Bindi's rejection of Berlusconi's dehumanization is emblematic of Italian feminists' increasingly vocal resistance to a social and political climate of unapologetic sexism; Italian translations of Gilman's work are part of this resistance. Yet this flamboyant example of silencing and objectification is not so different from that which women endure elsewhere, including in the United States. Attending to such social and political contexts and historicizing recovery work in Gilman studies illuminates the forces that shape scholars' choices and methodologies. More important, it demonstrates how and why this recovery matters and helps to explain why Gilman, even with her myriad flaws exposed, remains such a compelling figure for feminists of today.

GILMAN REDISCOVERED: RECOVERING THE PUBLISHED WRITING

During her long life, Gilman published an impressive quantity of material, including eight novels, close to two hundred short stories, nearly five hundred poems, eleven book-length nonfiction works, a vast number of articles, and an autobiography, along with a variety of other pieces. Some of this writing appeared in her journal, the *Forerunner*, which she edited and for which she wrote all of the content between 1909 and 1916. Although the recovery of this prolific output is still underway, scholars in a range of disciplines have brought a considerable number of these works back into print.[6]

Three publications stand out as Gilman's best-known and were the first to capture scholars' attention in the second half of the twentieth century. *Women and Economics*, a nonfiction treatise that traced the source of the inequality of the sexes to women's economic dependence on men, was originally published in 1898 and recovered in 1966. "The Yellow Wall-Paper," an 1892 short story of a woman objectified by both marriage and medical science who is denied full bodily autonomy and (some argue) driven mad as a result, was recovered for a wide audience in 1973.[7] And the 1915 utopian novel *Herland*, featuring a society without men or gender roles where women are free to develop their human strengths and aptitudes, was recovered in 1979. These texts offer accessible treatments of some of second-wave feminism's central concerns, including "the politics of gender relations, of housework, and of childcare." It is thus not surprising that they were attractive to critics and historians working in that era. Gilman "was rediscovered during" this period, argues Cynthia Davis, "largely for her insights into gender politics and issues that remain unresolved decades after her death."[8]

The first of these works to be recovered in the modern era, *Women and Economics*, was reissued by Carl Degler in 1966. Sensing "the emergent tenor of the times in the years immediately following the publication of Betty Friedan's *The Feminine Mystique* in 1963," Degler recognized, according to Michael Kimmel and Amy Aronson, that the "increasingly politicized feminist intellectuals" leading the women's movement sought "foremothers, mentors who had been there before, wrestled with the same issues." Although parts of Gilman's treatise had long since gone out of date, its central argument linking the inequality of the sexes to women's economic dependence on men unfortunately remained valid and was a topic of great concern to second-wave feminists.[9]

Preceding Degler's edition of *Women and Economics* by a mere three years, the Presidential Commission on the Status of Women (PCSW) had published a report calling for equal pay for equal work and work of comparable value (Gilman herself had given a lecture, "Equal Pay for Equal Work," in London in 1899).[10] The resulting Equal Pay Act did not sufficiently address the problem, leading some members of the commission to found the National Organization for Women in 1966. To this day, US women earn less than men for comparable work, and the disparity is wider still for women of color.[11] When Degler recovered *Women and Economics*, he confirmed that Gilman's aim was "to achieve full equality for women in an industrial society." The book had much to say, Degler insisted, "about and to women today."[12] Degler's reissue coincided with an upsurge of feminist literary criticism that represented part of the second wave's intellectual arm; studies such as Mary Ellman's pioneering *Thinking about Women* (1965) and Kate Millet's *Sexual Politics* (1969), echoing Gilman, challenged the sexist paradigms and assumptions that shaped gendered power relations, including the economic inequality that Gilman sought to eradicate through her work.

A reissue of "The Yellow Wall-Paper" appeared seven years later, in 1973; this story was one of the early titles published by the Feminist Press, which had been founded a mere three years before "by a women's collective intent on restoring to print women writers of high literary quality."[13] In her afterword to this edition, Elaine Hedges highlighted the contextual forces that shaped recovery work in Gilman studies: "with the new growth of the feminist movement, Charlotte Perkins Gilman is being rediscovered." Recognizing Gilman as "one of America's foremost feminists," Hedges highlighted the ways that Gilman's short story "directly confronted the sexual politics of the male-female, husband-wife relationship" that was such a flash point for second-wave activists. Gilman's indictment of the twin male-dominated institutions of marriage and medicine spoke with great urgency to feminists of the early 1970s. Hedges elsewhere remarks on the telling fact of the story's reappearance in the same year that the Supreme Court issued its verdict in *Roe v. Wade*, legalizing abortion in the United States.[14]

The issues of women's health and bodily and reproductive self-determination were clearly at the forefront of many minds that year, which also saw the first professionally published edition of the Boston Women's Health Book Collective's *Our Bodies, Ourselves*. Scholars' commitment to understanding these issues in historical perspective was confirmed in such publications as Carroll Smith-Rosenberg's foundational essay "The Hysterical Woman: Sex Roles and Role Conflict in Nineteenth-Century America" (1972), Barbara Ehrenreich and Deirdre English's book *Complaints and Disorders: The Sexual Politics of Sickness* (1973), and Ann Douglas Wood's article "'The Fashionable Diseases': Women's Complaints and Their Treatment in Nineteenth-Century America" (1973).

During the ensuing six years, as the women's movement developed apace, readers were primed for Ann Lane's recovery of *Herland* in 1979. The best-known of Gilman's utopian works, it had never before been published in a freestanding edition, having appeared serially in the *Forerunner* in 1915. Pantheon's book jacket proclaimed the novel's enduring relevance as "A Lost Feminist Utopian Novel" that was "as on target today as when it was written sixty-five years ago." Like Degler and Hedges before her, Lane reinforced this in her introduction, where she highlighted Gilman's argument for women's "common humanity" with men. "A healthy social organism . . . requires the autonomy of women. That autonomy can be achieved only by women's collective action." Lane noted the inextricability for Gilman of writing and activism, effectively rendering *Herland* a call for "collective action" on the part of women and feminists in her own era. Such activism was still urgently needed; it was in 1979, for example, that the Equal Rights Amendment—written in Gilman's lifetime by Alice Paul and first introduced in Congress in 1923—failed to become part of the US Constitution because of an insufficient number of state ratifications (and remaining so to this day). "The crisis of gender inequality loomed large: . . . Gilman's utopia—in which self-sufficient women, free of patriarchal oppression, governed themselves—offered a liberating yet tantalizing fantasy, still far beyond the reach of readers."[15]

Just as Lane (through Gilman) issued this challenge to the staying power of patriarchy, so other feminist literary critics continued their activism in academia: in 1979 Sandra Gilbert and Susan Gubar published *The Madwoman in the Attic*, a study of female writers in the nineteenth century. Among this volume's many contributions was an early analysis of Gilman's work. "The Yellow Wall-Paper," the authors argued, serves as a meditation on female writers' "parallel confinements in texts, houses, and maternal female bodies." Introducing the 2000 reissue of their volume, Gilbert and Gubar aptly supply a framework for understanding both the imbrication of recovery with its sociopolitical context and the trajectory of second-wave recoveries in Gilman studies in particular. For feminists of the 1970s, they explain, "the personal was the political," and "the sexual was the textual."[16]

GILMAN UNCOVERED:
RECOVERING THE UNPUBLISHED WRITING

Although feminist activists and academics have followed varying and more nuanced paths since the second-wave era—Golden has astutely surveyed such developments in Gilman studies, so I will not rehash them here—critics' increasing attention to women's private and otherwise unpublished cultural production has certainly been fueled, at least in part, by the enduring idea that the personal is political. Of course, this scholarship has also established that such binary categories themselves force into a false dichotomy the shifting, complex nature of texts and self-representation, particularly for women, who have had limited and uneven access to conventional publication.

Focusing specifically on recovery work in early American studies, Theresa Strouth Gaul elucidates the forces driving scholars' ever-expanding recovery efforts. "Scholars working on women's writing have long understood that attending primarily to published artifacts like books excludes from view the majority of women writers, who did not have access to publication, produced their work in manuscript form, and wrote in genres traditionally considered to be private or appropriate for females." Although Gilman lived and worked in an era when women of her background could achieve publication with relative ease, Gaul's remarks are instructive for our understanding of both the constraints that remained on Gilman's voice and the ethos that surely contributed to the recovery of Gilman's so-called private writing.[17]

The majority of this private writing has now been published; predictably, this recovery seems to have been fueled by scholars' increasing interest in Gilman after her appearance on the scene as outlined above as well as by critics' commitment to historicizing their analyses and their recognition that private writing is worthy of analysis in its own right. The deep recovery of Gilman's unpublished work also indicates that the trajectory of her own life still resonates with feminists decades after her death. In 1988 Denise Knight began the process of recovering Gilman's diaries, which she published in a two-volume set in 1994; a single-volume abridged edition followed in 1998. Interest in recovering Gilman's correspondence began even earlier. In 1985, Juliet Langley published some letters by Gilman to her first love, Martha Luther, in *Trivia: A Journal of Ideas*, an important radical feminist journal founded in 1982. It is significant that Langley sought to document Gilman's relationship with Luther at that historical moment, when women were increasingly and publicly shaking off the compulsory heterosexuality of both mainstream culture and some segments of the early women's movement, as Adrienne Rich so eloquently argued in 1980. "Throughout her life," Langley writes, "Gilman struggled relentlessly to create a world in which women could live, love, and express themselves as fully as possible. Perhaps through these letters we will find the courage to realize, express, and live our own 'audacious fancies'"[18]

Like Langley, Mary Hill recognized the myriad ways Gilman's correspondence spoke to contemporary women. In 1995 she published *A Journey from Within*, a volume of Gilman's letters to her second husband, Houghton Gilman. This project had been in the works for many years, during which Hill admits her views of the letters evolved, a process that occurred alongside successive waves of feminist activism in American culture. The letters are complex, contradictory, and subtly crafted texts that illustrate Gilman's attempts to negotiate "almost every women's issue she publicly discussed."[19]

Among the most prominent of these issues is "work-family reconciliation," long a concern of women's and workers' rights advocates and one that was at the forefront of feminist discourse during the years in which Hill was working with Gilman's correspondence (as it still is today). Gilman's letters, like much of her other writing, document the anguish caused by her inability to balance personal and political, private and public, body and mind—her desires as lover, wife, and mother with those as intellectual, writer, and world worker. Although much of Gilman's work aimed to challenge the idea that such categories had to be separate or oppositional, her strategy, as Davis argues throughout her biography of Gilman, seems to have been to continually suppress the individual in favor of the public self, at great personal cost. This struggle, which so captivated Hill in her recovery of Gilman's letters, remains as relevant as ever: a half century after the advent of feminism's second wave, Stephanie Coontz has shown, "When family and work obligations collide, mothers remain much more likely than fathers to cut back or drop out of work. But unlike the situation in the 1960s, this is not because most people believe this is the preferable order of things. Rather, it is often a reasonable response to the fact that our political and economic institutions lag way behind our personal ideals." Coontz notes, "This is where the political gets really personal."[20]

Certainly, Gilman's attempts to make her personal ideals compatible with what she perceived as her public duties (and with the extremely limiting political and economic institutions of her day) are starkly evident in the more comprehensive volume *The Selected Letters of Charlotte Perkins Gilman*, which Denise Knight and I published in 2009. Recent developments in epistolary studies provided us with a framework for appreciating the "performative, fictive, and textual dimensions" of Gilman's letters, in which Gilman negotiated the tensions between aspiration and limitation.[21] Although our study of the letters (initiated in 1990) benefited from recent insights in the scholarship on recovery and epistolarity, however, it generally took shape in response to an early third-wave moment in which we sought to explore Gilman's "mixed legacy"— complicating the stories that scholars tell about her, we pointed out—as well as to address a range of issues that remain unresolved in our present moment.[22]

A case that exemplifies both of these impulses concerns the letter that Gilman wrote to her physician, the neurologist S. Weir Mitchell, in 1887, before she departed for Philadelphia to take his rest cure. This letter, long sought by Gilman scholars but recovered only in 2004, provides a trove of information about the uses to which Gilman put the epistolary form and reveals substantial biographical details. It also enriches our framework for interpreting Gilman's best-known work of published fiction, "The Yellow Wall-Paper," and speaks directly to some of the most nettlesome problems facing women's rights advocates in the twenty-first century.

Written in 1890 and published in 1892, "The Yellow Wall-Paper" is a haunting account of a woman apparently driven mad by Victorian gender norms and their enforcement in medical treatment for so-called hysterical women; in particular, the story, though not reproducing the full regimen of the rest cure, critiques its disregard for the patient's perspective and its silencing of women. Although it is a work of fiction, the story is informed by Gilman's autobiographical experience with an illness that plagued her off and on for her entire life and with the treatment for that illness that she received at Mitchell's hands. At issue—in the story and, I would argue, in Gilman's letter to Mitchell—is a crucial question that faced women of the late-nineteenth century, when traditional Victorian gender roles still held sway and when the medical profession was in its ascendance: Who had the right to speak about a woman's experience of illness? Put more generally: Who had the authority to pronounce meaning about women's bodies and health?[23] Gilman's relationship with Mitchell is widely discussed in the scholarship, as is the fact that Mitchell merited explicit (and unflattering) mention in "The Yellow Wall-Paper." Although the question of who might have been the true target of Gilman's critique in the story is beyond the scope of this chapter (and there could even be more than one target), the interpretive value of Gilman's letter to Mitchell is difficult to ignore.[24]

On April 19, 1887, preparing to leave her Providence, Rhode Island, home for Mitchell's Philadelphia sanitarium, Gilman wrote in her diary, "Snowed yesterday. Cold night. Wintry this morning. . . . Take baby to Mary's. . . . Come over home. . . . Begin to write an account of myself for the doctor." In her autobiography, Gilman claimed that before her visit to Mitchell she sent him "a long letter giving 'the history of the case' in a way a modern psychologist would have appreciated. Dr. Mitchell only thought it proved self-conceit." Mitchell was known for his authoritarian stance and his heavy-handed methods of mastering the patient's will. His assumption that women ought to defer to their physicians' authority was commonly cited: "Wise women choose their doctors and trust them. The wisest ask the fewest questions."[25]

The letter itself, however, eluded scholars for decades; some even considered it apocryphal until it was found to be residing quietly among Zona Gale's papers at the Wisconsin Historical Society. Discovered first by Davis and shortly thereafter by Knight, the sixteen-page letter opens with Gilman's professed desire "to make you acquainted with all the facts of the case, that you may form a deeper judgment than from mere casual examination" (see figure 9.2). Those "facts" include a detailed outline of her family tree and the health history of her parents and grandparents, followed by an even more thorough physical and "mental history" of herself. This letter reveals a great deal about who is authorized to tell the story of Gilman's illness and in what manner: one's sex and professional status determine this authority as well as the social and literary conventions that govern its articulation. Throughout the letter Gilman called attention to Mitchell's medical clout. "I understand," she told him confidently, "you are the first authority on nervous diseases. . . . There is something the matter with my head. No one here knows or believes or cares. . . . But you will know." She deferred to and depended on his status and knowledge as her physician.[26]

In contrast, Gilman presented *herself* in the letter as one beholden to him and in need of his expertise. "Excuse me if I write unnessary [*sic*] facts," she offered in the first paragraph, "it is through ignorance." She ended the letter by saying, "Forgive the length. I know it isn't what I should have written but I can't do better now. . . . I am all alone in the house or I couldn't write this. *People* tire me frightfully. I'm running down like a clock—could go one [*sic*] scribbling now indefinitely—but the letters don't come right." An apologetic Gilman openly confessed her intellectual weaknesses. She was an aspiring author—"an artist of sufficient merit to earn an easy living when well." Nonetheless, she acknowledged that the letter "isn't what I should have writ-

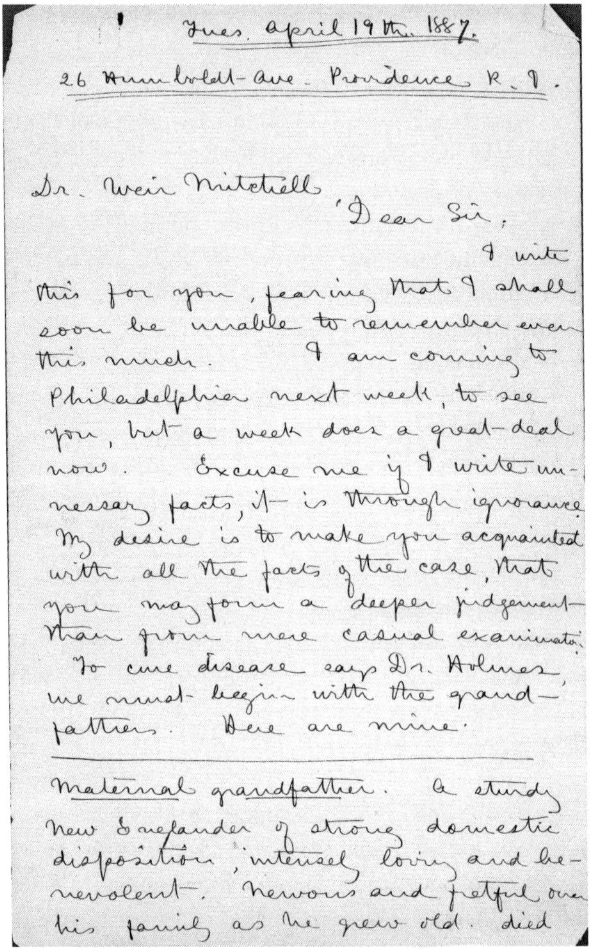
Tues. April 19th. 1887.
26 Humboldt Ave. Providence R. I.

Dr. Weir Mitchell
Dear Sir;
I write this for you, fearing that I shall soon be unable to remember even this much. I am coming to Philadelphia next week, to see you, but a week does a great deal now. Excuse me if I write unnessary facts, it is through ignorance. My desire is to make you acquainted with all the facts of the case, that you may form a deeper judgement than from mere casual examination. To cure disease says Dr. Holmes, we must begin with the grandfathers. Here are mine.

Maternal grandfather. A sturdy New Englander of strong domestic disposition, intensely loving and benevolent. Nervous and fretful over his family as he grew old. died

Figure 9.2. Charlotte Perkins Stetson [Gilman]'s letter to S. Weir Mitchell (Zona Gale Papers, Wisconsin Historical Society, Madison, WI, WHI-33389; used by permission)

ten," disparaging her words as "scribbling." At the end—the final line before her signature, which sounds a great deal like the narrator in "The Yellow Wall-Paper"—she revealed that she cannot even form the letters themselves.[27]

Yet even as she maligned her own account, Gilman asserted its authority and her entitlement to offer it. She indicated her familiarity with current medical theory. And she presumed to know what kinds of information Mitchell would need to collect in order to evaluate her case; she proposed to participate in the diagnostic process and implied that without her input Mitchell would conduct a "mere casual examination."[28] Gilman also seemed to be aware that she was not authorized to tell that story—hence the rhetorical manipulation positioning her as beholden to his expertise and higher status. If Mitchell did indeed dismiss her overture as "self-conceit," he was simply concurring with her on this point.

This letter, then, is centrally about the question of who has the authority to craft the narrative of Gilman's illness. Who was authorized to speak about the state of her body and her mind? Her letter to Mitchell not only bears witness to this struggle but also illuminates something important about the story that Gilman eventually published about her rest-cure experience. Although I generally concur with Knight's assertion that the letter does not "substantially change . . . our reading of Gilman," it does suggest to me that we might read her story "The Yellow Wall-Paper," written three years later, as another attempt at writing her case history.[29] Denied the right to write an account of her case in a medical context, she articulated it in fiction, which *was* seen as a legitimate venue for women in the 1890s and which allowed her the license to express herself through figurative means.

This dynamic has an explicit parallel in the story itself, in which the nervous narrator, being given something similar to a rest cure by her doctor-husband, is told that she should not write or think about her "condition," that he is the doctor and he knows all about it already. So instead, she says, "I will talk about the house." And what she does when talking about the house—something that as a woman she *would* have been authorized to speak about—is to describe, metaphorically, her imprisonment within a domestic role and to detail the progressive insanity it causes. Just as Gilman used the culturally acceptable medium of fiction to detail her "case," the narrator couches her own discussion of her condition in the nonthreatening language of domesticity.[30]

In her letter to Mitchell, Gilman highlighted her own position as the patient, but she also asserted the importance of the patient's knowledge of her own case and proposed the kind of cooperative doctor-patient relationship that is only today beginning to attain legitimacy in allopathic medicine.[31] This letter showcases her struggle to assert herself amid the constraints of the doctor-patient dynamic and Victorian gender ideology. It also lends weight to a reading of her best-known work of short fiction in which the story functions as a case history from the female patient's point of view. Whereas critics have long read the story itself as an indictment of the silencing and objectification of women who are denied bodily self-determination, the recently recovered letter to Mitchell illuminates an important dimension of "The Yellow Wall-Paper" and, even more significant, of Gilman's own biographical experience. The letter is evidence of her complex negotiation of medical discourse as well as her shrewd manipulation of rhetorical conventions (this time, of an epistolary nature) to accomplish her goals. It also invites us to consider the degree to which such power dynamics haunt the medical encounter or otherwise shape women's health issues in our own time.

Today the US medical profession, though not yet sufficiently integrated by sex (let alone other demographic factors such as race and socioeconomic background), is no longer such a bastion of male authority. According to the American Medical Women's Association, "the number of women choosing careers in medicine has grown substantially" in the last century, although "there has not been a commensurate increase in the percentage of women in senior leadership positions." Likewise, women now seek admission to medical schools in equal numbers with men, but women have not achieved parity in establishing practices subsequent to that education. In the medical encounter, too, there has been substantial but not sufficient change. Patient-centered decision making is gaining credibility. Susan Scherman has argued that we still need "a feminist ethics of health care" that "examines patient autonomy in [its] social and political dimensions" and identifies the gendered power relations that continue to shape female patients' conversations and relations with health-care professionals.[32]

In a recent study of women's health and public policy, Karen Baird celebrates the fact that women's health has now been recognized as a topic worthy of serious attention by policy makers: "by the late 1980s and early '90s," she observes, "calls for women's rights and equality were no longer considered to be the anthems of radical women['s] liberationists; they had become accepted, legitimate concerns that government needed to address and enforce when appropriate."[33]

If the doctor-patient dyad no longer necessarily functions, as it did so often in Gilman's time, to silence women and deny them self-determination, the same cannot be said for women's representation in the halls of the very government, celebrated by Baird, that sets health-care policy. Throughout the period in which Knight and I worked to recover and publish Gilman's selected letters, we suffered repeated reminders that women's bodily autonomy remains imperiled, despite substantial gains. The 1995 Beijing Declaration of the United Nations' Fourth World Conference on Women did include an "explicit recognition and reaffirmation" that women's right "to control all aspects of their health, in particular their own fertility, is basic to their empowerment"; this built on the earlier Convention on the Elimination of All Forms of Discrimination against Women (CEDAW), which since 1979 had required signatory states to "take all appropriate measures to eliminate discrimination against women in the field of health care in order to ensure, on a basis of equality of men and women, access to health care services, including those related to family planning."[34]

But the United States has (in)famously refused to join the 189 countries that, at the date of this writing, have signed on to CEDAW. In 1999 Senator Jesse Helms "bragged from the Senate floor" that he "did not intend to be pushed around by discourteous, demanding women" supporting the initiative, whom he'd previously described as "'radical feminists' with an 'antifamily agenda.'" It is significant that one reason for the opposition to CEDAW among American lawmakers is that it "might be used to encourage equal representation in Washington, where the US Congress and all executive agencies are exempt from affirmative action laws."[35]

Today, seven years since the *Selected Letters* were published, the issues raised by Gilman's letter to Mitchell remain as relevant as ever. Women still often lack a place at the table among the shapers of women's health policy, and their voices are still actively discredited and suppressed. A prominent example is the 2012 hearing of the House Committee on Oversight and Government Reform on the topic of insurance coverage for contraceptives. No women were among those impaneled by the committee to decide the issue, "prompting some women members of Congress to walk out of the hearing in protest." Senator Patty Murray of Washington state described the incident as "like stepping into a time machine and going back 50 years"; echoing Murray, Senator Jeanne Shaheen of New Hampshire noted that "here we are in 2012 and a House committee would hold a hearing on women's health and deny women the ability to share their perspective." California Senator Barbara Boxer's grandson said it best, on examining a photograph of the hearing: "It's all dudes."[36] This was, of course, the hearing at which Sandra Fluke was prevented from testifying; her protests made her the target of self-professed misogynist Rush Limbaugh, who called her a "slut" and a "prostitute" in an obvious attempt to further stifle her voice. "Because it happened in Congress," Fluke pronounced in her speech at the Democratic National Convention later that year, "people noticed. But it happens all the time. Many women are shut out and silenced" when their bodies and health are at issue.[37]

What makes Fluke's example so striking is its very typicality—it does, as she said, happen all the time. Despite the public outcry over the silencing of women both at this hearing and afterward over Limbaugh's airwaves, it has happened again and again. Witness the recent debate over Texas Senate Bill 5, an attempt by lawmakers to curtail women's constitutional right to terminate a pregnancy safely and legally. "The optics in the room were inescapable," noted Katha Pollitt. "Here was a bunch of prosperous and powerful and utterly confident middle-aged white men champing at the bit to tell women, mostly young and poor, many of color, many already with kids, what they could do with their bodies." Ironically, Senator Wendy Davis's eleven-hour filibuster of the bill indicated women's lack of a voice in the senate chamber, a fact expressed by other means when Senator Leticia Van de Putte, whose attempts to speak were repeatedly ignored, was forced to ask, "Mr. President, parliamentary inquiry. At what point must a female senator raise her hand or her voice to be recognized over the male colleagues in the room?"[38]

Parliamentary procedure such as that used in the Texas Senate is intended to maintain order and fairness, yet Davis and Van de Putte used sanctioned rhetorical acts, the filibuster and the parliamentary inquiry, precisely to highlight the lack of fairness in the government's handling of women's health issues. Indeed, they did so in part to protest women's silencing in the decision making on matters that directly affect them on the most visceral level. Unlike Gilman (and the narrator of "The Yellow Wall-Paper"), they had access to such rhetorical avenues and did not have to resort to "genres traditionally considered to be private or appropriate for females."[39]

Yet their assertive and public speech acts point to the same problem highlighted by the silencing of Sandra Fluke: women still must struggle for the right to speak about, let alone maintain full ownership of, their bodies. It is no wonder that Gilman's work persists as meaningful to feminists and that her private writing has caught and maintained their attention as well. Recovered documents like Gilman's letter to Mitchell speak to concerns in our own time, just as they illuminate the challenges that Gilman faced during her life. The very fact that women and feminists are still fighting these battles goes a long way to explaining why her life and work remain interesting to contemporary readers.

TRANSNATIONAL GILMAN: TRANSLATION AS RECOVERY

The 2010 Gilman conference in Rome documented "the continued relevance of Gilman's vision for contemporary feminisms"—both within and beyond the United States.[40] The increasing interest in Gilman abroad and the concomitant proliferation of translations of her work demand that scholars expand our definition of recovery to accommodate analysis of these texts as part of the phenomenon. Such analysis will also help to illuminate "the critical role of translation in the formation and transformation of feminist movements and politics" that is increasingly a concern of feminist translation studies.[41] Gilman's work has been translated into at least thirteen languages: Chinese, Danish, Dutch, Farsi, French, German, Hebrew, Italian, Japanese, Norwegian, Spanish, Swedish, and Turkish. Scholars around the world are making significant contributions to Gilman studies, some of them inherent in and some enabled by these translations. The focus of this final section is the recovery of Gilman's work in Italy, where feminists have been purposeful and explicit in employing this work to serve their needs in the present day.

In her own time, of course, Gilman likewise achieved an international audience: four of her nonfiction works were published in translation, along with several of her poems. *Women and Economics* had the farthest reach, appearing in Dutch, German, Hungarian, Italian, Japanese, Norwegian, Polish, and Russian; it was also excerpted in Danish. She boasted deservedly in her autobiography that her journal the *Forerunner* had readers "as far afield as India and Australia." Cynthia Davis notes, "On behalf of women's rights" Gilman "crossed the Atlantic several times" and "Nearly everywhere she traveled in Europe, she exulted in her international reputation and in the admiration of her fans." When Gilman served as an invited "speaker-at-large" at the International Council of Women Quinquennial in Berlin, the "turnout for her one talk at the conference was so large that she had to repeat it in a second hall for the overflow crowd."[42]

American suffragist Carrie Chapman Catt confirmed the transatlantic reach of Gilman's influence, crediting her work "with utterly revolutionizing the attitude of mind of the entire country, indeed of other countries, as to woman's place." Davis takes pains to point out, of course, that, while "Gilman devoted much of her life to theorizing about 'the world' and the service necessary on its behalf," a good portion of her international travel after the first decade of the twentieth century was undertaken "to offset her flagging national reputation." Similarly, although benefit to the world was a crucial aim of Gilman's philosophy of activism, as her tolerance for difference narrowed she became disenchanted with the world she had formerly idealized. During her final decades, "she swapped her always vaguely defined project of uplifting humanity via 'world service' for an investment in specifying the kinds of humans she considered worthy, or unworthy, of uplift." Her shrinking enthusiasm for the world beyond the United States certainly was evident in her account of a ten-day visit to Italy in 1904, for which, she archly reports, her daughter "had arranged an itinerary of appalling completeness."[43]

Italians of Gilman's time would have had access to one of her works in translation: *Women and Economics* appeared there in 1902, a mere "few years after its publication in the United States," Anna Scacchi points out. She notes that today, however, "Gilman is little known" in Italy.[44] Although there is no modern edition of *Women and Economics*, "The Yellow Wall-Paper" and *Herland* were important to Italian feminists in the second-wave era. It is illuminating to consider the social context of such recoveries. The first Italian translation of "The Yellow Wall-Paper," appearing in 1973, packaged the story as a horror tale; the second, however, came out in 1976 as one of the first titles published by the feminist press La Tartaruga, founded in 1975 by Laura Lepetit.[45]

As in the United States, in Italy this was a period of tumult over issues of women's bodily autonomy and their rights in marriage. To provide merely one example: La Tartaruga's edition was in production at the same time that Italians were in the process of overturning the Roman law of *patria potestas* (literally, "paternal power"); it had left Italian women "virtually without rights in their own homes, having no say in the upbringing of their children or where they live, and lacking rights to share family property." It also had required a woman to take her husband's surname and permitted a girl to marry as young as age fourteen—twelve, if she was pregnant. Laura Moschini points out that the "father's power" over the family remained the law of the land until 1975, when "sex equality in the family [was] sanctioned" by new legislation; of course, as Moschini also takes pains to confirm, the new laws assured "formal but not actual equality between sexes."[46]

It was in such a context that the first Italian translation of *Herland* was published in 1980, just a year after Ann Lane's American edition. It is not surprising that an all-women's utopia such as Gilman's would appear at that time, when women's reproductive and sexual rights were at the forefront of much public discourse. A 1976 protest march in Rome with fifty thousand participants called for abortion on demand; even though abortion was legalized shortly thereafter, it remains a source of conflict in Italy, particularly considering the influence wielded by the Vatican. In the same year, the case of Claudia Caputi provided a harsh reminder that women still lacked legal protection from sexual assault and other forms of violence: Caputi was gang-raped twice, the second time in retaliation for reporting the first; she was also slashed with razors in an attempt to silence her. Within hours of the second attack, fifteen thousand women mobilized to protest the law enforcement and legal corruption that both sanctioned this violence and further victimized Caputi. A commentator years later noted, "This was the first incarnation of Take Back the Night" in Italy.[47]

Moschini has noted that this second-wave period in Italy was characterized by "a great reflection on the emancipation of women" urged by feminist activists and academics; the difficulty lay then, as it lies now, in applying that theory and in enforcing the legislative advances that have been made. Although a few Gilman translations appeared during the 1970s and 1980s, in her review of this literature Scacchi points out that Gilman subsequently "was forgotten for more than two decades."[48] Aside from one appearance of "The Yellow Wall-Paper" in a 1989 anthology of horror stories, no new Italian translations of Gilman's work appeared until 2007, and most appeared later than that. Michela Marzano confirms that after the significant gains and consciousness-raising of the second-wave decades, there have been "more and more systematic attacks on the victories won by feminism. . . . Women are rescaled to remind them that their 'natural' place is next to a man. . . . Speech is reserved for men. Women should be content to be beautiful and silent."[49]

The recent resurgence of feminism in Italy is characterized by increasingly pointed critiques such as Marzano's, and the recovery of Gilman seems to be riding the crest of this wave. In the last five years a new rediscovery of Gilman has begun, and there is, as Michael Hill has observed, "a small but growing collection of translations" of her work into Italian.[50] Most notable are the three separate anthologies of Gilman's short fiction: one edited in 2008 by Marcella Romeo, another in 2010 by Ilaria Police, and finally, Scacchi's long-awaited 2011 collection, which includes both a detailed scholarly introduction and a translation of *Herland*.

One glaring absence is that there is no modern Italian edition of *Women and Economics*. Moschini has argued that such a translation is sorely needed: the allocation of financial resources "is not," she reminds us, "a neutral instrument . . . ; on the contrary, it reflects the distribution of power existing in society." She notes that "some Italian public administration offices are now beginning to implement gender budgeting"—financial reforms intended to allocate resources more equitably between men and women—"and that is the reason it is important that these administrators be supported by a *gender analysis* of the context in which they operate" and by Gilman's "innovative . . . economic theory."[51]

In other words, translating Gilman's work is valuable in part because it can raise public consciousness about enacting social change. In the absence of a translation that would bring Italians to Gilman's economic theory, Moschini has taken Gilman's economic theory to Italians—"stress[ing] the importance and topicality of . . . Gilman's ideas," for example, at the National Meeting on Gender Budgeting held in Rome in 2006. The administrations and municipalities that are enacting financial reforms "are well aware," Moschini notes, "of the work to be done[,] . . . of the difficulties to be faced before public politics can overcome gender inequalities: for this reason it is important that Charlotte Perkins Gilman's belief, and her proposals, be accessed, investigated, and implemented—even with a 100-year delay."[52]

Moschini's activism is one sign among many that the recovery and translation of Gilman's work is not merely an intellectual exercise. Although critics strive to be appropriately mindful of Gilman's many ideological liabilities, the building urgency among Italian feminist scholars to produce translations of her work suggests, Chloé Avril notes, that Gilman "still has the power to shake us out of complacency and certainty" about having achieved meaningful sexual equality and about the blind spots that remain within contemporary Western feminism. In her recent Gilman anthology, Scacchi explains that Gilman's aim was "to write with a purpose," and Gilman's work provides women with "models for change"; in making Gilman's writing accessible, the translators give readers new "narrative structures through which to imagine their lives."[53]

The recent Italian upsurge of interest in recovering Gilman is a hopeful sign; it accompanies the recent revival of feminism in general. In taking stock of the work that lies ahead for feminist activists and academics, Moschini considers "the Italian resistance to reconsidering the traditional idea of women and family," which she traces "back, as Charlotte Perkins Gilman asserted after having analysed the female condition and society in the Western world, to the fact that *family*, *home*, and *mother* are still considered sacred and inalterable institutions. This mentality constitutes *the* obstacle to the active participation of [Italian] women in productive and social political actions." Some other aspects of this problem are women's sexual objectification—Rubygate, the recent controversy concerning former Prime Minister Silvio Berlusconi's dealings with an underage prostitute, is only the tip of the proverbial iceberg—and violence against women, which remains deeply intractable in Italian culture.[54] But while the Italians have Berlusconi, they also have the formidable prosecutor Ilda Boccassini, who presided over Berlusconi's sex charges. The Sciarpa Bianca (White Scarf) marches in 2011 protested the objectification of women, and the participants described themselves (possibly in reference to the then-popular American-imported TV show *Desperate Housewives*) as "neither desperate, nor housewives." One of the protesters affirmed, in fact, the frequently repeated fact that Berlusconi "reinvigorated the women's movement."[55] It is particularly telling that Scacchi's publisher chose a senator, Vittoria Franco, to write the preface to Scacchi's new Italian edition of *Herland* and Gilman's short fiction. Franco, like Gilman, is a feminist philosopher and longtime activist for social justice. Reviewer Bruna Bianchi confirms of Scacchi's volume, "The importance of these writings . . . lies not so much in their content, . . . but in the very act of imagining, in the ability to look beyond the present." Rediscovering Gilman's work during these troubled times, she predicts, will lead readers "to rediscover the creative impulse of feminism."[56]

Although an appropriately theorized analysis of the Gilman translations themselves is beyond the scope of this project, this work will be necessary if we are to understand how, when, and where these translations have appeared and how they function *as* translations within the larger field of Gilman studies. Sujit Mukherjee's book *Translation as Discovery* "demonstrate[s] how the act of making a translation or even the process of reading one [can] become a moment of revelatory literary discovery." Feminist translation theory suggests that such acts of translation are neither objective nor neutral, shaped, as Michael Cronin puts it, more by "ideology" than by "linguistics or aesthetics." And Olga Castro points out that translators have a "double (con)textual responsibility," with duties toward both the original source and the "(con)texts" in which the translation will be read.[57] In making Gilman's works available to a global audience, translators, engaging with and shaped by such contexts, facilitate recovery not only by bringing more people into the conversation but also by decentering North American perspectives in Gilman scholarship.

Translations of Gilman's work are therefore an important part of the recovery that has fueled the field since the second-wave era of feminism. Although a good deal remains to be done to bring the great variety of her output to the awareness of contemporary readers, there now exists a significant body of recovered work, representing her published and unpublished writing, appearing in a variety of languages, and appealing to a diverse readership. The more scholars learn about Gilman, and the more they discover about just how mixed her legacy is, the more complex their relationship with her becomes. Historicizing recovery in Gilman studies—*placing* recovery in its myriad contexts—helps to illuminate that relationship as well as to shed light on why the demand for such recovery remains as strong as ever.

After all, when Hillary Clinton proclaimed in her 1995 address to the Fourth World Conference on Women that "women's rights are human rights," what so electrified audiences around the world was the very fact that it was still necessary to assert such a thing. More than a decade later, in 2009, Italian political scientist Sofia Ventura used what was by then familiar language to counter the proposed candidacy of television showgirls in European parliamentary elections, asserting (in words quite reminiscent of Gilman's), "Women are not playthings to be used as decoys, nor are they fragile creatures in need of protection and nurturing by generous, paternal overlords; women are, quite simply, people."[58] Gilman's writings spoke to such issues in her day, just as they continue to do in ours; her work reveals a great deal about her biography and the time in which she lived, but what we do with it also tells us about ourselves.

ACKNOWLEDGMENTS

I am grateful to Jennifer Lunden, Laura Moschini, and Anna Scacchi for their generous comments on earlier versions of this essay. For producing the illustrations I thank the Wisconsin Historical Society and Hollis Haywood at the University of New England. I also thank the Wisconsin Historical Society and Donzelli Press for granting me permission to use the images.

NOTES

1. Portions of this essay originated in that keynote address: Jennifer S. Tuttle, "'Scrappy, Imperfect, Desperately Earnest': Recovering the Work of Charlotte Perkins Gilman," paper presented at the "Women and Polis: Charlotte Perkins Gilman Today" conference, Rome, October 22, 2010. I thank Cristina Giorcelli,

Laura Moschini, and Anna Scacchi for inviting me and inspiring my thinking on the project.

2. Elaine Showalter, ed., "Introduction: The Feminist Critical Revolution," in *The New Feminist Criticism: Essays on Women, Literature and Theory* (New York: Pantheon, 1985), 3; Catherine J. Golden, "Looking Backward: Rereading Gilman in the Early Twenty-First Century," in *Charlotte Perkins Gilman: New Texts, New Contexts*, ed. Jennifer S. Tuttle and Carol Farley Kessler (Columbus: Ohio State University Press, 2011), 46, 50.

3. Charlotte Perkins Gilman, *The Selected Letters of Charlotte Perkins Gilman*, ed. Denise D. Knight and Jennifer S. Tuttle (Tuscaloosa: University of Alabama Press, 2009), 293.

4. Charlotte Perkins Gilman, *Women and Economics: A Study of the Economic Relation between Men and Women as a Factor in Social Evolution* (1898; repr., New York: Prometheus Books, 1994), 49.

5. Sylvia Poggoli, "Italian Women Assail Berlusconi for Sexist Remarks," NPR, October 28, 2009, http://m.npr.org/story/114242303; Chiara Saraceno, "Affront to Rosy Bindi Exposes the 'Philosophy of the Exploiter,'" trans. Wendell Ricketts, *Una Vita Vagabonda*, February 3, 2010, http://unavitavagabonda.wordpress.com/?s=bindi.

6. For a more detailed discussion of this recovery work, see Jennifer S. Tuttle and Carol Farley Kessler, eds., "Introduction," in *Charlotte Perkins Gilman: New Texts, New Contexts* (Columbus: Ohio State University Press, 2011), 2–4. Much of the material in this section of the chapter appeared previously in this source, and I thank the Ohio State University Press for allowing me to build upon it here.

7. This is in no way meant to diminish the importance of the story's inclusion the previous year in Gail Thain Parker's historical anthology *The Oven Birds: American Women on Womanhood, 1820–1920*, which traced a genealogy of American feminism. The Feminist Press edition of the story, however, packaged as a single-text reprint with Elaine Hedges's afterword and marketed to the scholarly and pedagogical arm of the women's movement, obtained a higher profile. The story had, in fact, remained in print throughout the twentieth century, but many of the anthologies in which it appeared framed it as a horror story. Ann Lane has argued that the second wave of the women's movement provided an audience that was prepared to appreciate what the Feminist Press edition offered. Ann Lane, ed., *The Charlotte Perkins Gilman Reader*, 2nd ed. (Charlottesville: University Press of Virginia, 1999), x.

8. Cynthia J. Davis, *Charlotte Perkins Gilman: A Biography* (Stanford, CA: Stanford University Press, 2010), xii, 345.

9. Michael Kimmel and Amy Aronson, "Introduction," in *Women and Economics: A Study of the Economic Relation between Men and Women as a Factor in Social Evolution*, by Charlotte Perkins Gilman (1898; repr., Berkeley: University of

California Press, 1998), vii, viii. This introduction discusses the dynamic relation-ship between the reissues of *Women and Economics* and the historical moments in which they have appeared. See also Jennifer S. Tuttle, "Women and Econom-ics," in *American History through Literature, 1870–1920*, ed. Tom Quirk and Gary Scharnhorst (Detroit, MI: Scribner's, 2006): 3:1203–7.

10. Davis, *Biography*, 228.

11. In 2010 the National Organization for Women reported, "For full-time, year-round workers, women are paid on average only 78 percent of what men are paid. . . . These wage gaps stubbornly remain despite the passage of the Equal Pay Act in 1963 and a variety of legislation prohibiting employment discrimina-tion." National Organization for Women, "Women Deserve Equal Pay," http://www.now.org/issues/economic/factsheet.html.

12. Carl N. Degler, ed., "Introduction," in *Women and Economics: A Study of the Economic Relation between Men and Women as a Factor in Social Evolution*, by Charlotte Perkins Gilman (1898; repr., New York: Harper, 1966), vii–viii.

13. The Feminist Press confirms the explicit link between recovery and ac-tivism, reminding us that publishers have always partnered with scholars in such efforts: "we began," the staff of the press explain, "as a crucial publishing compo-nent of second wave feminism, reprinting feminist classics by writers such as Zora Neale Hurston and Charlotte Perkins Gilman, and providing much-needed texts for the developing field of women's studies." Feminist Press, "About FP," http://www.feministpress.org/about-fp.

14. Elaine R. Hedges, "Afterword," in *The Yellow Wall-Paper*, by Charlotte Per-kins Gilman, 1892 (New York: Feminist Press, 1996), 37, 39; Elaine R. Hedges, "'Out at Last'?: 'The Yellow Wallpaper' after Two Decades of Feminist Criticism," in *The Captive Imagination: A Casebook on The Yellow Wallpaper*, ed. Catherine J. Golden (New York: Feminist Press, 1992), 327–28.

15. Ann J. Lane, "Introduction," in *Herland*, by Charlotte Perkins Gilman (1915; repr., New York: Pantheon, 1979), xi; Tuttle and Kessler, "Introduction," 15–16. According to Davis, *Biography*, 474n67, Gilman in fact opposed the Equal Rights Amendment.

16. Sandra M. Gilbert and Susan Gubar, *The Madwoman in the Attic: The Woman Writer and the Nineteenth-Century Literary Imagination*, 2nd ed. (New Haven, CT: Yale University Press, 2000), xlii, 89.

17. Theresa Strouth Gaul, "Recovering Recovery: Early American Women and *Legacy*'s Future," *Legacy: A Journal of American Women Writers* 26, no. 2 (2009): 265. Gilman also produced a large quantity of public, unpublished work, her lec-tures most prominent among them; these have yet to find their way into print. In addition, it is important to mention her detective novel, *Unpunished*, composed in 1929, which she tried and failed to publish during her lifetime. The 1997 recov-ered edition of this work notes the continued relevance of the novel's indictment

of intimate partner violence. Catherine J. Golden and Denise D. Knight, "Afterword," in *Unpunished: A Novel*, by Charlotte Perkins Gilman (New York: Feminist Press, 1997), 222–23. Six years earlier the novel was recognized as still compelling: as in the post–Nineteenth Amendment era in which it was composed, in the early 1990s, "we are being told that women's struggle is over" and "existing gains are being threatened." Lillian S. Robinson, "Killing Patriarchy: Charlotte Perkins Gilman, the Murder Mystery, and Post-Feminist Propaganda," *Tulsa Studies in Women's Literature* 10, no. 2 (1991): 283.

18. Adrienne Rich, "Compulsory Heterosexuality and Lesbian Existence," *Signs* 5, no. 4 (Summer 1980): 631–60; Juliette A. Langley, "Audacious Fancies: A Collection of Letters from Charlotte Perkins Gilman to Martha Luther," *Trivia: A Journal of Ideas* 6 (Winter 1985): 68–69.

19. Mary A. Hill, ed., "Introduction," in *A Journey from Within: The Love Letters of Charlotte Perkins Gilman, 1897–1900* (Lewisburg, PA: Bucknell University Press, 1995), 17, 28. In her 1980 Gilman biography, Hill remarked on her plans to publish further on Gilman's correspondence. Mary A. Hill, *Charlotte Perkins Gilman: The Making of a Radical Feminist, 1860–1896* (Philadelphia, PA: Temple University Press, 1980), ix.

20. Ariane Hegewisch and Janet Gornick, *Statutory Routes to Workplace Flexibility in Cross-National Perspective* (Washington, DC: Institute for Women's Policy Research, 2008), viii; Stephanie Coontz, "Why Gender Equality Stalled," *New York Times*, February 16, 2013. http://www.nytimes.com/2013/02/17/opinion/sunday/why-gender-equality-stalled.html?pagewanted=1&_r=1&hp&.

21. William Merrill Decker, *Epistolary Practices: Letter Writing in America before Telecommunications* (Chapel Hill: University of North Carolina Press, 1998), 4.

22. Catherine J. Golden and Joanna Schneider Zangrando, eds., "Introduction," in *The Mixed Legacy of Charlotte Perkins Gilman*, (Newark: University of Delaware Press, 2000), 12; Denise Knight and Jennifer S. Tuttle, eds., "Introduction," In *The Selected Letters of Charlotte Perkins Gilman* (Tuscaloosa: University of Alabama Press, 2009), xxii.

23. The scholarship on Gilman's engagement with medical discourse in "The Yellow Wall-Paper" is vast. In addition to the work of Elaine Hedges cited above, some foundational studies are Catherine J. Golden, "'Overwriting' the Rest Cure: Charlotte Perkins Gilman's Literary Escape from S. Weir Mitchell's Fictionalization of Women," in *Critical Essays on Charlotte Perkins Gilman*, ed. Joanne B. Karpinski (New York: G. K. Hall, 1992), 144–58; Suzanne Poirier, "The Weir Mitchell Rest Cure: Doctor and Patients," *Women's Studies* 10, no. 1 (1983): 15–40; Paula Treichler, "Escaping the Sentence: Diagnosis and Discourse in 'The Yellow Wallpaper,'" *Tulsa Studies in Women's Literature* 3, no. 1–2 (1984): 61–77; and Ann Douglas Wood, "'The Fashionable Diseases': Women's Complaints and Their Treatment in Nineteenth-Century America," *Journal of Interdisciplinary History* 4, no. 1 (1973): 25–52. No-

table recent work on the topic includes Cynthia J. Davis, *Bodily and Narrative Forms: The Influence of Medicine on American Literature, 1845–1915* (Stanford, CA: Stanford University Press, 2000), 122–53; Helen Lefkowitz Horowitz, *Wild Unrest: Charlotte Perkins Gilman and the Making of "The Yellow Wall-Paper"* (New York: Oxford University Press, 2010); Denise D. Knight, "'All the Facts of the Case': Gilman's Lost Letter to Dr. S. Weir Mitchell," *American Literary Realism* 37, no. 3 (2005): 259–77; Denise Knight, "'I Am Getting Angry Enough to Do Something Desperate': The Question of Female 'Madness,'" in *"The Yellow Wall-Paper" by Charlotte Perkins Gilman: A Dual-Text Critical Edition*, ed. Shawn St. Jean (Athens: Ohio University Press, 2006), 73–87; and Jane F. Thrailkill, "Doctoring 'The Yellow Wallpaper,'" *English Literary History* 69, no. 2 (Summer 2002): 525–66. All these works inform my own thinking here.

24. Although the story seems most overtly to criticize Mitchell, it might have actually been an attack on Gilman's first husband, Charles Walter Stetson. Denise D. Knight, "'Only a Husband's Opinion': Walter Stetson's View of Gilman's 'The Yellow Wall-Paper'; An Inscription," *American Literary Realism* 36, no. 1 (2003): 86–87.

25. Charlotte Perkins Gilman, *The Diaries of Charlotte Perkins Gilman*, ed Denise D. Knight (Charlottesville: University of Virginia Press, 1994), 1:385; Charlotte Perkins Gilman, *The Living of Charlotte Perkins Gilman: An Autobiography* (1935; repr., Madison: University of Wisconsin Press, 1990), 95; S. Weir Mitchell, *Doctor and Patient* (Philadelphia, PA: Lippincott, 1888), 48.

26. Gilman, *Selected Letters*, 45, 47, 49–50.

27. Ibid., 45, 49, 50.

28. Knight asserts that Gilman "proposes to aid S. Weir Mitchell in making a diagnosis." Knight's rhetorical analysis of the letter indicates that in it Gilman was "attempting to reclaim her identity, to advance an agenda, and to illustrate her self-worth." Knight, "All the Facts of the Case," 264, 268.

29. Ibid., 271.

30. Charlotte Perkins Gilman, *The Yellow Wall-Paper*, ed. Elaine R. Hedges (1892; repr., New York: Feminist Press, 1996), 11. There is still a clear need for further feminist scholarship on such sexuo-textual power dynamics when even the most welcome and legitimate of calls for greater historical precision in accounts of Mitchell's rest cure can effectively reinscribe Mitchell as the sole authority in the encounter. Gilman used the language (and the license) of fiction to comment on her experience of illness, but this "literary representation" of the treatment remains suspect because it is an inaccurate portrayal of the "highly orchestrated regimen established by Mitchell." Michael Blackie, "Reading the Rest Cure," *Arizona Quarterly* 60, no. 2 (Summer 2004): 79.

31. For an excellent discussion of Gilman's engagement with medical discourse beyond "The Yellow Wall-Paper," see Martha J. Cutter, "The Writer as Doctor:

New Models of Medical Discourse in Charlotte Perkins Gilman's Later Fiction," *Literature and Medicine* 20, no. 2 (2001): 151–82.

32. American Medical Women's Association, "AMWA's History of Success," http://www.amwa-doc.org/about-amwa/history; Molly Carnes, Claudia Morrissey, and Stacie E. Geller, "Women's Health and Women's Leadership in Academic Medicine: Hitting the Same Glass Ceiling?" *Journal of Women's Health* 17, no. 9 (2008): 1454, http://www.ncbi.nlm.nih.gov/pmc/articles/PMC2586600/; Susan Scherman, with Voices from the Network, "Introduction," in *The Politics of Women's Health: Exploring Agency and Autonomy*, ed. Susan Scherman and the Feminist Health Care Ethics Research Network (Philadelphia, PA: Temple University Press, 1998), 13; Susan Scherman, "A Relational Approach to Autonomy in Health Care," in *The Politics of Women's Health: Exploring Agency and Autonomy*, ed. Susan Scherman and the Feminist Health Care Ethics Research Network (Philadelphia, PA: Temple University Press, 1998), 44.

33. Karen L. Baird, *Beyond Reproduction: Women's Health, Activism, and Public Policy* (Cranbury, NJ: Associated University Presses, 2009), 26.

34. United Nations, "Beijing Declaration and Platform for Action," Fourth World Conference on Women, Beijing, September 4–15, 1995, http://www.un.org/womenwatch/daw/beijing/pdf/BDPfA%20E.pdf; United Nations, "Convention on the Elimination of All Forms of Discrimination against Women," http://www.un.org/womenwatch/daw/cedaw/text/econvention.htm#intro.

35. Lisa Baldez, "U.S. Drops the Ball on Women's Rights," CNN Opinion, March 8, 2013, http://www.cnn.com/2013/03/08/opinion/baldez-womens-equality-treaty; Ellen Chesler, "Introduction," in *Where Human Rights Begin: Health, Sexuality, and Women in the New Millennium*, ed. Wendy Chavkin and Ellen Chesler (New Brunswick, NJ: Rutgers University Press, 2005), 14, 15.

36. Sunlen Miller, "Birth-Control Hearing Was 'Like Stepping into a Time Machine,'" ABC News, February 17, 2012, http://abcnews.go.com/blogs/politics/2012/02/birth-control-hearing-was-like-stepping-into-a-time-machine/.

37. Sandra Fluke, "Sandra Fluke's Speech: Full Text from the Democratic National Convention," *National Journal*, September 5, 2012, http://www.nationaljournal.com/conventions-speeches/sandra-fluke-s-speech-full-text-from-the-democratic-national-convention-20120905.

38. Katha Pollitt, "Wendy Davis, Superhero," *Nation*, June 26, 2013, http://www.thenation.com/blogs/katha-pollitt#; Leticia Van de Putte, "Leticia Van de Putte Asks What Women Need to Do to Be Heard in the Texas Legislature," YouTube, June 25, 2013, http://www.youtube.com/watch?v=yPntuZ7jmGY. Although Davis's filibuster succeeded in blocking the passage of Senate Bill 5, the nearly identical House Bill 2 was signed into law soon afterward. A Supreme Court challenge to some provisions of this law, *Whole Woman's Health v. Hellerstedt*, is cur-

rently underway. There, at least, women have a place at the table, and there, too, they refuse to be silenced. The March 2, 2016, discussion of the case was notable in this respect: "There was something wonderful and symbolic," writes Dahlia Lithwick, "about [Chief Justice John] Roberts losing almost complete control over the court's indignant women, who are just not inclined to play nice anymore." Dahlia Lithwick, *Slate*, March 2016.

39. Gaul, "Recovering Recovery," 265.

40. Cristina Giorcelli, Laura Moschini, and Anna Scacchi, "Donne e polis: Charlotte Perkins Gilman oggi," prospectus of the "Women and Polis: Charlotte Perkins Gilman Today" conference, Rome, October 22–23, 2010.

41. Olga Castro and Emek Ergun. "CFP: Feminist Translation Studies." WMST-L, July 18, 2013.

42. Gilman, *Living*, 305; Cynthia J. Davis, "Abroad Yet Narrow: Charlotte Perkins Gilman's Transatlantic World," paper presented at the Transatlantic Women II Conference, Florence, Italy, June 6–9, 2013; Davis, *Biography*, 276.

43. Davis, *Biography*, 368–69; Davis, "Abroad Yet Narrow"; Gilman, *Living*, 299.

44. Anna Scacchi, ed., "Una donna vittoriana a Utopia," in *La terra delle donne: Herland e altri racconti* (Rome: Donzelli, 2011), xxvii. The quotations in the original Italian are *a pochi anni dalla pubblicazione negli Stati Uniti* and *Gilman e poco nota in Italia*.

45. Charlotte Perkins Gilman, *La carta gialla*, ed. and trans. Bibi Tomasi and Laura McMurphy (Milan: La Tartaruga, 1976). The first edition was *Le signore dell'orrore* [Ladies of Horror], ed. Seon Manley and Gogo Lewis, trans. Lisa Morpurgo (Milan: Loganesi, 1973).

46. Correspondent in Rome, "New Family Law Gives Italian Wives Equality," *Sydney Morning Herald*, May 1, 1975, http://news.google.com/newspapers?nid=1301&dat=19750501&id=NvpjAAAAIBAJ&sjid=YeYDAAAAIBAJ&pg=3024,78125; Laura Moschini, "The Economic Proposals of Charlotte Perkins Gilman and Gender Budgeting in Italy," *International Review of Sociology* 19, no. 3 (2009): 434.

47. "Take Back the Night, Brooklyn, 2010," Rad-Sauce, December 29, 2012, http://ninjabikeslut.tumblr.com/post/39187523125/in-1976-claudia-caputi-a-17-year-old-woman-was.

48. Moschini, "Economic Proposals," 434; Scacchi, "Una donna," xviii. The original Italian is *ma poi Gilman e stata dimenticata per piu di due decenni*.

49. Michela Marzano, "The Humiliation of Women: The Situation in Italy," *TransEuropa* 9 (May 10, 2010): 18. According to studies cited in 2013 by Rashida Manjoo, the United Nations reporter on violence against women, "53 percent of women appearing on television in Italy didn't speak, while 46 percent of them 'were associated with issues such as sex, fashion, and beauty, and only 2 percent

issues of social commitment and professionalism.'" Nicole Winfield, "Italy Tries to Reduce Violence against Women," *Yahoo News*, May 2, 2013, http://news.yahoo .com/italy-tries-reduce-violence-against-women-113833126.html.

50. Michael R. Hill, ed., "Introduction: Charlotte Perkins Gilman on the Sociology of Families, Marriages, and Children," in *Families, Marriages, and Children* (New Brunswick, NJ: Transaction, 2011), xi.

51. Moschini, "Economic Proposals," 437, 443.

52. Ibid., 435, 443.

53. Chloé Avril, *The Feminist Utopian Novels of Charlotte Perkins Gilman: Themes of Sexuality, Marriage, and Motherhood* (Lewiston, NY: Edwin Mellen, 2008), 34; Scacchi, "Una donna," xxxi. The original Italian phrases are *scrivere con uno scopo, modelli per cambiare*, and *che offra alle lettrici strutture narrative diverse sulle quali immaginare le proprie vite.*

54. Moschini, "Economic Proposals," 436. In May 2013, "Italy's lower chamber of parliament ratified a European anti-domestic violence convention on the same day that the latest victim was buried: a 15-year-old girl beaten, stabbed 20 times, and burned alive, allegedly by her boyfriend." Winfield, "Italy Tries to Reduce." However, "politicians were criticized for not taking the issue more seriously after only a handful turned up to debate about the treaty"—the chamber was "nearly empty." Naomi O'Leary, "Brutal Murder of Teenager Overshadows Italy['s] Women's Rights Vote," *Reuters*, May 28, 2013, http://uk.reuters.com/article/2013/05/28/ uk-italy-women-idUKBRE94R0TW20130528.

55. Ben Marshall, "The Rise of Women in Italy," *Stylist*, http://www.stylist .co.uk/life/the-rise-of-women-in-italy#image-rotator-1.

56. Franco is the author of *Care Ragazze: Un Promemoria* [Dear Girls: A Reminder] (Rome: Donzelli, 2010), in which she reminds younger generations of women about what progress has been made but also what remains to be done. Bruna Bianchi, Review of *La terra delle donne: Herland e altri racconti, (1891– 1916)*, ed. and trans. Anna Scacchi *Deportate, esuli, profughe* 20 (July 2012), 222. The original Italian is *L'importanza di queste scritture . . . non risiede tanto nel loro contenuto, . . . ma nell'atto stesso dell'immaginare, nella capacità di guardare oltre il presente* and *a riscoprire l'impulso progettuale del femminismo.*

57. Harish Trivedi, "Introduction," in *Translation as Recovery*, by Sujit Mukherjee (Delhi: Pencraft, 2009), 11; Olga Castro, "(Re-)Examining Horizons in Feminist Translation Studies: Towards a Third Wave?," trans. Mark Andrews, *MonTI* 1 (2009): trans; Michael Cronin, "Ideology and Translation," in *Encyclopedia of Literary Translation into English*, ed. Olive Classe (London: Fitzroy Dearborn, 2000), 695; Olga Castro, "Talking at Cross-Purposes?: The Missing Link between Feminist Linguistics and Translation Studies," *Gender and Language* 7, no. 1 (2013): 35.

58. Patrick E. Tyler, "Hillary Clinton, in China, Details Abuse of Women,"

New York Times, September 6, 1995, http://www.nytimes.com/1995/09/06/world/
hillary-clinton-in-china-details-abuse-of-women.html; Marzano, "Humiliation of
Women," 18.

WORKS CITED

American Medical Women's Association. "AMWA's History of Success." http://
    www.amwa-doc.org/about-amwa/history.
Avril, Chloé. *The Feminist Utopian Novels of Charlotte Perkins Gilman: Themes
    of Sexuality, Marriage, and Motherhood*. Lewiston, NY: Edwin Mellen, 2008.
Baird, Karen L. *Beyond Reproduction: Women's Health, Activism, and Public Policy*.
    Cranbury, NJ: Associated University Presses, 2009.
Baldez, Lisa. "U.S. Drops the Ball on Women's Rights." CNN Opinion, March 8,
    2013. http://www.cnn.com/2013/03/08/opinion/baldez-womens-equality-treaty.
Bianchi, Bruna. Review of *La terra delle donne: Herland e altri racconti (1891–
    1916)*, edited and translated by Anna Scacchi. *Deportate, esuli, profughe* 20
    (July 2012): 219–22.
Blackie, Michael. "Reading the Rest Cure." *Arizona Quarterly* 60, no. 2 (Sum-
    mer 2004): 57–85.
Carnes, Molly, Claudia Morrissey, and Stacie E. Geller. "Women's Health and
    Women's Leadership in Academic Medicine: Hitting the Same Glass Ceiling?"
    Journal of Women's Health 17, no. 9 (2008): 1453–62. http://www.ncbi.nlm.nih
    .gov/pmc/articles/PMC2586600/.
Castro, Olga. "(Re-)Examining Horizons in Feminist Translation Studies: Towards
    a Third Wave?" Translated by Mark Andrews. *MonTI* [Monographs in Trans-
    lation and Interpreting] 1 (2009): 1trans–17trans.
———. "Talking at Cross-Purposes?: The Missing Link between Feminist Lin-
    guistics and Translation Studies." *Gender and Language* 7, no. 1 (2013): 35–58.
Castro, Olga, and Emek Ergun. "CFP: Feminist Translation Studies." WMST-L
    [Women's Studies Listserv], July 18, 2013.
Chesler, Ellen. "Introduction." In *Where Human Rights Begin: Health, Sexuality,
    and Women in the New Millennium*, edited by Wendy Chavkin and Ellen Ches-
    ler, 1–34. New Brunswick, NJ: Rutgers University Press, 2005.
Coontz, Stephanie. "Why Gender Equality Stalled." *New York Times*, February 16,
    2013. http://www.nytimes.com/2013/02/17/opinion/sunday/why-gender-equality
    -stalled.html?pagewanted=1&_r=1&hp&.
Correspondent in Rome. "New Family Law Gives Italian Wives Equality." *Sydney
    Morning Herald*, May 1, 1975. http://news.google.com/newspapers?nid=1301
    &dat=19750501&id=NvpjAAAAIBAJ&sjid=YeYDAAAAIBAJ&pg=3024,78125.
Cronin, Michael. "Ideology and Translation." In *Encyclopedia of Literary Trans-*

lation into English, edited by Olive Classe, 694–96. London: Fitzroy Dearborn, 2000.

Cutter, Martha J. "The Writer as Doctor: New Models of Medical Discourse in Charlotte Perkins Gilman's Later Fiction." *Literature and Medicine* 20, no. 2 (2001): 151–82.

Davis, Cynthia J. "Abroad Yet Narrow: Charlotte Perkins Gilman's Transatlantic World." Paper presented at the Transatlantic Women II Conference, Florence, Italy, June 6–9, 2013.

———. *Bodily and Narrative Forms: The Influence of Medicine on American Literature, 1845–1915*. Stanford: Stanford University Press, 2000.

———. *Charlotte Perkins Gilman: A Biography*. Stanford, CA: Stanford University Press, 2010.

Decker, William Merrill. *Epistolary Practices: Letter Writing in America before Telecommunications*. Chapel Hill: University of North Carolina Press, 1998.

Degler, Carl N., ed. "Introduction." In *Women and Economics: A Study of the Economic Relation between Men and Women as a Factor in Social Evolution*, by Charlotte Perkins Gilman, 1898, vi–xxxv. New York: Harper, 1966.

Feminist Press. "About FP." http://www.feministpress.org/about-fp.

———. "About FP: History." http://www.feministpress.org/about-fp/history.

Fluke, Sandra. "Sandra Fluke's Speech: Full Text from the Democratic National Convention." *National Journal*, September 5, 2012. http://www.nationaljournal .com/conventions-speeches/sandra-fluke-s-speech-full-text-from-the-democratic -national-convention-20120905.

Gaul, Theresa Strouth. "Recovering Recovery: Early American Women and *Legacy*'s Future." *Legacy: A Journal of American Women Writers* 26, no. 2 (2009): 262–83.

Gilbert, Sandra M., and Susan Gubar. *The Madwoman in the Attic: The Woman Writer and the Nineteenth-Century Literary Imagination*. 2nd ed. New Haven, CT: Yale University Press, 2000.

Gilman, Charlotte Perkins. *The Diaries of Charlotte Perkins Gilman*. 2 vols. Edited by Denise D. Knight. Charlottesville: University of Virginia Press, 1994.

———. *Herland*. 1915. Edited by Ann J. Lane. New York: Pantheon, 1979.

———. *La carta gialla*. Edited and translated by Bibi Tomasi and Laura McMurphy. Milan: La Tartaruga, 1976.

———. *La terra delle donne: Herland e altri racconti (1891–1916)*. Edited and translated by Anna Scacchi. Rome: Donzelli, 2011.

———. *The Living of Charlotte Perkins Gilman: An Autobiography*. 1935. Madison: University of Wisconsin Press, 1990.

———. *The Selected Letters of Charlotte Perkins Gilman*. Edited by Denise D. Knight and Jennifer S. Tuttle. Tuscaloosa: University of Alabama Press, 2009.

———. *Women and Economics: A Study of the Economic Relation between Men and Women as a Factor in Social Evolution*. 1898. New York: Prometheus Books, 1994.

———. *The Yellow Wall-Paper*. 1892. Edited by Elaine R. Hedges. New York: Feminist Press, 1996.

Giorcelli, Cristina, Laura Moschini, and Anna Scacchi. "Donne e polis: Charlotte Perkins Gilman oggi." Prospectus of the "Women and Polis: Charlotte Perkins Gilman Today" conference, Rome, October 22–23, 2010.

Golden, Catherine J. "Looking Backward: Rereading Gilman in the Early Twenty-First Century." In *Charlotte Perkins Gilman: New Texts, New Contexts*, edited by Jennifer S. Tuttle and Carol Farley Kessler, 44–67. Columbus: Ohio State University Press, 2011.

———. "'Overwriting' the Rest Cure: Charlotte Perkins Gilman's Literary Escape from S. Weir Mitchell's Fictionalization of Women." In *Critical Essays on Charlotte Perkins Gilman*, ed. Joanne B. Karpinski, 144–58. New York: G. K. Hall, 1992.

Golden, Catherine J., and Denise D. Knight. "Afterword." In *Unpunished: A Novel*, by Charlotte Perkins Gilman, 213–40. New York: Feminist Press, 1997.

Golden, Catherine J., and Joanna Schneider Zangrando, eds. "Introduction." In *The Mixed Legacy of Charlotte Perkins Gilman*, 11–22. Newark: University of Delaware Press, 2000.

Hedges, Elaine R. "Afterword." In *The Yellow Wall-Paper*, by Charlotte Perkins Gilman, 1892, 37–62. New York: Feminist Press, 1996.

———. "'Out at Last'?: 'The Yellow Wallpaper' after Two Decades of Feminist Criticism." In *The Captive Imagination: A Casebook on The Yellow Wallpaper*, edited by Catherine J. Golden, 319–34. New York: Feminist Press, 1992.

Hegewisch, Ariane, and Janet C. Gornick. *Statutory Routes to Workplace Flexibility in Cross-National Perspective*. Washington, DC: Institute for Women's Policy Research, 2008.

Hill, Mary A. *Charlotte Perkins Gilman: The Making of a Radical Feminist, 1860–1896*. Philadelphia, PA: Temple University Press, 1980.

———, ed. "Introduction." In *A Journey from Within: The Love Letters of Charlotte Perkins Gilman, 1897–1900*, 17–35. Lewisburg, PA: Bucknell University Press, 1995.

Hill, Michael R., ed. "Introduction: Charlotte Perkins Gilman on the Sociology of Families, Marriages, and Children." In *Families, Marriages, and Children*, xi–xxi. New Brunswick, NJ: Transaction, 2011.

Horowitz, Helen Lefkowitz. *Wild Unrest: Charlotte Perkins Gilman and the Making of "The Yellow Wall-Paper."* New York: Oxford University Press, 2010.

Kimmel, Michael, and Amy Aronson. "Introduction." In *Women and Economics: A Study of the Economic Relation between Men and Women as a Factor in So-*

cial Evolution, by Charlotte Perkins Gilman, 1898, vii–lxx. Berkeley: University of California Press, 1998.

Knight, Denise D. "'All the Facts of the Case': Gilman's Lost Letter to Dr. S. Weir Mitchell." *American Literary Realism* 37, no. 3 (2005): 259–77.

———. "'I Am Getting Angry Enough to Do Something Desperate': The Question of Female 'Madness.'" In *"The Yellow Wall-Paper" by Charlotte Perkins Gilman: A Dual-Text Critical Edition,* edited by Shawn St. Jean, 73–87. Athens: Ohio University Press, 2006.

———. "'Only a Husband's Opinion': Walter Stetson's View of Gilman's 'The Yellow Wall-Paper'; An Inscription." *American Literary Realism* 36, no. 1 (2003): 86–87.

Knight, Denise D., and Jennifer S. Tuttle, eds. "Introduction." In *The Selected Letters of Charlotte Perkins Gilman,* xv–xxii. Tuscaloosa: University of Alabama Press, 2009.

Lane, Ann J., ed. *The Charlotte Perkins Gilman Reader.* Charlottesville: University Press of Virginia, 1999.

———. "Introduction." In *Herland,* by Charlotte Perkins Gilman, 1915, v–xxiii. New York: Pantheon, 1979.

Langley, Juliet A. "Audacious Fancies: A Collection of Letters from Charlotte Perkins Gilman to Martha Luther." *Trivia: A Journal of Ideas* 6 (Winter 1985): 52–69.

Marshall, Ben. "The Rise of Women in Italy." *Stylist.* http://www.stylist.co.uk/life/the-rise-of-women-in-italy#image-rotator-1.

Marzano, Michela. "The Humiliation of Women: The Situation in Italy." *Trans-Europa* 9 (May 10, 2010): 18–19.

Miller, Sunlen. "Birth-Control Hearing Was 'Like Stepping into a Time Machine.'" ABC News, February 17, 2012. http://abcnews.go.com/blogs/politics/2012/02/birth-control-hearing-was-like-stepping-into a-time-machine/.

Mitchell, S. Weir. *Doctor and Patient.* Philadelphia, PA: Lippincott, 1888.

Moschini, Laura. "The Economic Proposals of Charlotte Perkins Gilman and Gender Budgeting in Italy." *International Review of Sociology* 19, no. 3 (2009): 433–46.

National Organization for Women. "Women Deserve Equal Pay." http://www.now.org/issues/economic/factsheet.html.

O'Leary, Naomi. "Brutal Murder of Teenager Overshadows Italy['s] Women's Rights Vote." Reuters, May 28, 2013. http://uk.reuters.com/article/2013/05/28/uk-italy-women-idUKBRE94R0TW20130528.

Poggoli, Sylvia. "Italian Women Assail Berlusconi for Sexist Remarks." NPR, October 28, 2009. http://m.npr.org/story/114242303.

Pollitt, Katha. "Wendy Davis, Superhero." *Nation,* June 26, 2013. http://www.thenation.com/blogs/katha-pollitt#.

Poirier, Suzanne. "The Weir Mitchell Rest Cure: Doctor and Patients." *Women's Studies* 10, no. 1 (1983): 15–40.

Rich, Adrienne. "Compulsory Heterosexuality and Lesbian Existence." *Signs* 5, no. 4 (Summer 1980): 631–60.

Robinson, Lillian S. "Killing Patriarchy: Charlotte Perkins Gilman, the Murder Mystery, and Post-Feminist Propaganda." *Tulsa Studies in Women's Literature* 10, no. 2 (1991): 273–85.

Saraceno, Chiara. "Affront to Rosy Bindi Exposes the 'Philosophy of the Exploiter.'" Translated by Wendell Ricketts. *Una Vita Vagabonda*, February 3, 2010. http://unavitavagabonda.wordpress.com/?s=bindi.

Scacchi, Anna, ed. and trans. "Una donna vittoriana a Utopia." In *La terra delle donne: Herland e altri racconti (1891–1916)*, xvii–xxxii. Rome: Donzelli, 2011.

Scherman, Susan. "A Relational Approach to Autonomy in Health Care." In *The Politics of Women's Health: Exploring Agency and Autonomy*, edited by Susan Scherman and the Feminist Health Care Ethics Research Network, 19–47. Philadelphia, PA: Temple University Press, 1998.

Scherman, Susan, with Voices from the Network. "Introduction." In *The Politics of Women's Health: Exploring Agency and Autonomy*, edited by Susan Scherman and the Feminist Health Care Ethics Research Network, 1–18. Philadelphia, PA: Temple University Press, 1998.

Showalter, Elaine, ed. "Introduction: The Feminist Critical Revolution." In *The New Feminist Criticism: Essays on Women, Literature and Theory*, 3–17. New York: Pantheon, 1985.

"Take Back the Night, Brooklyn, 2010." Rad-Sauce, December 29, 2012. http://ninjabikeslut.tumblr.com/post/39187523125/in-1976-claudia-caputi-a-17-year-old-woman-was.

Thrailkill, Jane F. "Doctoring 'The Yellow Wallpaper.'" *English Literary History* 69, no. 2 (Summer 2002): 525–66.

Treichler, Paula. "Escaping the Sentence: Diagnosis and Discourse in 'The Yellow Wallpaper.'" *Tulsa Studies in Women's Literature* 3, no. 1–2 (1984): 61–77.

Trivedi, Harish. "Introduction." In *Translation as Recovery*, by Sujit Mukherjee, 11–18. Delhi: Pencraft, 2009.

Tuttle, Jennifer S. "Women and Economics." In *American History through Literature, 1870–1920*, Vol. 3, edited by Tom Quirk and Gary Scharnhorst, 1203–7. Detroit, MI: Scribner's, 2006.

Tuttle, Jennifer S., and Carol Farley Kessler, eds. "Introduction." In *Charlotte Perkins Gilman: New Texts, New Contexts*, 1–24. Columbus: Ohio State University Press, 2011.

Tyler, Patrick E. "Hillary Clinton, in China, Details Abuse of Women." *New York Times*, September 6, 1995. http://www.nytimes.com/1995/09/06/world/hillary-clinton-in-china-details-abuse-of-women.html.

United Nations. "Beijing Declaration and Platform for Action." Fourth World Conference on Women, Beijing, September 4–15, 1995. http://www.un.org/womenwatch/daw/beijing/pdf/BDPfA%20E.pdf.

United Nations. "Convention on the Elimination of All Forms of Discrimination against Women." http://www.un.org/womenwatch/daw/cedaw/text/econvention.htm#intro.

Van de Putte, Leticia. "Leticia Van de Putte Asks What Women Need to Do to Be Heard in the Texas Legislature." YouTube, June 25, 2013. http://www.youtube.com/watch?v=yPntuZ7jmGY.

Winfield, Nicole. "Italy Tries to Reduce Violence against Women." Yahoo News, May 2, 2013. http://news.yahoo.com/italy-tries-reduce-violence-against-women-113833126.html.

"The Women's Movement in Italy." Libcom, August 14, 2009. http://libcom.org/library/19-womens-movement-italy.

Wood, Ann Douglas. "'The Fashionable Diseases': Women's Complaints and Their Treatment in Nineteenth-Century America." *Journal of Interdisciplinary History* 4, no. 1 (1973): 25–52.

Contributors

Jill Bergman is a professor emerita at the University of Montana, where she taught courses in American literature and women's studies. She is the author of *The Motherless Child in the Novels of Pauline Hopkins* (2012) and the coeditor of *Our Sisters' Keepers: Nineteenth-Century Benevolence Literature by American Women* (2005). Her work on American female writers has also appeared in numerous journals and collections.

Peter Betjemann is an associate professor and the director of the master's program in English at Oregon State University; since 2009 he has served as the executive director of the Charlotte Perkins Gilman Society. His work, *Talking Shop: The Language of Craft in an Age of Consumption* (2011), reads nineteenth- and early twentieth-century literature in its decorative, material, and visual contexts. He publishes on authors including Charlotte Perkins Gilman, Willa Cather, Henry James, and Nathaniel Hawthorne in such journals as *Word and Image*, *American Literary Realism*, *Nineteenth-Century Prose*, and *The Journal of Design History*, and he is currently writing a book about nineteenth-century paintings that depict scenes from literature.

Sari Edelstein is an assistant professor of English at the University of Massachusetts Boston. She is the author of *Between the Novel and the News: The Emergence of American Women's Writing* (2014), and her essays have appeared in journals, including *Studies in American Fiction*, *Legacy*, *ESQ: A Journal of the American Renaissance*, and *American Literature*. She is currently writing a book about American literature and the making of age.

Catherine J. Golden is a professor of English at Skidmore College in Saratoga Springs, New York, where she specializes in Victorian literature and culture. She is the author of *Posting It: The Victorian Revolution in Letter Writing*, the winner of the 2010 DeLong Book History Prize from the Society for the History of Authorship, Reading, and Publishing. She is also the author of *Images of the Woman Reader in Victorian British and American Fiction* (2003) and the editor or coeditor of five additional books, including *Charlotte Perkins Gilman's The Yellow Wall-Paper: A Sourcebook and Critical Edition* (2004), and *Book Illustrated: Text, Image, and Culture, 1770–1930* (2000). She is a founding member of the Charlotte Perkins Gilman Society and served as its executive director from 1998 to 2002. She is currently writing a book on the Victorian illustrated book from the serial to the graphic novel.

Brady Harrison is a professor of English at the University of Montana. He is the author of *Agent of Empire: William Walker and the Imperial Self in American Literature* (2004) and the editor or coeditor of a number of books, most recently *These Living Songs: Reading Montana Poetry* (2014) and *Punk Rock Warlord: The Life and Work of Joe Strummer* (2014). His articles, essays, and fiction have appeared in journals and books in the United States, Canada, Mexico, Puerto Rico, England, France, Germany, and Australia.

Denise D. Knight is the distinguished teaching professor emerita of nineteenth-century American literature at the State University of New York College at Cortland. She is the author of *Charlotte Perkins Gilman: A Study of the Short Fiction* (1997), the editor of the two-volume *The Diaries of Charlotte Perkins Gilman* (1994), and the editor of collections of Gilman's fiction and later poetry. She is the coeditor of *The Selected Letters of Charlotte Perkins Gilman* (2009) with Jennifer S. Tuttle, of *Charlotte Perkins Gilman's In This Our World and Uncollected Poems* (2012) with Gary Scharnhorst, and of *Charlotte Perkins Gilman and Her Contemporaries* (2004) and *Approaches to Teaching Charlotte Perkins Gilman's "The Yellow Wall-Paper"* (2003) with Cynthia J. Davis. She has published more than thirty articles and essays on Gilman.

Gary Scharnhorst is a distinguished professor emeritus at the University of New Mexico, the editor of the journal *American Literary Realism*, and the editor in alternating years of the research annual *American Literary Scholarship*. He has published numerous books and articles on a broad range of writers, books, and subjects in American literature.

William C. Snyder is a professor of English at Saint Vincent College in Latrobe, Pennsylvania. His 1984 dissertation was a cross-disciplinary exploration of the affinities between nineteenth-century painting and perceptual process and the poetry and theory of William Wordsworth. In the intervening decades he has made numerous presentations on his investigation of the relation of visual art to verbal art while teaching composition and literature courses. He has published articles in several composition journals, as well as in *European Romantic Review* and *Women's Studies*.

Jennifer S. Tuttle is the Dorothy M. Healy Professor of Literature and Health at the University of New England, where she also serves as the faculty director of the Maine Women Writers Collection. She is the editor of the first modern reissue of Gilman's 1911 novel *The Crux* (2002), the coeditor of *The Selected Letters of Charlotte Perkins Gilman* (2009) with Denise D. Knight, and the coeditor of *Charlotte Perkins Gilman: New Texts, New Contexts* (2011) with Carol Farley Kessler. A particular focus of her work has been recovering Gilman's associations with the US West. Her other published work concerns María Amparo Ruiz de Burton, S. Weir Mitchell, Elizabeth Stuart Phelps, and Owen Wister.

Index